Tanakh Companion

the book of
Samuel

Edited by **Nathaniel Helfgot**

Contributors:

Avraham Weiss

David Silber

Hayyim Angel

Jack Bieler

Joshua Berman

Leeor Gottlieb

Nathaniel Helfgot

Shmuel Herzfeld

Yehuda Felix

Ben Yehuda Press

Bible study in the spirit of modern and open Orthodox Judaism

THE TANAKH COMPANION TO THE BOOK OF SAMUEL
©2006 Yeshivat Chovevei Torah Rabbinical School. All rights reserved.
No part of this book may be used or reproduced in any manner whatsoever
without written permission except in the case of brief quotations embodied
in critical articles and reviews.

Published by Ben Yehuda Press
430 Kensington Road
Teaneck, NJ 07666

http://www.BenYehudaPress.com

For permission to reprint, including distribution of the material in this
book as part of a synagogue or school newsletter, please contact:
Permissions, Ben Yehuda Press,
430 Kensington Road, Teaneck, NJ 07666.
permissions@BenYehudaPress.com.

Ben Yehuda Press books may be purchased for educational, business or sales
promotional use. For information, please contact:
Special Markets, Ben Yehuda Press,
430 Kensington Road, Teaneck, NJ 07666.
markets@BenYehudaPress.com.

ISBN 0-9769862-4-8

Library of Congress Control Number: 2006929435

Acknowledgements: Map of Saul's Kingdom (p. 71) reprinted from The Graphic
Bible by Lewis Browne by the kind permission of the Lewis Browne Estate.
©1928 by Lewis Browne. Copyright renewed 1956.

06 07 08 09   / 10 9 8 7 6 5 4 3

In Memory of

Samuel Mitchell Newman

שמואל מנחם נוימן

born
June 3, 1955

הלך לעולמו
October 21 , 1989

dedicated by
**Ann and Bertram Newman
and their family**

וְהָיְתָה נֶפֶשׁ אֲדֹנִי צְרוּרָה בִּצְרוֹר הַחַיִּים
אֶת יי אֱלֹהֶיךָ

*" May his soul be bound
in the bond of life "*

– I Samuel 25:29

Acknowledgements:

For making the book possible: Adina Weinstein, whose transcription services turned the *ba'al peh* into *be-ktav;* Ariella Grossman, Samuel Grossman, Yael Grossman, Judika Illes, and B.J. Yudelson for their eyes like eagles'; and Shuli Boxer and Daniela Weiss for their patient assistance.

A special thank you to the contributors who suffered the editors wrestling with their words in a format not of their first choosing — who turned out to be as kind and helpful in their correspondence as they are brilliant in their lectures.

People who read the fine print at the back of books are likely to notice typographical and other errors elsewhere in the text. You know who you are. Let us know, too. Future editions will acknowledge by name everyone who lets us know about a previously unnoticed error at corrections@BenYehudaPress.com

Note: This volume contains large swaths of the original Hebrew text which includes the name of God, and should be treated with the proper dignity and respect with which one handles any holy book.

Table of Contents

YCT Tanakh Companion

Introduction

Rabbi Nathaniel Helfgot

In the early 1990's the Yaacov Herzog Teachers Institute, affiliated with the renowned Yeshivat Har Eztion in Alon Shvut, Israel, began holding an annual program of study days, or *yemei iyun*, for Israeli teachers of the Bible. These study days showcased the outstanding teachers and scholars of Bible who formed the core of the faculty of the Institute and were led by Rabbi Yoel Bin Nun, a highly creative and original thinker and teacher whose methodology and Torah quickly spread throughout the religious-Zionist world and beyond.

Amongst the faculty of that early group were leading Bible educators in the religious-Zionist world including Rabbi Mordechai Breuer, Rabbi Mordechai Sabato and Rabbi Yaaqov Medan, recently appointed *rosh yeshiva* of Yeshivat Har Etzion.

These study days quickly grew. From hosting 150-200 people, the study days have expanded to include close to 2,000 teachers and lay people who annually spend three days of intensive study of Bible in Alon Shvut during the summer months. A fourth day is devoted to full day *tiyulim* (hikes) with "a Bible in hand." These visits are made to areas where many of the major Biblical episodes occurred, encouraging in-depth study and discussion.

At the same time, the Yaacov Herzog institute began publishing *Megadim*, a journal of Modern Orthodox Tanakh scholarship. Today *Megadim* is a highly respected paragon of the integration of traditional and modern study of Bible in the context of profound religious commitment and sensitivity.

In 2002, New York City's Yeshivat Chovevei Torah (YCT), the open Orthodox Rabbinical School, imported the model of the *yemei iyun* study days to the shores of the United States. YCT, led by its founder, Rabbi Avi Weiss, and its *rosh yeshiva*, Rabbi Dov Linzer, began hosting a similar, though more modest, two day conference of intense Bible study. Held annually in New Jersey, this event has proven to be a great success and has expanded in recent years to incorporate a new element – a third day devoted to the in-depth study of Jewish thought. Hundreds of educators and interested lay people from all over the United States come and participate in intensive, all-day learning.

The *Yemei Iyun* have in the past benefited from the support of a number of educational organizations including the Jewish Agency for Israel, the Coalition for the Advancement of Jewish Education, the Lookstein Center for Jewish Education in the Diaspora and the Academy for Torah Initiatives and Directions (ATID). We thank them for their past cooperation and support. This past year YCT has been proud to work directly with the former Yaacov Herzog Teachers Institute, now the fully-accredited Yaacov Herzog Teachers College, as partners in sponsoring the *Yemei Iyun*.

Last year at the close of the YCT *Yemei Iyun*, my good friends, Larry and Eve Yudelson, founders and directors of Ben Yehuda Press, approached me with the idea for the volume that is before you. The idea was to give the general public a taste of the outstanding classes and beautiful and profound Torah learning that take place during the event. It is only due to Larry and Eve's hard work, dedication and skill that this project has come to fruition. They performed most of the editing, structuring and refining that turned a disparate series of classes into a cohesive and delightful read. With great care, skill, and most of all love, they have shepherded this book through its gestation and labor pains. Well done! *Yasher Kochakhem!*

The essays included in this volume are lightly edited transcripts of the oral presentations delivered at the Yemei Iyun on the Book of Samuel during the last three years. **As such, the essays should be read in that light, not as full-blown academic treatments of the topics at hand. Rather, these are popular presentations of profound and sophisticated ideas that help us appreciate and understand this fascinating book of the Bible.** Many of the essays have thus retained elements of their oral nature, in an attempt to bestow upon readers a sense of shared learning. To that end, we have kept the footnotes and scholarly apparatus to a minimum. Indeed, that is the thrust of the title. This book is to serve as a companion to the in-depth textual study.

For that reason, we have printed large portions of the texts under discussion in both the Hebrew original and an English translation (based on the 1917 JPS translation).

Finally, a few words about the underlying methodology shared by most of the authors in this volume. In short, the methodology employed by the authors (and the one that dominates most sophisticated Modern-Orthodox Bible study both here and in Israel) has been appropriately termed by my esteemed teacher, Rabbi Shalom Carmy, "the literary-theological method to the study of the Bible."

This approach makes systematic use of all the literary tools and methods that have come to the fore in the last hundred years while maintaining a firm control of all the classical exegetical literature. This study not only builds upon the insights of *Midrash* and classical exegesis, but strives to engage the text directly as well, in order to tease out the profound religious meaning of the text. The primary, though not exclusive, goal is one of apprehending the plain sense of the text, *peshuto shel mikra*. In that vein, this approach makes judicious use of the entire range of insights that have emerged from the archaeological and historical study of the Biblical and ancient Near-Eastern world—filtered through the prism of a religious world-view.

This type of study makes consistent use of techniques such as: close reading, patterning, intertextuality and self-reference in the text, literary echoes, enveloping, development of character, word-plays, parallelism and chiastic structure, plot development and a whole host of other literary tools that can be brought to bear on the text of the *Tanakh*.

This approach has moved *Tanakh* study from a primarily atomistic focus on the individual verse and commentary, to identifying entire literary units and narratives. The structure of entire episodes, and in legal sections whole units, has become a major sub-field in the study of *Tanakh*, an enterprise that was by and large not undertaken by the classical commentators. In addition, this has led to an appreciation of the structure and order of entire Biblical books, yielding wonderful insights relating to both form, content, and interdependence.

Through this methodology, recurring themes, motifs and overarching meta-concepts underlying *Tanakh* as a whole have been fruitfully uncovered. For the narrative books of the Bible, the focus becomes one of careful character study.

Each and every one of the literary methods and techniques, including the "overview" approach to Biblical books, has some precedents in various classical Jewish commentators, the *Rishonim*. The systematic use of the entire phalanx of techniques and methods is a direct byproduct of integrating many of the best and most sophisticated literary readings and sensibilities in approaching our sacred texts.

This methodology, which has sparked such wide interest in and excitement for the study of *Tanakh* in many of our circles, is unapologetically predicated on the perspective that "The Bible speaks in the language of human beings." This perspective, fiercely held to by a wide swath of classical Jewish scholars, including *Rishonim* and later *Achronim*[1], while fully committed to Torah as the word of the living God, understands that He, in His infinite wisdom chose to make known His will to mankind within a specific historical context in terms understandable to the human ear and heart. He chose to make His will known in the form of the written word, in the form of literature in its broadest definition.

It is a particular pleasure to thank all the outstanding teachers and scholars who agreed to share their presentations with us and incorporate them into this companion volume to the study of the Book of Samuel. It is and always has been a pleasure to work with this roster of individuals, which reads as a veritable *Who's Who* of the top teachers of Bible in our community today. May we all go from strength to strength and may the work of our hands find favor in the eyes of the Lord and in the eyes of man.

Rabbi Nathaniel Helfgot
Chair, Departments of Bible and Jewish Thought
Yeshivat Chovevei Torah Rabbinical School

---

1 *Achronim*, literally meaning "the final ones," refers to the rabbinic sages since the mid-16th century, in contrast to their predecessors who are designated the *Rishonim*, literally "the first." An extensive glossary and bibliography of traditional Jewish sources referred to in this book can be found online at http://www.BenYehudaPress/yct/biblio/

The Birth of Samuel and the Birth of Kingship
I Samuel 1:1-2:10

based on a lecture by **Rabbi David Silber**

The Book of Samuel is about the concept of kingship. Whereas the books of Kings and Chronicles deal with specific kings, the Book of Samuel[1] is primarily about the monarchy as an institution. It implicitly addresses the question: Is the monarchy a good or bad development for the Jewish people?

The Prophet Samuel holds a negative view of kingship, for a variety of reasons which he makes very clear. Nonetheless, he anoints Saul and David, the two kings who appear in the book. Willingly or unwillingly, Samuel is the kingmaker. That the leader who adamantly opposes the monarchy is the one responsible for its institution is one of the many paradoxes of the Book of Samuel.

But what is God's opinion on the subject? The answer to this central question can be found through a close reading[2] of the introductory sections of the Book of Samuel.

So let's start at the beginning:

I Samuel 1

1 Now there was a certain man of Ramathaim-zophim, of the hill-country of Ephraim, and his name was Elkanah,

א וַיְהִי אִישׁ אֶחָד מִן-הָרָמָתַיִם צוֹפִים-מֵהַר אֶפְרָיִם: וּשְׁמוֹ אֶלְקָנָה

---

[1]   It is important to note that Books I and II of Samuel are really two parts of one book. The split is a late non-Jewish division. Recognizing both sections of Samuel as one literary construct is very important, as the careers of Samuel, Saul and David are all thematically connected.

[2]   Let me note at the outset that I'm going to explicate what we call *peshat* (the unadorned narrative) and see what the text actually is saying. How others have understood this material is very important, but not my subject matter for the present.

the son of Jeroham, the son of Elihu, the son of Tohu, the son of Zuph, an Ephraimite.	בֶּן-יְרֹחָם בֶּן-אֱלִיהוּא בֶּן-תֹּחוּ בֶן-צוּף-אֶפְרָתִי.
2 And he had two wives: the name of the first was Hannah, and the name of the second Peninah; and Peninah had children, but Hannah had no children.	ב וְלוֹ שְׁתֵּי נָשִׁים-שֵׁם אַחַת חַנָּה וְשֵׁם הַשֵּׁנִית פְּנִנָּה: וַיְהִי לִפְנִנָּה יְלָדִים וּלְחַנָּה אֵין יְלָדִים.
3 And this man went up out of his city from year to year to worship and to sacrifice unto the LORD of hosts in Shiloh. And the two sons of Eli, Chofni and Pinchas, were there as priests unto the LORD.	ג וְעָלָה הָאִישׁ הַהוּא מֵעִירוֹ מִיָּמִים יָמִימָה לְהִשְׁתַּחֲוֹת וְלִזְבֹּחַ לַיי צְבָאוֹת בְּשִׁלֹה: וְשָׁם שְׁנֵי בְנֵי-עֵלִי חָפְנִי וּפִנְחָס כֹּהֲנִים לַיי.

The book begins with Samuel's father, Elkanah, of whom we learn two things. First, he has two wives, Hannah and Peninah, one of whom has children and one of whom does not. Second, he is a pious individual who regularly worships God at Shiloh. What is the significance of these two points in understanding Samuel the man and Samuel the book?

The Two Wives Club

Genesis twice tells of men who marry a second woman when their original wives are barren: Abram is given Hagar by Sarai,[3] and Jacob is given Bilhah by Rachel.[4] Sarai and Rachel both seek to become mothers through their slave women.

We don't know if Hannah's story is similar. Certainly, in Genesis two wives are a prescription for domestic disaster. It does not work out any differently for Elkanah:

I Samuel 1

4 It came to pass upon a day, when Elkanah sacrificed, that he gave portions to Peninah his wife, and to all her sons and her daughters.	ד וַיְהִי הַיּוֹם וַיִּזְבַּח אֶלְקָנָה: וְנָתַן לִפְנִנָּה אִשְׁתּוֹ וּלְכָל-בָּנֶיהָ וּבְנוֹתֶיהָ מָנוֹת.

---

3 Genesis 16:2
4 Genesis 30:3

5 but to Hannah he gave a double portion; for he loved Hannah, but the LORD had shut up her womb.

6 And her rival vexed her sore, to make her fret, because the LORD had closed up her womb.

7 And as he did so year by year, when she went up to the house of the LORD, so she vexed her; therefore she wept, and would not eat.

ה וּלְחַנָּה יִתֵּן מָנָה אַחַת אַפָּיִם: כִּי אֶת-חַנָּה אָהֵב וַיי סָגַר רַחְמָהּ.

ו וְכִעֲסַתָּה צָרָתָהּ גַּם-כַּעַס בַּעֲבוּר הַרְעִמָהּ: כִּי-סָגַר יי בְּעַד רַחְמָהּ.

ז וְכֵן יַעֲשֶׂה שָׁנָה בְשָׁנָה מִדֵּי עֲלֹתָהּ בְּבֵית יי–כֵּן תַּכְעִסֶנָּה: וַתִּבְכֶּה וְלֹא תֹאכַל.

When Elkanah offers sacrifices during his pilgrimage to Shiloh, he brings back portions for his family. He tenders a double portion to Hannah, clearly favoring her over Peninah. This is reminiscent of the favoritism in the story of Jacob, Rachel and Leah. But Jacob loved Rachel best from the start, only ending up with two wives because of his father-in-law's trickery. With Elkanah, however, there is no reason to believe that his own dysfunctional family is not of his own making.

Verse six is difficult, but the gist is that Hannah's *tzarah*, the rival wife, made her very angry and the text adds "because the Lord had closed up her womb." It sounds as if Peninah is taunting Hannah about her child-lessness. Like Jacob of old, Elkanah markedly demonstrates his favoritism and contributes to the friction in the family.

The next verse is very instructive. Elkanah did this every year. It was a ritual: He would give Hannah a double portion; Peninah would get angry about the favoritism and taunt her rival. Every time he went to sacrifice, Peninah would bother Hannah.

In verse 7, the term *shanah be-shanah*, year by year, referring to something done periodically, actually has a parallel in this little story: the phrase, *u-miyamim yamimah* in verse 3, which we have also translated as "year by year." Literally, it means something like "from days by days," but it means "periodically." The term has an important resonance that we will examine later in this lecture.

This returns us to the question we raised above: What is the significance of Elkanah's regular worship at Shiloh?

There is a hint in verse 3, when the text adds that Chofni and Pinchas were ministering to God in Shiloh. Why are they mentioned here? If the purpose is to introduce the story's characters, we should be told instead about Eli, the primary Priest of Shiloh. After all, he speaks to Hannah a few verses later, while Chofni and Pinchas don't really figure into the story until the next chapter. No, there is something about Chofni and Pinchas that is a key to understanding Elkanah's regular pilgrimage.

What should we be noticing? What do we know about Chofni and Pinchas? The next chapter tells us:

I Samuel 2

12 Now the sons of Eli were base men; they knew not the LORD.

יב וּבְנֵי עֵלִי בְּנֵי בְלִיָּעַל: לֹא יָדְעוּ אֶת-יְיָ.

They are wicked people. The second chapter spells out the details. But for now, the text tells us that wicked priests run the show in Shiloh – the central place of worship. That's the import of highlighting the role of Chofni and Pinchas.

God or Status Quo in Shiloh

Understanding Shiloh tells us something about Elkanah, whose regular worship there is central to his identity.

Elkanah wants to serve God, but his very service reinforces the bad atmosphere that Chofni and Pinchas create at Shiloh.

Is Elkanah really to blame for their actions? Where else could he go to worship? This raises the very interesting question about participation in institutions that are not perfect – and no institution is perfect. All institutions fall short of the mark. (My belief is that they fail by their very nature.) On the other hand, institutions serve a purpose. This is one of the issues that this story raises, and it is an issue central to the combined books of Judges, Samuel and Kings. The problem of the relationship between the Jewish people and God is ultimately not solved by the institution of the monarchy.

The point here, though, is that there's imperfect – and then there's rotten to the core. Shiloh is rotten to the core.

Shiloh's rottenness is made quite clear in chapter two. After Eli rebukes Chofni and Pinchas in his mild way, it says they did not obey God, because God wants to kill them. This is very striking. God wants Shiloh destroyed:

I Samuel 2

25 If one man sin against another,
God shall judge him; but if a man
sin against the LORD, who shall
entreat for him? But they (Chofni
and Pinchas) did not listen to the
voice of their father, because the
LORD desired to slay them.

כה אִם-יֶחֱטָא אִישׁ לְאִישׁ וּפִלְלוֹ
אֱלֹהִים וְאִם לַיי יֶחֱטָא-אִישׁ מִי
יִתְפַּלֶּל-לוֹ: וְלֹא יִשְׁמְעוּ לְקוֹל
אֲבִיהֶם כִּי-חָפֵץ יְי לַהֲמִיתָם.

The general philosophical question of whether or not to work within the system does not apply here. God is saying that the current system, Shiloh under Chofni and Pinchas, is no good at all.

The Crimes of Chofni and Pinchas

In a very real way, Chofni and Pinchas and their corruption simply continue the bankrupt moral climate present at the end of Judges.

The crimes of Chofni and Pinchas are described in two places in the Book of Samuel. The first mention[5] describes how, when well-intentioned Jews would come to bring sacrifices, Chofni and Pinchas would send a representative with a three-pronged fork to demand and take the specific portions they wanted.

Remember, when the Torah speaks about the Priestly gifts, *matnot ki-hunah*, it is always about priests *receiving* gifts. It never discusses priests *taking*. The Talmud goes even further, explaining that the priest is not even allowed to give the *appearance* of taking.[6] He is supposed to wait until after the animal is sacrificed and the incense is burned on the altar. Only then may a priest gather up his priestly portion.

But in Shiloh, they take too much and they take too soon. They steal from the people and they steal from God.

The other sin that Chofni and Pinchas commit is the one that we are told comes to the attention of Eli:

I Samuel 2

22 Now Eli was very old; and he
heard all that his sons did unto
all Israel, and how that they lay
with the women that did service
at the door of the tent of meeting.

כב וְעֵלִי זָקֵן מְאֹד: וְשָׁמַע אֵת
כָּל-אֲשֶׁר יַעֲשׂוּן בָּנָיו לְכָל-יִשְׂרָאֵל
וְאֵת אֲשֶׁר-יִשְׁכְּבוּן אֶת-הַנָּשִׁים
הַצֹּבְאוֹת פֶּתַח אֹהֶל מוֹעֵד.

---

5   I Samuel 2:13-17
6   Chullin 133a

This is a different abuse of power: raping the women who would gather before the Tabernacle. This is the sort of sin people like to talk about, so this is the abuse that comes to Eli's attention. (He never has firsthand knowledge of anything.) However, the abuse described directly by the text is financial: the grabbing of sacrifices.

Interestingly, Eli's sons' behavior with the women in front of the Tabernacle is quite similar to the description of Shiloh at the end of the Book of Judges.

Looking back to Judges

Generally, when we read Samuel we think of the corruption of Shiloh in terms of the events that follow in consequence of that corruption: the displacement of Eli by Samuel, and of Shiloh by Jerusalem. But really, the significance of Shiloh in the opening chapters of this story is established by looking at the precipitate events in the Book of Judges.[7]

Judges is essentially a book that has three parts. The first part is really a continuation of the Book of Joshua. The middle part is the sequence of judges ending with Samson. Then there's an epilogue to the Book of Judges which consists of five chapters, 17 through 21, telling two stories. The final story of the Book of Judges is, of course, the story of *pilegesh be-Give'ah*, the Concubine of Give'ah.

In brief: A man traveling with his wife/concubine is attacked by the people of Give'ah from the tribe of Benjamin. They kidnap and rape his wife. At this point, the man cuts her body into twelve pieces and sends it all around Israel.

Everybody is terribly shocked, and a civil war breaks out as the rest of Israel attacks the tribe of Benjamin. After the third battle, the tribe of Benjamin is almost annihilated. Not just the men, but the women, too. Israel begins to have second thoughts, and they want to repopulate the tribe of Benjamin. But they can't. They have taken an oath not to give their daughters to Benjamin.[8]

---

7   Depending on how one orders the books of the Tanakh, which is far from self-evident, one thing that's clear is that the Book of Samuel has deep connections to the Book of Judges. In our Tanakh, one follows the other. One can make a good case, however, that the Book of Ruth is actually intended to be placed between the Book of Judges and the Book of Samuel (as it is in some Christian traditions). In any event, without a question, Samuel and Judges have deep connections.

8   Judges 21:1

It turns out that one town, Yaveish Gile'ad, did not participate in the oath. At this point, the people dispatch the army to punish Yaveish Gile'ad, and in the process, they kidnap four hundred women whom they hand over to the tribe of Benjamin. They think they've solved the problem, but it turns out there are not enough women from Yaveish Gile'ad to go around for all the men of Benjamin.

So in the last chapter in the Book of Judges, we see:

Judges 21

15 And the people repented them for Benjamin, because that the LORD had made a breach in the tribes of Israel.

טו וְהָעָם נִחָם לְבִנְיָמִן: כִּי-עָשָׂה יְיָ פֶּרֶץ בְּשִׁבְטֵי יִשְׂרָאֵל.

16 Then the elders of the congregation said: 'What shall we do for wives for them that remain, seeing the women are destroyed out of Benjamin?'

טז וַיֹּאמְרוּ זִקְנֵי הָעֵדָה מַה-נַּעֲשֶׂה לַנּוֹתָרִים לְנָשִׁים: כִּי-נִשְׁמְדָה מִבִּנְיָמִן אִשָּׁה.

Subsequently, the elders get together and propose a plan:

Judges 21

19 And they said: 'Behold, there is the feast of the LORD **from year to year** in Shiloh, which is on the north of Beth-el, on the east side of the highway that goeth up from Beth-el to Shechem, and on the south of Lebonah.'

יט וַיֹּאמְרוּ הִנֵּה חַג-יְיָ בְּשִׁלוֹ מִיָּמִים יָמִימָה אֲשֶׁר מִצְפוֹנָה לְבֵית-אֵל מִזְרְחָה הַשֶּׁמֶשׁ לִמְסִלָּה הָעֹלָה מִבֵּית-אֵל שְׁכֶמָה: וּמִנֶּגֶב לִלְבוֹנָה.

Note the phrase "from year to year," *mi-yamim yamimah*, which we have already seen in I Samuel 1:3 – which comes only nine verses later in the Tanakh. The repetition of this phrase links the period at the end of the book Judges and the beginning of the Book of Samuel.

The passage continues:

Judges 21

20 And they commanded the children of Benjamin, saying: 'Go and lie in wait in the vineyards

כ וִיצוּ (וַיְצַוּוּ) אֶת-בְּנֵי בִנְיָמִן לֵאמֹר: לְכוּ וַאֲרַבְתֶּם בַּכְּרָמִים.

21 and see, and, behold, if the daughters of Shiloh come out to dance in the dances, then come out of the vineyards, and catch every man a wife for himself from the daughters of Shiloh, and go to the land of Benjamin.

22 And it shall be, when their fathers or their brethren come to strive with us, that we will say to them: Grant them graciously to us; because each man took not his wife in battle; neither did you give them to them, that you should now be guilty.'

כא וּרְאִיתֶם וְהִנֵּה אִם-יֵצְאוּ בְנוֹת-שִׁילוֹ לָחוּל בַּמְּחֹלוֹת וִיצָאתֶם מִן-הַכְּרָמִים וַחֲטַפְתֶּם לָכֶם אִישׁ אִשְׁתּוֹ מִבְּנוֹת שִׁילוֹ: וַהֲלַכְתֶּם אֶרֶץ בִּנְיָמִן.

כב וְהָיָה כִּי-יָבֹאוּ אֲבוֹתָם אוֹ אֲחֵיהֶם לרוב (לָרִיב) אֵלֵינוּ וְאָמַרְנוּ אֲלֵיהֶם חָנּוּנוּ אוֹתָם כִּי לֹא לָקַחְנוּ אִישׁ אִשְׁתּוֹ בַּמִּלְחָמָה: כִּי לֹא אַתֶּם נְתַתֶּם לָהֶם כָּעֵת תֶּאְשָׁמוּ.

Rather than break their oath and give their daughters outright to Benjamin,[9] the elders decided that the Benjaminites should kidnap *en m*

---

9 Why wasn't *hatarat nedarim*, the nullification of vows, used by the elders to alter the situation and allow the marriages? The answer is that *hatarat nedarim* doesn't exist in Tanakh. You won't find it. There is one case of "so-called *hatarat nedarim*" in Tanakh to my knowledge, which appears in the Book of Samuel. It appears when Saul vows to kill his son (I Samuel 14:24-27). There it is not termed *hatarat nedarim*. The people simply say, forget about it, it's not happening, *va-yifdu et Yonatan* (I Samuel 14:44-45). But as the Mishnah (Chagia 1:8) says, *heter nedarim porchin be-avir*, the rite of anulling vows "hangs in the air" without real textual foundation. In the text, the whole idea of an oath, *shevuah* – and probably a vow, *neder,* too – is that it is truly binding.

As far as the vow of Jephthah in Judges 11:30-31, the Talmud suggests that Jephthah could have gotten out of it. He could have gone to Pinchas, the head priest of the time. Or the people could have prevented Jephthah from going through with it the way they prevented Saul. Maybe they should have. But I wouldn't call it *hatarat nidarim*, exactly. Jephthah's mistake was taking the *neder* in the first place. It's very clear that whereas Jephthah didn't think that it would be his daughter who would come out to greet him, his words were: "The one who comes to greet me after the war, I will sacrifice to God." (*"Asher yetzei me-daltei beiti li-krati"* – Judges 11:31.) Who did he *think* was going to greet him? This type of language refers to a person. So Jephthah obviously intends all along to bring a human sacrifice. Typically, the very flaw that a judge exhibits is the identical flaw as that of the people he opposes. This is another theme of the Book of Judges. Jephthah fights Ammon and Moab, who are known for human sacrifice. So, in the case of Jephthah, it's the flaw of Moab. In the case of Gideon, it's the flaw of Midian. Each judge shares the flaw of his greatest enemy.

---

many women from Shiloh during a festival. There was probably some kind of wine festival, *mi-yamim yamimah*, probably right around *Tu B'Av*, the mid-summer full moon.

Wait a minute. Why was there a civil war in the first place? From the supposed moral outrage over the rape of one concubine.[10] And how does it end? With the sanctioned kidnap and rape of hundreds of women. And where does this occur? In the one holy place, the Temple at Shiloh. As the final verse of Judges says: "In those days there was no king in Israel, and every man did that which was right in his own eyes."[11]

Clearly, Shiloh is redolent of hypocrisy and violence even before Chofni and Pinchas take over.

And that's how the Book of Samuel begins, with the well-meaning, but inept, Elkanah, who favors one of his two wives and repeats that mistake year by year, *shanah be-shanah*. He wants to serve God, but at the worst place in the world, Shiloh, the place of utter corruption. And he does it, *mi-yamim yamimah*, regularly.

Hannah's Choice

Of course, Elkanah is a foil for Hannah. It is Hannah who is our hero.

Hannah conducts herself differently from Elkanah. She prefers to stay home. And when her husband drags her along to Shiloh, she serves God in a different way. She doesn't perform the ritual forms of devotion of bowing down and sacrificing, which are forms of worship, but not worship itself.

Hannah has a different way, a different path.

Hannah's outlook is given voice by her son fourteen chapters later.

Samuel says to Saul, "Why did you disobey the word of God and take the animals of Amalek?" Saul answers, "I took them to sacrifice." Samuel replies, "Has the Lord as great delight in burnt-offerings and sacrifices, as in listening to the voice of the Lord? Behold, to obey is better than sacrifice, and to listen better than the fat of rams."[12]

Samuel and Hannah believe that rituals are very important when they express something real. When they *substitute* for something real, they express nothing. In fact, they become actual idolatry, having become an end in themselves rather than a means to worship God. Hannah opts out of

---

10   If you read the story carefully, as Nachmanides notes in his Torah commentary, no one is really outraged.

11   Judges 21:25

12   I Samuel 15:22-23

participating, because her experience of Shiloh is one of witnessing empty practice.

Hannah is surrounded by good people. Elkanah is a good man, devoted to God and to his beloved Hannah. However, he understands nothing. He really means well, but he does not understand that everything he is doing actually hurts Hannah. And that is important to the story.

Similarly, Eli the priest, understands nothing. Eli is a good and holy man. He cares about the glory of God. (From a literary standpoint, that is part of the greatness of the Book of Samuel: the portraits of even the minor characters are wonderful. Eli could have been presented as an evil man; He is not.)

Eli means so well that his blessing means something, too. He blesses Hannah at the end, "May God bless you, my daughter."[13]

Eli's problem is that he is blind about everything important in his life. Hannah, by contrast, sees perfectly. She understands everything. That is the point of the story.

Samson: More help from outside the system

The story of Hannah clearly refers to another story from Judges: the birth of Samson.

Both stories begin with childless women, both have sons whose hair goes uncut, and both boys go on to redeem the nation of Israel. Samson's story is found in Judges Chapter 13 and is the *haftarah* read in synagogue along with Naso, Numbers 6:1-21, the story of the *nazir*.

Samson's story begins:

Judges 13

1 And the children of Israel again did that which was evil in the sight of the LORD; and the LORD delivered them into the hand of the Philistines forty years.

א וַיֹּסִפוּ בְּנֵי יִשְׂרָאֵל לַעֲשׂוֹת הָרַע בְּעֵינֵי יְיָ: וַיִּתְּנֵם יְיָ בְּיַד־פְּלִשְׁתִּים אַרְבָּעִים שָׁנָה.

2 And there was a certain man of Zorah, of the family of the Danites, whose name was Manoach; and his wife was barren, and bore not.

ב וַיְהִי אִישׁ אֶחָד מִצָּרְעָה מִמִּשְׁפַּחַת הַדָּנִי וּשְׁמוֹ מָנוֹחַ: וְאִשְׁתּוֹ עֲקָרָה וְלֹא יָלָדָה.

---

13   I Samuel 1:17

3 And the angel of the LORD appeared to the woman, and said to her: 'Behold now, you are barren, and have not borne; but you shall conceive, and bear a son.

ג וַיֵּרָא מַלְאַךְ-יְיָ אֶל-הָאִשָּׁה: וַיֹּאמֶר אֵלֶיהָ הִנֵּה-נָא אַתְּ-עֲקָרָה וְלֹא יָלַדְתְּ וְהָרִית וְיָלַדְתְּ בֵּן.

4 Now therefore beware, I pray you, and drink no wine nor strong drink, and eat not any unclean thing.

ד וְעַתָּה הִשָּׁמְרִי נָא וְאַל-תִּשְׁתִּי יַיִן וְשֵׁכָר: וְאַל-תֹּאכְלִי כָּל-טָמֵא.

5 For, lo, you shall conceive, and bear a son; and no razor shall come upon his head; for the child shall be a Nazirite unto God from the womb; and he shall begin to save Israel out of the hand of the Philistines.'

ה כִּי הִנָּךְ הָרָה וְיָלַדְתְּ בֵּן וּמוֹרָה לֹא-יַעֲלֶה עַל-רֹאשׁוֹ-כִּי-נְזִיר אֱלֹהִים יִהְיֶה הַנַּעַר מִן-הַבָּטֶן: וְהוּא יָחֵל לְהוֹשִׁיעַ אֶת- יִשְׂרָאֵל-מִיַּד פְּלִשְׁתִּים .

Elkanah finds a parallel in the character Manoach, Samson's father. Both represent their existing cultures and both have no interest in change. Elkanah is happy with Shiloh. It is only Hannah who sees a problem and prays for change. And the angel ignores Manoach, who represents the status quo — and speaks only to his wife.

And, of course, in these two stories Samuel and Samson are parallel characters. Hannah promises that no razor will touch Samuel's head,[14] the same vow as for a *nazir*.

Salvation Without Prayer

There is something very strange about the story of Samson. Throughout the Book of Judges, there is a pattern which repeats: Israel sins; Israel is punished through the attack of an adversary; Israel cries out to God; and God sends a deliverer. This pattern appears seven or eight times in Judges.

Patterns bring into focus those things that don't fit, and the prelude to Samson is an example of this.

Here, Israel sins and God hands Israel over to the Philistines. That fits the pattern. Then God sends an angel to the woman to tell her that her son will save Israel. That also fits, but something is still missing.

What is missing is the third step: Israel crying out to God.

---

14   I Samuel 1:11

This absence is even more striking because of how the pattern has played out just a couple of chapters earlier: Israel worships foreign gods and then God hands them over to various enemies.

In this time just *before* Samson, in Judges 10:10, the Israelites cry out to God. God has a long answer[15] which can be paraphrased as: "Listen, you know, this entire book you have been calling out to Me, and I have been saving you. I am getting sick of it. Why don't you call out to those other gods that you worship all the time? I have had enough."

And Israel replies, "We have sinned. *Chatanu.* Do whatever you want but save us this one time."[16] And they get rid of their foreign gods. (Note that God was suffering with Israel.)[17] And then, just two verses later, Jepthah comes on the scene to save Israel.

But here in chapter 13, Israel is not praying at all. There is no mention of crying out to God. Nonetheless, God proactively sends an angel to Mrs. Manoach.

Why aren't the Israelites crying out to God? And why does God nonetheless send help? Why is the pattern broken?

Importantly, Israel no longer has any interest in being saved. We see this later on in the story, when the men of Judah actually want to hand Samson over to the Philistines. They tell him, "Don't you know that the Philistines are our rulers? What are you making trouble for?"[18]

In essence, it isn't God who breaks the pattern by sending a savior out of sequence; it is Israel who breaks the pattern by losing the desire to be delivered! Israel is content to be ruled by Philistines.

So God is very unhappy. God's people are no longer turning to God for redemption.

Another question about Samson: Why must the deliverer of Israel be a *nazir*? The other heroes of Judges are not Nazirites. Why does Samson break that pattern, too?

And why is he such a strange type of *nazir*? According to the Torah, one becomes a *nazir* by vowing to take on specific restrictions for a limited period of time.[19] Numbers spends more time describing the *completion* of one's time as a *nazir* than it does describing what it is to *be* one.

What is different about Samson's *nizirut*? First, it's imposed from without, as opposed to the biblical version of *nizirut* as an oath one takes upon oneself. Also, Samson's status spans his entire life. In the Torah,

---

15 Judges 10:11-14
16 Judges 10:15
17 Judges 10:16
18 Judges 15:11
19 Numbers 6:2-8

nizirut is a temporary status undertaken for a limited time. This status is imposed on Samson from the womb and forever.

The Meaning of Samson

In the Samson narrative, the Jews don't deserve to be saved and God has no interest in saving them. God's interest is simply to vanquish God's enemies. And that is why God goes to the woman and *not* the man.(Note that God totally ignores Manoach. He is worse than Elkanah.) Manoach represents the prevailing culture — which has absolutely no interest in change.

The striking failure of Israel to pray for redemption is paralleled by the childless couple who do not pray to God for a child. Usually, childless couples turn to God. We see this with Abram, Isaac, Jacob... and Hannah later on. Up until this point, the genre suggests that those in need of help turn to God.

But these people have no problem. They're happy with the status quo. It's only God who is unhappy. So God chooses somebody from outside the community, the ultimate *nazir*. Samson is not the normal religious Jew who doesn't drink wine or cut his hair, but someone completely and totally outside the community — not just for thirty days, but from conception.

Barren Matriarchs, Fruitful Prayer

In contrast to Mrs. Manoach, Hannah is not happy with the status quo. And she is not waiting for the oblivious Elkanah to wake up and start praying on her behalf. Hannah approaches God herself, essentially bypassing the whole apparatus of Shiloh. What this whole story is really about is Hannah's prayer. She stands in Shiloh and she's praying. Eli has never seen this before. What's she doing there? This is a place of sacrifice and bowing down, but with Hannah it's not just a prayer, it's a prayer without sound. "Her voice was not heard."[20]

In Tanakh, each story plays off other stories. So when Hannah prays for children, it plays off the genre of the childless couple, a genre prominent in Genesis.

Three of the four matriarchs, Sarah, Rebeccah and Rachel, have problems producing children. The only one with spontaneous pregnancies is Leah. And the narrative goes out of its way to explain Leah's fecundity: "God saw that Leah was hated, so He opened her womb, and Rachel was

---

20   I Samuel 1:13

barren."[21] The matriarchs always wait for children. It's part of being in the covenantal relationship with God: In Genesis, the blessing is always deferred and only received after much struggle.

Let us look closely at the different ways the struggle with infertility plays out in Genesis. In the first instance, we have Abram.[22] His name means "great father," only he has no successor. When God says, "Don't worry Abram, I'll give you a very great reward,"[23] Abram's answer is: "Oh, Lord, what will you give me? Eliezer of Damascus is going to inherit me."[24]

One word stands out in this little prayer, "me." For Abram, it's about "me," not "us." Abram uses the wrong two letter word. Abram mistakenly believes that his destiny is not bound up with Sarai at all; that is why he calls her his "sister."[25]

Ultimately, Abram has to come to understand that the covenant is about the *two* of them; it's about Sarai's child, too, and that is why the chosen son is Isaac and *not* Ishmael. But for now, Sarai gives Abram her slave to get children. It backfires, of course, but it is Sarai's idea.

In the second instance, Rebeccah and Isaac have no child. "And Isaac entreated the Lord for his wife, because she was barren; and the Lord let Himself be entreated of him, and Rebeccah his wife conceived."[26] The midrash[27] expounds that each pray in a different corner, but the text simply states that Isaac prays for them both. Isaac prays for his wife. Rebeccah does not pray for herself. (Rebeccah does other things, but she does not pray. She tries to find answers in other ways.)

Rachel is the most pro-active. First, she gives her servant, Bilhah, to Jacob.[28] Then, she trades time with Jacob for mandrakes, which are some kind of fertility pill.[29] In my view, the story of stealing Laban's *teraphim*[30] is also an attempt to have a child. (The *teraphim* work, as the mandrakes do, but with a sting. This attempt reminds one of Macbeth's witches, who tell the truth but deceive at the same time.) Jacob curses "whoever" has stolen the *teraphim*, and Rachel dies in childbirth.

21   Genesis 29:31
22   Abram and Sarai's names do not change until Genesis 17:5 for Abraham, and Genesis 17:15 for Sarah.
23   Genesis 15:1
24   Genesis 15:2
25   Genesis 12:13
26   Genesis 25:21
27   Rashi on Genesis 25:21
28   Genesis 30:3
29   Genesis 30:14
30   Genesis 31:19

Supporting the view that the *teraphim* were used to produce a child for her, Rachel names the child "Ben On"[31], son of my *aven*, my "iniquity." And, of course, those who know Tanakh, and especially the Book of Samuel, understand very well that there is a byword in Tanakh with the word *aven*. It is combined with another word, *teraphim*. In fact you have it here in the Book of Samuel:

I Samuel 15

23 For rebellion is as the sin of witchcraft, and stubbornness is as **idolatry and teraphim**. Because you have rejected the word of the LORD, He has also rejected you from being king.

כג כִּי חַטַּאת-קֶסֶם מֶרִי וְאָוֶן
וּתְרָפִים הַפְצַר: יַעַן מָאַסְתָּ
אֶת-דְּבַר יי וַיִּמְאָסְךָ מִמֶּלֶךְ.

Of course, Saul is Rachel's great, great, great grandson. Not just biologically, but he takes after her as the person who goes to the *ba'alat ov*, the ghost diviner, when he consults the Witch of Endor.[32] He dabbles in the same magical activities as Rachel.

So if you look at all these stories in Genesis, there is a clear difference from Hannah: The women don't pray for themselves. In fact, when Rachel goes to Jacob and says, *havah li banim*,[33] "give me children," Nachmanides explains that she is asking Jacob to "give me children through prayer." In other words, she goes to Jacob to have him pray.

Hannah, in contradistinction, tries to help herself. Her husband does not understand the problem. For him, life is beautiful, everything is great, and Hannah has his love. He doesn't see the problem, so he's not going to try to find a solution. Only Hannah understands the problem.

Unlike the matriarchs, Hannah has to take matters into her own hands and approach God personally. Unfortunately, the place of worship where she finds herself is very corrupt, indeed.

Hannah's Prayer

This sets the stage for understanding the importance of Hannah's prayer. Unlike Elkanah, Hannah goes to Shiloh reluctantly. And when she goes, it's not to bow and sacrifice.[34] She does not participate in the

---

31   Genesis 35:18
32   I Samuel 28:7
33   Genesis 30:1
34   I Samuel 1:3

forms of worship which are appropriate to Shiloh; rather, Hannah actually prays.

With that background to Hannah, Shiloh, and the book as a whole, we can begin examining Hannah's prayer–the central piece of the pre-history of Samuel–which is the *haftarah*, the prophetic reading, for Rosh Hashanah:

I Samuel 1

10 And she [Hannah] was in bitterness of soul–and prayed unto the LORD, and wept sore.

י וְהִיא מָרַת נָפֶשׁ: וַתִּתְפַּלֵּל עַל-יי וּבָכֹה תִבְכֶּה.

11 And she vowed a vow, and said: O LORD of hosts, if You will indeed look on the affliction of Your handmaid, and remember me, and not forget Your handmaid, but will give to Your handmaid a man-child, then I will give him to the LORD all the days of his life, and there shall no razor come upon his head.

יא וַתִּדֹּר נֶדֶר וַתֹּאמַר יי צְבָאוֹת אִם-רָאֹה תִרְאֶה בָּעֳנִי אֲמָתֶךָ וּזְכַרְתַּנִי וְלֹא-תִשְׁכַּח אֶת-אֲמָתֶךָ וְנָתַתָּה לַאֲמָתְךָ זֶרַע אֲנָשִׁים: וּנְתַתִּיו לַיי כָּל-יְמֵי חַיָּיו וּמוֹרָה לֹא-יַעֲלֶה עַל-רֹאשׁוֹ.

What is the nature of this oath that Hannah makes – to give her child away to God all the days of his life? It is very peculiar. Presumably she wants to have a child for herself. So why is she offering to give the child away?

And what happens after the boy is born, weaned, and brought to Shiloh? Hannah prays again, a very famous prayer. In fact, I had to memorize it as a child. It is the first ten verses of the second chapter and is composed after Samuel is born. The curious thing about this poem is that it seems to bear no relationship whatsoever to childbirth:

I Samuel 2

1 And Hannah prayed, and said: my heart exults in the LORD, my horn is exalted in the LORD; my mouth is enlarged over mine enemies; because I rejoice in Your salvation.

א וַתִּתְפַּלֵּל חַנָּה וַתֹּאמַר עָלַץ לִבִּי בַּיי רָמָה קַרְנִי בַּיי: רָחַב פִּי עַל-אוֹיְבַי כִּי שָׂמַאֽין-קָדוֹשׁ כַּיי כִּי אֵחְתִּי בִּישׁוּעָתֶךָ.

2 There is none holy as the
LORD, for there is none
beside You; neither is there
any rock like our God.

ב אֵין־קָדוֹשׁ כַּיי כִּי אֵין בִּלְתֶּךָ׃
וְאֵין צוּר כֵּאלֹהֵינוּ׃

3 Multiply not exceeding proud
talk; let not arrogancy come out
of your mouth; for the LORD
is a God of knowledge, and by
Him actions are weighed.

ג אַל־תַּרְבּוּ תְדַבְּרוּ גְּבֹהָה גְבֹהָה
יֵצֵא עָתָק מִפִּיכֶם׃ כִּי אֵל דֵּעוֹת
יְיָ וְלֹא (וְלוֹ) נִתְכְּנוּ עֲלִלוֹת׃

4 The bows of the mighty men are
broken, and they that stumbled
are girded with strength.

ד קֶשֶׁת גִּבֹּרִים חַתִּים׃
וְנִכְשָׁלִים אָזְרוּ חָיִל׃

5 They that were full have hired
out themselves for bread; and
they that were hungry have
ceased; while the barren has
borne seven, she that had many
children has languished.

ה שְׂבֵעִים בַּלֶּחֶם נִשְׂכָּרוּ וּרְעֵבִים
חָדֵלּוּ׃ עַד־עֲקָרָה יָלְדָה שִׁבְעָה
וְרַבַּת בָּנִים אֻמְלָלָה׃

6 The LORD kills, and makes
alive; He brings down to
the grave, and brings up.

ו יְיָ מֵמִית וּמְחַיֶּה׃ מוֹרִיד שְׁאוֹל וַיָּעַל׃

7 The LORD makes poor,
and makes rich; He brings
low, He also lifts up.

ז יְיָ מוֹרִישׁ וּמַעֲשִׁיר׃
מַשְׁפִּיל אַף־מְרוֹמֵם׃

8 He raises up the poor out of the
dust, He lifts up the needy from
the dung-hill, to make them sit
with princes, and inherit the
throne of glory; for the pillars of
the earth are the LORD'S, and
He has set the world upon them.

ח מֵקִים מֵעָפָר דָּל מֵאַשְׁפֹּת יָרִים
אֶבְיוֹן לְהוֹשִׁיב עִם־נְדִיבִים וְכִסֵּא
כָבוֹד יַנְחִלֵם׃ כִּי לַיי מְצֻקֵי
אֶרֶץ וַיָּשֶׁת עֲלֵיהֶם תֵּבֵל׃

9 He will keep the feet of His holy
ones, but the wicked shall be put
to silence in darkness; for not
by strength shall man prevail.

ט רַגְלֵי חֲסִידָו יִשְׁמֹר וּרְשָׁעִים בַּחשֶׁךְ
יִדָּמּוּ׃ כִּי־לֹא בְכֹחַ יִגְבַּר־אִישׁ׃

10 They that strive with the LORD
shall be broken to pieces; against
them will He thunder in heaven;
the LORD will judge the ends
of the earth; and He will give
strength unto His king, and
exalt the horn of His anointed.

י יְיָ יֵחַתּוּ מְרִיבָו עָלָו בַּשָּׁמַיִם יַרְעֵם
יְיָ יָדִין אַפְסֵי־אָרֶץ׃ וְיִתֶּן־עֹז
לְמַלְכּוֹ וְיָרֵם קֶרֶן מְשִׁיחוֹ׃

What does any of this have to do with having a child? There is one reference to a woman who has children.[35] But in its totality, the basic idea of Hannah's prayer seems to be that God destroys the arrogant, the proud, and the mighty, and that God raises up the lowly, the poor, the needy, and the hungry.

And then the last verse: "God will judge the ends of the earth and He will give strength to His king." What in the world does it have to do with the fact that God answered Hannah's prayer for a baby?

An additional question is: Why is this here in the first place? (This is a very important question in general: Why does the particular book choose to include this material? It is an especially good question for the Tanakh, which is so sparse in detail. Why something is included and something else left out is always an important question.)

It appears that the story of Hannah is not simply about a woman who wants to have a child. Actually, Hannah wants something else.

As I see it, what Hannah really wants is to change the world.

Her prayer is the clue. It is not a prayer for a baby; it is about something very different. Hannah's message is that God is the true King. God's will is that the powerful and the haughty should not oppress those who are impoverished and weak. People graced with power should not abuse it.[36]

Hannah prays for a kingdom on earth which reflects the heavenly kingdom. What Hannah is calling for is explicit in the reference to *malko*, to God's king. It is actually a request for kingship—one that reflects the true kingship of God.

This is why we read this on Rosh Hashanah. The basic theme of Rosh Hashanah is God's kingship. The *haftarah* reminds us that our job here on earth is to reflect the kingship of heaven on earth.

Hannah's prayer for God to give "strength to His king" is a direct rebuke to the present rulers who are not reflecting God's kingship. Who are these rulers in the beginning of the Book of Samuel? That would be Chofni and Pinchas, as the priests to God, who are (not coincidentally) described right after Hannah's prayer as Eli's worthless sons.

This is a particularly sharp description, given the fact that when Eli confronts Hannah and says to her, "You are drunk, leave the holy precincts." Hannah's response is:

---

35   I Samuel 2:5
36   This is also, of course, the basic message of the Bible. It is the story of the Exodus. God is particularly concerned about those who don't have power, the disenfranchised.

I Samuel 1

16 Count not your handmaid
for a **wicked woman**: for out
of the abundance of my
complaint and my vexation
have I spoken until now.

טז אַל-תִּתֵּן אֶת-אֲמָתְךָ לִפְנֵי
בַּת-בְּלִיָּעַל: כִּי-מֵרֹב
שִׂיחִי וְכַעְסִי דִּבַּרְתִּי עַד-הֵנָּה.

The English "wicked woman" in Hebrew is the same phrase, *bat beliya'al,* that is applied to Eli's sons. You can see that the text is almost saying to us, Hannah is not a *bat beliya'al,* but someone else *is.* Perhaps Eli should be looking a little closer to home.

I am suggesting that Hannah's request is not for herself.

Hannah walks into Shiloh and she sees something very wrong with the place. This is not the proper Temple. God's footstool here on earth does not reflect Hannah's values. There is a stink of corruption that pervades from the last days of the Book of Judges and infects the priests, too. She prays to God to remove this evil impediment and, in its stead, place a true king who reflects the true values of God.

As a woman, Hannah is powerless. Women have no power in the Book of Samuel or any other place in Tanakh either, I would add. But they see clearly.

(The book of Samuel actually introduces us to an interesting category, the so-called "wise woman," the *ishah chokhamah,* who appears three times in the book.[37] Hannah does not fit exactly into the category of the wise woman. What is common to all three stories is that in each, case the

---

37   The first of these wise women is, of course, Avigayil, *tovat sekhel* (I Samuel 25:3). She's described as a clever woman. Avigayil stops David from killing her husband Naval and the whole plantation. "Don't do it. It would be a mistake for you," she says. "It will ruin you." And David says, "Thank God that you came and stopped me, because I would have killed him. I would have massacred them all."

The second wise woman is the woman from Teko'ah that Yo'av sends to David to convince him to allow Absalom to return (II Samuel 14:2). She tells a story about a woman who has lost a child and the fellow who wants to kill the other child. It is an allegory for David, and she succeeds in getting David to say, "Let him return."

Then there is the woman in Avel Ma'akhah in the story of Sheva Ben Bikhri (II Samuel 20:16). When the city is surrounded by Yo'av and his army threatening to kill the whole town, because Sheva Ben Bikhri has run to the city, the woman stands by the city wall and says, "Will you destroy an entire city?" (II Samuel 20:19) "God forbid," says Yo'av, "just Sheva Ben Bikhri." She says, "Wait back there." And they throw Sheva's head over the wall to Yo'av.

woman wants to avert bloodshed. That is why I think Hannah is not a "wise woman" in the narrow sense. One gets the impression in reading Hannah's prayer, actually, that she would not mind seeing a little bloodshed.)

Hannah's language is very strong. She is not only interested in raising up the lowly, she wants the powerful destroyed. There is no question about it. She is very angry.

Clear Vision

Hannah's clarity of vision recalls the woman in Genesis who has a clear perception of how the blessing is supposed to proceed: Rebeccah.

Why does Rebeccah favor Jacob? Isaac clearly plans to bless Esau. Apologetics and creative exegesis notwithstanding, he is going to give Esau the one and only blessing. One can ask whether this insight stems from something intrinsic about women, or does their reduced status allow them to see more clearly? I don't personally believe that Rebeccah has this insight simply because she is a woman. I believe it's something else.

The Book of Samuel, certainly, is not about men versus women; it is about people who have power and people who don't. People who have power never understand anything because they are entrenched, busy figuring out how to retain their power.

In the Book of Samuel, women have no power; neither do prophets. They have no power, no armies. But they have vision; it is their lack of power that allows them to see clearly. And that is the story of Hannah.

Vision and Change

Hannah sees perfectly, like no one else can. Elkanah cannot see. Eli is quite blind about his own sons and about her. Only Hannah sees clearly, but she hasn't the power to change anything.

So Hannah's prayer is not for a child alone; it is for a champion: "Give me a child to send to the center of power[38] and I will change everything."

Because Hannah's prayer is not really about personal fulfillment, Elkanah's attempt to console her does not work:

I Samuel 1

8 And Elkanah her husband said to her: 'Hannah, why do you weep?

ח וַיֹּאמֶר לָהּ אֶלְקָנָה אִישָׁהּ
חַנָּה לָמֶה תִבְכִּי

---

38   When Samuel is sent to Shiloh he actually sleeps next to the Ark, "*Beheikhal Hashem*" (I Samuel 3:3).

And why do you not eat? And why is your heart grieved? Am not I better to you than ten sons?'

וְלָמֶה לֹא תֹאכְלִי וְלָמֶה יֵרַע לְבָבֵךְ: הֲלוֹא אָנֹכִי טוֹב לָךְ מֵעֲשָׂרָה בָּנִים?

The answer is no, he is not better. Actually, she does not answer him. She thinks to herself, "Yes, he does love me, he loves me so much, but my distress is not about anything personal; it is about business."

If it were a matter of someone to love her, she would not be giving away her child. Hannah wants someone to transform the tabernacle, to transform Jewish life. She seeks the destruction of a corrupt institution, and hopes to replace Shiloh with kingship. The book of Samuel begins with the priesthood being destroyed as a political force. From that point on, the priests have no political power.

The Book of Samuel offers two replacements for the priest. The first, Samuel himself, occupies one chapter. Samuel is the Prophet King. That is the Samuel of chapter seven. He actually leads, and he brings victory through religious reformation and prayer. Carrying on his mother's tradition, he is included in Psalms with the great men of prayer:

Psalm 99

6 Moses and Aaron among His priests, and Samuel among them that call upon His name, did call upon the LORD, and He answered them.

ו מֹשֶׁה וְאַהֲרֹן בְּכֹהֲנָיו וּשְׁמוּאֵל בְּקֹרְאֵי שְׁמוֹ: קֹרִאים אֶל-יְיָ וְהוּא יַעֲנֵם.

But Samuel can't work as a long-term replacement for the priest. When Samuel becomes old, the people approach him requesting a king.

Thus is instituted the second replacement for Shiloh, kingship, which Samuel begrudgingly establishes because God instructs him to do so. Monarchy, the form of leadership which persists for the rest of Tanakh, has positive and negative aspects, but the leader arises from and represents the people. The king is the exact opposite of the *nazir*, who functions outside the community. The king is chosen, says the Torah, from "amongst his brothers."[39]

In the Samson story, God proactively chooses someone from outside the fold to fight God's battles. There is no one else. Samson is responsible to God alone. He is not advocating for the strengthening of the Jewish community in any way.

---

39   Deuteronomy 17:15

There is never a suggestion that Samson is a long term answer to anything. He actually dies in the process of killing the enemy. A *nazir*, by definition, has no continuity. Whether Samuel is technically a *nazir* or not is not the point. Samuel has no direct continuity—his sons do not inherit his status—but he *is* instrumental in passing on the leadership of the people and in creating institutions.

In the Book of Judges, the people are unable to resolve their own problems. And when they try, it's a disaster. It is anarchy, and it is an anarchy that persists into the first pages of the Book of Samuel. "There was no king in Israel; each man did what was right in his own heart" (Judges 21:25).

So, the book of Samuel begins with a woman's prayer for reinventing the central institution of the Jewish people. Hannah asks for the institution of kingship, which she sees as ultimately reflecting the will of God.

The story of Hannah is the story of the woman who has no child. It plays off the Genesis stories of barren women. It plays off the story of Mr. and Mrs. Manoach, who see no problem and no solution. In contrast, Hannah sees what must be done and works toward effective change.

By once again turning to God for help, Hannah is answered with the birth of Samuel. Hannah has leveled her best shot at those in power, and her prayer is answered in the dawning of a new era in Jewish history.

YCT Tanakh Companion

Hannah, the Mother of Prayer
I Samuel 1:1-2:10

Rabbi Dr. Yehuda Felix

Why do we read the story of Hannah[1] on Rosh Hashanah? The standard explanation is that Hannah's prayer for a child echoes a motif from the day's Torah portion, which tells how Sarah was granted a child at age 90.

This explanation falls short, however. Sarah is mentioned in the Rosh Hashanah Torah reading only as an adjunct to the story of the binding of Isaac, the *Akeidah*, which is an essential theme of Rosh Hashanah. The blowing of the shofar, the ram's horn, recalls the ram that was offered by Abraham in Isaac's stead. Reference to the *Akeidah* recurs throughout the holiday liturgy. So why should the *haftarah* reading from the prophets be linked to Sarah's story, which is ancillary to that of Isaac?

Actually, the story of Hannah is, on its own merit, profoundly linked to the themes of Divine majesty and human prayer which underlie the Jewish New Year.

Let us turn to the book in which the prayer appears, the Book of Samuel.

Era of Samuel as a Turning Point

The material covered in Samuel could have been included in either the Book of Judges (Eli and Samuel are both judges) or the Book of Kings (Saul and David are discussed at length). Why then do we have a unique book for Samuel?

It may help to recall that the Book of Judges concludes with two terrible stories depicting the degradation of Israelite society.

One tale tells of the idol of Micah,[2] and the other about the concubine of Give'ah.[3] These stories combine bloodshed and idolatry. The underlying

1   I Samuel 1:1-2:10
2   Judges 17-18
3   Judges 19-21

message of the book of Judges is its picture of complete anarchy: "In those days, there was no king in Israel, and each man did what was good in his eyes."[4]

According to the commentary of Abarbanel, Samuel may, in fact, not chronologically belong at the end of this dark period. He states that the two terrible stories could have taken place any time at all during the period of Judges. Nevertheless, the very fact that it is placed after Judges in the canon encourages a comparison between the time of the Judges, the morally lowest period in the history of Israel, and the more elevated era of the first Prophets, which Abarbanel considers the highest attained by Israel. Samuel, David, and Saul bring Israel to the highest levels she ever enjoys as a nation – spiritually and materially.[5]

Samuel's uniqueness is mentioned even in Psalms. "Moses and Aaron were among His priests, and Samuel was among those who called upon His name; they called upon the Lord, and He answered them."[6] Here, Samuel is likened to Moses and Aaron. It is as if the Psalmist has put them on a scale – on one side Samuel, on the other side Moses and Aaron.

Moses was of course unique,[7] but regarding the quality of calling the name of God – a special kind of prophecy – Samuel is on the same level as Moses and Aaron.

The *haftarah* reading for Rosh Hashanah constitutes the introduction to Samuel the book as well as to Samuel the prophet. It encompasses the entire first chapter and the first ten verses from the second chapter. (This is according to the standard chapter divisions, which are of Christian origin. In the traditional Jewish division, our present selection comprises the complete initial portion).

This excerpt introduces Samuel. We might assume that Samuel's rise is due to the fact that Israel has hit bottom and needs leadership. But that is is not the whole story.

To understand Samuel and his time, we need to understand his forebears – remembering that the Talmud says that every human being is brought forth by the efforts of three partners: his father, his mother and the Blessed Holy One.[8] Each one contributes to the new creature.

---

4   Judges 21:25
5   This point can be debated, with some suggesting that Solomon's era, when the Temple was built and the largest empire maintained, was the peak.
6   Psalms 99:6
7   "And there has not arisen a prophet since in Israel like unto Moses, whom the LORD knew face to face" (Deuteronomy 34:10)
8   Nidah 31a

Elkanah: Father of Education

Samuel's father is Elkanah, a name which translates to "God acquired." Does it mean that he acquired God? Or that God acquired him? Really, it can be understood both ways. God and Elkanah acquired each other.

What is Elkanah's nature? What makes him unique? The consensus from Rabbinic sources is that the answer lies in the realm of education, in *chinukh*.

Look at the first verse:

I Samuel 1

1 And there was a certain man of Ramatayim-tzophim, of the hill-country of Ephraim, and his name was Elkanah, the son of Jeroham, the son of Elihu, the son of Tohu, the son of Zuph, an Ephrathite.

א וַיְהִי אִישׁ אֶחָד מִן־הָרָמָתַיִם צוֹפִים־מֵהַר אֶפְרָיִם: וּשְׁמוֹ אֶלְקָנָה בֶּן־יְרֹחָם בֶּן־אֱלִיהוּא בֶּן־תֹּחוּ בֶן־צוּף־אֶפְרָתִי.

Each word indicates something special about Elkanah.

We start with what we have translated as "And," which in Hebrew is the conjunctive letter *vav* (ו), the *vav ha-chibur*. Why begin a book with the conjunction "and"? This beginning highlights the connection (and the contrast) between Judges and Samuel.

That first word – *va-yehi* in Hebrew, translated "and there was" – carries a message whenever it appears, according to the Talmud. It denotes an era that is either very sad or very happy.[9]

It makes sense. *Va-yehi*, "was," is a form of the general word for existence. And the reality of our existence is always either happiness or trouble. Usually, they are mixed together.[10] That is life. Here, at the beginning of Samuel, *va-yehi* comes to indicate a time of happiness, in contrast with the anarchy of Judges.

The second word in Hebrew is "*ish*," meaning "man." Here's a general rule for understanding Tanakh: If the "man" referred to is not directly described as evil,[11] then the word "*ish*" always denotes a positive personality.

---

9   Megillah 10b

10   There is the idea of "rejoice in fear," *gilu biriada,* Psalms 2:11. Some have suggested the corollary, that when you are afraid, you should "fear in joy," *tiradu be-gilah*. Similarly, at a wedding we always remember sadness, the destruction of Jerusalem, when we break the wedding glass.

11   e.g. Esther 7:6

The words "*ish*" and its plural, "*anashim*," are even sometimes interpreted as "angels."

The third word, "*echad*," literally means "one" (thus the translation here as a "certain" man), but it often means unique, or special. There is a famous example in Genesis, when Abraham and Sarah go to the land of the Philistines. The Philistine king, Avimelekh, says "One of the people (*achad ha'am*) might have lain with your wife."[12] As Rashi explains in his commentary, *echad* here is not "one." It does not mean "one from among the people." It connotes the most unique one of the people – *me-yuchad she-be'am* – the king is speaking about himself!

The next two words seemingly denote a place: "*Ramatayim-Tzofim*." But as the Midrash notes, the literal meaning of *ramatayim*, "the high places," can apply to people as well. In other words, Elkanah comes from elevated stock.

The word *tzofim* denotes a real place in Jerusalem, Mt. Scopus, from where you can see the Temple Mount. The Hebrew word *tzofeh* relates to vision, *scopus* in Latin. The word can also be used as a metaphor for seers, or prophets.

So Samuel's father Elkanah came from a very special family. The text goes on to list the names of Elkanah's ancestors, culminating with his great-great-grandfather. Another general principle in studying Tanakh is that if a righteous person's ancestors are mentioned, we can assume that they were also righteous. (Conversely, if one of the mentioned ancestors was evil, and the text traces his lineage, then the descendants are to be considered evil as well.)

From here we see that Elkanah was from a righteous family.

What about their geographical origins? Is there any significance to Elkanah being described as hailing from "the hill-country of Ephraim," in addition to being tagged "an Ephraimite?" Most of the classic commentaries say the repetition of Ephraim is meant to teach something about Samuel besides his geographical origins. There is a deeper meaning to be gleaned.

Abarbanel explains that "*Ephrati*" means important.[13]

In short, every word in this first verse indicates that Elkanah is someone very important.

---

12   Genesis 26:10. "And Avimelekh said, What have you done to us? One of the people might easily have lain with your wife, and you would have brought guilt upon us."

13   Compare 1 Kings 11:26 וְיָרָבְעָם בֶּן-נְבָט אֶפְרָתִי "And Jeroboam the son of Nebat, an Ephraimite," and I Samuel 17:12 וְדָוִד בֶּן-אִישׁ אֶפְרָתִי "David was the son of that Ephrathite."

Why is Elkanah so important? My argument is that Samuel's father is a pioneer of moral education.

The evidence is in two details in this first chapter. (Small details are very important in education.) One concerns pilgrimage:

I Samuel 1

3 And this man went up out of his city from year to year to worship and to sacrifice unto the LORD of hosts in Shiloh. And the two sons of Eli, Chofni and Pinchas, were priests there to the LORD.	ג וְעָלָה הָאִישׁ הַהוּא מֵעִירוֹ מִיָּמִים יָמִימָה לְהִשְׁתַּחֲוֹת וְלִזְבֹּחַ לַיי צְבָאוֹת בְּשִׁלֹה: וְשָׁם שְׁנֵי בְנֵי־ עֵלִי חָפְנִי וּפִנְחָסכֹּהֲנִים לַיי.

What are Eli's sons doing here, in the story of Elkanah and Hannah?

There is an argument among the Sages about how many times a Jew must go to worship at the Temple. One tradition held that one should visit three times a year, as written in the Torah:[14] The other view was that the visit was required only once a year.

Elkanah probably went three times a year. He seems to have made a decision *not* to take his family and his small children to Shiloh for every pilgrimage. In Shiloh, the sons of Eli, the main priests, set a negative example and Elkanah didn't want his children to be influenced by bad role models. On the other hand, he brought his family along at least once a year, hoping that the atmosphere in Shiloh would still give them a very good experience.

Facing the dilemma of whether or not to take his family to Shiloh, Elkanah decided that once a year was appropriate, but three times was excessive. Elkanah concerned himself with these small details. All of us make these kinds of decisions. Where should we send our children to school? Which pre-school? Which university?

We call Elkanah the father of Jewish education not just because he cares about his own family's religious instruction, but because he considers the broader community. Our Sages understood the phrase "year by year," in describing Elkanah's trip to Shiloh, to mean that each year he took another route. He doesn't repeat his path. Why? His aim is to reach as many people as possible, to bring different people to Shiloh to participate in, and be influenced by, the holy worship.

---

14   Exodus 23:17. "Three times in the year all your males shall appear before the Lord your God."

This second important detail pertains to Samuel, who later goes "around"[15] among the people before returning to Ramah, someplace near Jerusalem.

I Samuel 7

15 And Samuel judged Israel all the days of his life.

16 And he went from year to year around to Beth-el, and Gilgal, and Mizpah; and he judged Israel in all those places.

17 And his return was to Ramah, for there was his house; and there he judged Israel; and he built there an altar to the LORD.

טו וַיִּשְׁפֹּט שְׁמוּאֵל אֶת-
יִשְׂרָאֵל כֹּל יְמֵי חַיָּיו.

טז וְהָלַךְ מִדֵּי שָׁנָה בְּשָׁנָה וְסָבַב בֵּית-
אֵל וְהַגִּלְגָּל וְהַמִּצְפָּה: וְשָׁפַט אֶת-
יִשְׂרָאֵל–אֵת כָּל-הַמְּקוֹמוֹת הָאֵלֶּה.

יז וּתְשֻׁבָתוֹ הָרָמָתָה כִּי-שָׁם
בֵּיתוֹ וְשָׁם שָׁפָט אֶת-יִשְׂרָאֵל:
וַיִּבֶן-שָׁם מִזְבֵּחַ לַיי.

Samuel learned this behavior from the dedication of his father El-kanah.

This is a necessary attribute of educators: teachers must be prepared to meet students halfway – where they are – without waiting to be approached by them. An educator, like a judge, has a responsibility to go amongst the people and mix with them.

I remember the best teacher at my elementary school went between the desks and looked at what we were doing. Today, it is much more sophisticated. Now we look into the special needs of each child. Every child is different. And every person is different. A good leader – and an educator is a spiritual leader – must mingle among the people that are his students.

That describes not only Elkanah, but Samuel too, who learned this from his father.

Unfortunately, the lesson was not passed on to Samuel's children:

I Samuel 8

1 And it came to pass, when Samuel was old, that he made his sons judges over Israel.

א וַיְהִי כַּאֲשֶׁר זָקֵן שְׁמוּאֵל: וַיָּשֶׂם
אֶת-בָּנָיו שֹׁפְטִים לְיִשְׂרָאֵל.

---

15   I Samuel 7:16

2 Now the name of his first-born was Joel; and the name of his second, Abijah; they were judges in Beer-sheba.

3 And his sons walked not in his ways, but turned aside after lucre, and took bribes, and perverted justice.

ב וַיְהִי שֶׁם-בְּנוֹ הַבְּכוֹר יוֹאֵל וְשֵׁם מִשְׁנֵהוּ אֲבִיָּה: שֹׁפְטִים בִּבְאֵר שָׁבַע.

ג וְלֹא-הָלְכוּ בָנָיו בִּדְרָכָו וַיִּטּוּ אַחֲרֵי הַבָּצַע: וַיִּקְחוּ-שֹׁחַד-וַיַּטּוּ מִשְׁפָּט.

In a passage defending the questionable behavior of various Biblical characters, the Talmud says, "Whoever says that the sons of Samuel sinned, he is mistaken."[16] The Talmud explains that although Samuel's sons did not follow in his ways, we should not assume that they sinned.

So why, according to this apologetic reading[17], are Samuel's sons rebuked? It is because they did not follow in the path of their grandfather, Elkanah, and their father, Samuel, who walked the roads of the countryside, traveling from place to place to bring people to Shiloh. But the grandsons of Elkanah, the sons of Samuel, did not travel the same road. (The Talmud suggests that they found it more profitable to set up shop in one place and force people to come to them. Additionally, because they viewed their leadership position as an opportunity to profit from real estate, they are accused by the text of chasing lucre and taking bribes.)

But as we heard, Samuel went about the paths and judged the people.[18] As an educator, Elkanah successfully taught Samuel to follow in his footsteps.

Hannah: Mother of Prayer

If Elkanah is the father of teaching Torah, Hannah is the "mother of prayer." From Hannah, says the Talmud, we learn how to pray.[19]

"Prayer" for the Talmud is specifically the standing, silent devotion, the eighteen benedictions of the *Shemoneh Esrei*. The rules of how we comport ourselves during this prayer – standing with legs together, being silent, but with moving lips – all this is learned from Hannah's behavior.

---

16 Shabbat 55b

17 This is the same passage which acquits numerous Biblical characters, among them Reuben and David, of their crimes.

18 I Samuel 7:16

19 Berachot, 31a

But I would like to emphasize that when we call Hannah the mother of prayer, it is not simply because she showed us the laws of prayer; rather, she illustrates its importance, modeling what prayer can accomplish.

Her prayer begins:

I Samuel 2

1 And Hannah prayed, and said: my heart exults in the LORD, my horn is exalted in the LORD; my mouth is enlarged over my enemies; because I rejoice in Your salvation.

א וַתִּתְפַּלֵּל חַנָּה וַתֹּאמַר עָלַץ לִבִּי
בַּיי רָמָה קַרְנִי בַּיי: רָחַב פִּי
עַל-אוֹיְבַי כִּי שָׂמַחְתִּי בִּישׁוּעָתֶךָ.

Her prayer is a beautiful song in ten verses.

Hannah as Prophetess

Hannah is numbered among the forty-eight prophets enumerated by our tradition.[20] But what is her prophecy? How can she be a prophetess without a prophecy!?[21]

Maimonides defines prophecy as "knowledge that reaches from God to man."[22] It is illumination which reaches the prophet directly. The Targum Yonatan and the Vilna Gaon both claim that the ten verses of Hannah's prayer *are* her prophecy. These commentaries teach that we should not view these verses as prayer at all, but rather as a prophecy that pertains for all time. They understood these verses as a divine message covering all of history from beginning to end. They both agree that each verse, each word, has relevance until the days of Messiah.[23]

But if Hannah's words are prophecy, why does the verse[24] say, "and Hannah **prayed**?"

---

20   Megillah 14a

21   About Sarah, Avraham's wife, it says: *Sarah, kol asher tomar elekha sh-emah bekola.* (Whatever Sarah says, you must listen to her voice.) And our Sages of blessed memory say: *ruach HaKodesh yesh ba-hen,* "There is the holy spirit in them" (the female prophets).

22   *"Madah ha-magi'ah me-Hashem el ha-'adam,"* Mishneh Torah *hilchot teshuvah* 3:8, frequently cited by R. Zvi Yehuda Kook in class.

23   *Meshikho* ("his anointed one") refers not only to the anointed kings in the book, Saul and David, but it is also a prophecy about the Messiah Ben David in the last days. Whether the prophecy starts with Adam or Abraham is a point of disagreement for these two interpreters.

24   I Samuel 2:1

Another way of understanding this is that she invented the power of prayer; she revealed to us the great strength and power of this practice. Using the language of Chasidic teachings, I would say that Hannah came to the world with a soul of prayer.

Prayer and prophecy are generally understood to be opposites. We offer prayer to God, and God sends prophecy to us. But Hannah had the unique ability to combine the two; whatever came from her soul was as prophecy. The author of this book called her prophecy "prayer" to tell us that Hannah is teaching us about the highest level of connection possible between God and human beings.

God's Role

Now we come to the the third partner, God. What is His task here? There is a very beautiful story in the midrash[25] which says that when Hannah was pregnant, "a heavenly voice exploded," *Bat kol haytah mefotzetzet*,[26] heralding Samuel's arrival. Every expectant mother of that generation was divinely inspired and said, "I am going to name my baby boy Samuel."

What are the Rabbis teaching us in this midrash? The message is: the end of the evil time had arrived. In the words found in Job, "Darkness has an end."[27]

It was known that a savior was required because the religious, political and social degeneration from the time of the Judges could no longer continue. The people felt uplifted by a Godly promise, that there would be an end to the darkness.

So why does Samuel come to the world at this specific time?

Samuel's arrival reflects the combination of three factors. He had a father who was a role model for education, a mother who was the soul of prayer, and God had finally decided that "the time had arrived for the darkness to end."

Thus Samuel.

Hannah and Rosh Hashanah

Now we can return to our original question: Why do we read this selection on the first day of Rosh Hashanah?

---

25   Midrash Shmuel (Buber) 3:4
26   According to Maimonides, *bat kol* (a voice from Heaven) may be similar to divine inspiration (*Ruach Ha-Kodesh*); it is the lowest form of prophecy – nevertheless, something gets heard in the world.
27   Job 28:3

What is the concept of Rosh Hashanah? Prayer. On Rosh Hashanah the additional prayer (*musaf*) is the largest one with the most impact. It includes many additions, including the repeated blowing of the shofar. We want God to hear the sound of our pleadings.

Hannah is the one who had the ability to communicate with God with the full range of giving and receiving. Prayer and prophecy.

Rosh Hashanah is rooted in prayer. The sound of the shofar itself is kind of prayer, a kind of crying. One of the themes of Hannah's prayer is kingship, and it is on this day that we crown God as our king.

On this day of prayer, right before *musaf*, the biggest prayer, we read the *haftarah*, to experience the epitome of prayer – a flow back and forth between us and God – the prayer of Hannah.

Anarchy and Monarchy Part One:
Samuel the Prophet King
I Samuel 8-13

based on a lecture by **Rabbi David Silber**

Most of the Book of Samuel concerns the establishment of the monarchy of Israel – the careers, both ultimately tragic, of Saul and David. There is a brief, happy interlude, however, in chapter 7, when Samuel holds sway as the Prophet King, leading the people through war and peace with God as his guide.

Then Samuel grows old and the people begin to wonder what will happen next. To reassure them, Samuel offers his sons as judges in his stead.

I Samuel 8	
1 And it came to pass, when Samuel was old, that he made his sons judges over Israel.	א וַיְהִי כַּאֲשֶׁר זָקֵן שְׁמוּאֵל: וַיָּשֶׂם אֶת-בָּנָיו שֹׁפְטִים לְיִשְׂרָאֵל.
2 Now the name of his first-born was Joel; and the name of his second, Aviyah; they were judges in Beer-sheba.	ב וַיְהִי שֶׁם-בְּנוֹ הַבְּכוֹר יוֹאֵל וְשֵׁם מִשְׁנֵהוּ אֲבִיָּה: שֹׁפְטִים בִּבְאֵר שָׁבַע.
3 And his sons walked not in his ways, but turned aside after lucre, and took bribes, and perverted justice.	ג וְלֹא-הָלְכוּ בָנָיו בִּדְרָכָו וַיִּטּוּ אַחֲרֵי הַבָּצַע: וַיִּקְחוּ-שֹׁחַד וַיַּטּוּ מִשְׁפָּט.

Unfortunately, Samuel's sons are corrupt. They take bribes. They pervert justice. They are not worthy successors.

I Samuel 8	
4 Then all the elders of Israel gathered themselves together, and came to Samuel unto Ramah.	ד וַיִּתְקַבְּצוּ כֹּל זִקְנֵי יִשְׂרָאֵל: וַיָּבֹאוּ אֶל-שְׁמוּאֵל הָרָמָתָה.

5 And they said to him: 'Behold, you are old, and your sons walk not in your ways; now make us a king to judge us like all the nations.'	ה וַיֹּאמְרוּ אֵלָיו הִנֵּה אַתָּה זָקַנְתָּ וּבָנֶיךָ לֹא הָלְכוּ בִּדְרָכֶיךָ: עַתָּה שִׂימָה-לָּנוּ מֶלֶךְ לְשָׁפְטֵנוּ כְּכָל-הַגּוֹיִם.

The specific spur for the people to request a king is Samuel's advanced age. The people are happy with Samuel; as long as he can lead them, they don't want a king. The people are telling Samuel: We like you very much, but we don't want your sons' leadership.[1] They ask instead for the institution of a monarchy.

But why? What guarantee is there that the son of the king will behave any better than the sons of Samuel? If Samuel's sons are problematic, why would the solution be a dynastic monarchy, rather than the search for a new prophetic leader?

Why should the corrupt descendants of David ultimately prove more satisfying to the people than the corrupt descendants of Samuel?

A king, however, is not a prophet, nor even his generation's religious exemplar. He is simply the son of the previous king. There will be good kings and bad kings. There will be many, many bad kings. But good or bad, a king is a king – he performs the function.

We must assume then, that the people were not looking to change the nature of *succession*, but rather, the nature of *leadership*. That is what angers Samuel. Until now, Israel, unlike other nations, has followed the paradigm of leadership established by Moses and continuing through Samuel, in which the most authentically religious person of each generation is chosen to serve as leader. The system produces great leaders, but at a heavy cost: A new talent search must be conducted in every generation, as it is virtually guaranteed that the son of the present ruler will not qualify. The death of the leader will always bring great instability. In asking for a king to rule them, the people are saying they want to trade authentic religious leadership for political stability.

Filling the Shoes

It is because of the importance of succession that clothing represents both kingship and the priesthood in the Book Samuel and beyond. The actual person filling the role and wearing the garments (royal or priestly)

---

1   Samuel, like the other fathers in the book of Samuel (Eli, David, Saul), is unaware that anything is wrong with his children (fathers' blindness to their children is a basic theme of the Book of Samuel).

is secondary. It is the *role* of king, or priest, symbolized by the clothes, that is important. The priesthood, in this way, mirrors the monarchy.

And, likewise, there are many bad priests.

In asking for kingship – a system of automatic transfer of power – the people are asking for somebody to wear the clothing and fill the job, even if that means that the one who is performing the role may not always be the ideal person.

Samuel is not convinced:

I Samuel 8

6 But the thing was evil in Samuel's eyes, when they said: 'Give us a king to judge us.' And Samuel prayed unto the LORD.

7 And the LORD said to Samuel: 'Hearken to the voice of the people in all that they say to you; for they have not rejected you, but they have rejected Me, that I should not be king over them.

8 According to all the works which they have done since the day that I brought them up out of Egypt even to this day, in that they have forsaken Me, and served other gods, so they also do to you.

9 Now **hearken to their voice**; but you shall earnestly forewarn them, and declare to them the manner of the king that shall reign over them.'

ו וַיֵּרַע הַדָּבָר בְּעֵינֵי שְׁמוּאֵל כַּאֲשֶׁר אָמְרוּ תְּנָה-לָּנוּ מֶלֶךְ לְשָׁפְטֵנוּ: וַיִּתְפַּלֵּל שְׁמוּאֵל אֶל יי.

ז וַיֹּאמֶר יי אֶל-שְׁמוּאֵל שְׁמַע בְּקוֹל הָעָם לְכֹל אֲשֶׁר-יֹאמְרוּ אֵלֶיךָ: כִּי לֹא אֹתְךָ מָאָסוּ כִּי-אֹתִי מָאֲסוּ מִמְּלֹךְ עֲלֵיהֶם.

ח כְּכָל-הַמַּעֲשִׂים אֲשֶׁר-עָשׂוּ מִיּוֹם הַעֲלֹתִי אוֹתָם מִמִּצְרַיִם וְעַד-הַיּוֹם הַזֶּה וַיַּעַזְבֻנִי וַיַּעַבְדוּ אֱלֹהִים אֲחֵרִים: כֵּן הֵמָּה עֹשִׂים גַּם-לָךְ.

ט וְעַתָּה שְׁמַע בְּקוֹלָם: אַךְ כִּי-הָעֵד תָּעִיד בָּהֶם וְהִגַּדְתָּ לָהֶם מִשְׁפַּט הַמֶּלֶךְ אֲשֶׁר יִמְלֹךְ עֲלֵיהֶם.

The people say to Samuel, "Give us a king, like all the nations." Samuel is very upset about this.

He turns to God and God's answer is: Give them what they want.

That's the first word and the last word of God. In the middle, God says to Samuel: I know how you feel – they have been doing this to Me for hundreds of years. But the bottom line remains, "hearken to their voice."

God gives permission for a king, but what is God's real feeling about kingship? It becomes very important for each king himself to figure this out; otherwise, his reign will be disastrous.

Job Requirements for Israelite Kings

If you look in the Torah for God's position on the role of kings, you won't find any discussion of what a king actually does. You find only a list of limitations placed upon the powers of the rulers of Israel:

Deuteronomy 17

14 When you come to the land which the LORD your God gives you, and shall possess it, and shall dwell there; and shall say: 'I will set a king over me, **like all the nations** that are round about me';

15 you shall set him king over you, whom the LORD your God shall choose; **one from among your brothers** shall you set king over you; you may not put a foreigner over you, who is not your brother.

16 Only he shall not multiply horses to himself, nor cause the people to return to Egypt, to the end that he should multiply horses; as the LORD has said to you: 'You shall henceforth return no more that way.'

17 Neither shall he multiply wives to himself, that his heart turn not away; neither shall he greatly multiply to himself silver and gold.

18 And it shall be, when he sits upon the throne of his kingdom, that he shall write himself a copy of this law in a book, out of that which is before the priests the Levites.

19 And it shall be with him, and he shall read therein all the days of his life; that he may learn to fear the LORD his God, to

יד כִּי-תָבֹא אֶל-הָאָרֶץ אֲשֶׁר יְיָ אֱלֹהֶיךָ נֹתֵן לָךְ וִירִשְׁתָּהּ וְיָשַׁבְתָּה בָּהּ: וְאָמַרְתָּ אָשִׂימָה עָלַי מֶלֶךְ כְּכָל-הַגּוֹיִם אֲשֶׁר סְבִיבֹתָי.

טו שׂוֹם תָּשִׂים עָלֶיךָ מֶלֶךְ אֲשֶׁר יִבְחַר יְיָ אֱלֹהֶיךָ בּוֹ: מִקֶּרֶב אַחֶיךָ תָּשִׂים עָלֶיךָ מֶלֶךְ לֹא תוּכַל לָתֵת עָלֶיךָ אִישׁ נָכְרִי אֲשֶׁר לֹא-אָחִיךָ הוּא.

טז רַק לֹא-יַרְבֶּה-לּוֹ סוּסִים וְלֹא-יָשִׁיב אֶת-הָעָם מִצְרַיְמָה לְמַעַן הַרְבּוֹת סוּס: וַיְיָ אָמַר לָכֶם לֹא תֹסִפוּן לָשׁוּב בַּדֶּרֶךְ הַזֶּה עוֹד.

יז וְלֹא יַרְבֶּה-לּוֹ נָשִׁים וְלֹא יָסוּר לְבָבוֹ: וְכֶסֶף וְזָהָב לֹא יַרְבֶּה-לּוֹ מְאֹד.

יח וְהָיָה כְשִׁבְתּוֹ עַל כִּסֵּא מַמְלַכְתּוֹ: וְכָתַב לוֹ אֶת-מִשְׁנֵה הַתּוֹרָה הַזֹּאת עַל-סֵפֶר מִלִּפְנֵי הַכֹּהֲנִים הַלְוִיִּם.

יט וְהָיְתָה עִמּוֹ וְקָרָא בוֹ כָּל-יְמֵי חַיָּיו: לְמַעַן יִלְמַד לְיִרְאָה אֶת-יְיָ אֱלֹהָיו

keep all the words of this law
and these statutes, to do them;

לִשְׁמֹר אֶת-כָּל-דִּבְרֵי הַתּוֹרָה הַזֹּאת
וְאֶת-הַחֻקִּים הָאֵלֶּה לַעֲשֹׂתָם.

20 that his heart be not lifted up
above his brothers, and that
he not turn aside from the
commandment, to the right
hand, or to the left; to the end
that he may prolong his days
in his kingdom, he and his
children, in the midst of Israel.

כ לְבִלְתִּי רוּם-לְבָבוֹ מֵאֶחָיו וּלְבִלְתִּי
סוּר מִן-הַמִּצְוָה יָמִין וּשְׂמֹאול:
לְמַעַן יַאֲרִיךְ יָמִים עַל-מַמְלַכְתּוֹ
הוּא וּבָנָיו בְּקֶרֶב יִשְׂרָאֵל.

The king should not acquire too much money, too many wives, nor too many horses. But the actual job requirements are never described in the Torah.

The Book of Samuel spells out two functions of the king: judging[2] the people in some capacity; and leading the army in battle.

Judging probably indicates a kind of leadership, not heading a court.[3] The judges in the Book of Judges are political and military leaders, not judicial figures. We never see Samson sitting in a court house.

The second task of kingship is fighting battles. So the king is a type of leader with both executive and martial obligations. That is what the people want.

The point is that the request for kingship is not a rejection of Samuel, but of the system he embodied. On the contrary, the people take the request to Samuel because they trust him as a ruler. They say: "We love you, but we want a different kind of institution and we want you to help create it."

Samuel might have given the people guidance for how to properly accomplish the institution of monarchy. Instead, he resists. It is God who says: "Do what they want."

God also says: "I commiserate with you, Samuel. You've been such a loyal servant. I know how you feel. They do this to Me also." God sympathizes with Samuel, but the bottom line is that He grants their request.

Samuel thinks the very act of asking for a king is sinful. As far as Samuel is concerned, Saul's requested kingship (the very name "Saul" means

---

2   David hears two cases during the course of the book: one from Nathan the Prophet (II Samuel 12:1-15); and one from the woman from Teko'ah (II Samuel 14:1-24). He also judges in the matter of the Give'onites (II Samuel 21:1-9).

3   My own view is that kingship does entail judging in some way in the Book of Kings, but others disagree with that.

"the one who was requested") was a noble experiment that failed. Samuel is blindsided when God responds to Saul's failure by asking Samuel to anoint another king:

I Samuel 16

1 And the LORD said to Samuel: 'How long will you mourn for Saul, seeing I have rejected him from being king over Israel? fill your horn with oil, and go, I will send you to Jesse of Bethlehem; for I have seen among his sons a king for Me.'

א וַיֹּאמֶר יְיָ אֶל-שְׁמוּאֵל עַד-מָתַי
אַתָּה מִתְאַבֵּל אֶל-שָׁאוּל וַאֲנִי
מְאַסְתִּיו מִמְּלֹךְ עַל-יִשְׂרָאֵל:
מַלֵּא קַרְנְךָ שֶׁמֶן וְלֵךְ אֶשְׁלָחֲךָ
אֶל-יִשַׁי בֵּית-הַלַּחְמִי כִּי-
רָאִיתִי בְּבָנָיו לִי מֶלֶךְ.

The Divine Perspective

And, in fact, God makes a point of actively choosing David "from amongst his brothers." From that standpoint, it seems that kingship is not something that is wrested from God. God is doing more than grudgingly going along with the desires of a flawed people. There's something about human kingship that God actually likes.

This question, by the way, transcends the Book of Samuel and is a question that becomes a running theme for Tanakh as a whole: What is the Bible's attitude, or perhaps attitudes, towards kingship? For example, at the end of the Book of Judges, the leitmotif of the last five chapters is:[4]

Judges 21

25 In those days there was no king in Israel; every man did that which was right in his own eyes.

כה בַּיָּמִים הָהֵם אֵין מֶלֶךְ בְּיִשְׂרָאֵל:
אִישׁ הַיָּשָׁר בְּעֵינָיו יַעֲשֶׂה.

Minimally, this means that kingship is at least a necessary evil. Without kingship we witness anarchy. People run all over the place doing whatever they want. Tribes seize land that doesn't belong to them, individuals call themselves priests, and so on. Running an effective government, one which includes all the people and allows for tribes to peace-ly live together, requires kingship. Some people assume that Samuel's

---

Also: Judges 17:6; 18:1;19:1

personal view is also the view of the Book of Samuel. I argue that this is probably not the case.

By the same token, wanting a king "like all the nations" is inherently problematic. One of the main themes of the Bible is that Israel is not like the other nations, nor should they try to be. [5]

But there is another argument that characterizes kingship as a fundamentally positive thing. Kingship can be seen as a manifestation of the people's urge to assume responsibility for themselves upon entering the land of Israel. As Nahmanides points out, the *mitzvah* of living in the Land of Israel is not just about physical residence, but about establishing the necessary religious and social structures. These include courts, a special sacred place chosen by God, and a king.

As spelled out in Deuteronomy, the king is the last piece in the structure. The people get together and say: "We are responsible for ourselves, we are ready to be a nation with our own stable, transferable government." It is a good thing. The idea of taking responsibility for oneself is arguably the basic idea of the Torah. That is why the worst thing any king can possibly do is take the people down to Egypt. This would be a big step towards slavery and away from responsibility. Egypt and autonomy are polar opposites. Egypt represents living someone else's agenda. Ideally, kingship is about making our own choices.

Unfortunately, returning to Egypt is what our beloved Solomon seems to have done, metaphorically, in the Book of Kings.

The Book of Kings is written by someone sitting in exile and tracing causal events back in time; to Manasseh, to Ahab, to Jeroboam, back to the beginning of the Book of Kings. And what is at the beginning of the Book of Kings? In the first two chapters David chooses Solomon, and Solomon eliminates his enemies. "And his kingdom was firmly established."[6] With Solomon's coronation, David's kingship is established as well. In the last verse of that chapter, the text tells us: "The kingdom was established in the hand of Solomon."[7] And in the very next verse:

---

5   Asking for a king "like all the nations" is certainly a troubling expression, but as we've seen, the concept of monarchy is introduced in the Torah. The people's petition to Samuel is not the first appearance of the idea of kingship in Tanakh. God says in the Torah (Deuteronomy 17:14) that one day the people will request a king.

6   1 Kings 2:12

7   1 Kings 2:46

1 Kings 3

1 And Solomon became allied
to Pharaoh king of Egypt by
marriage, and took Pharaoh's
daughter, and brought her
into the city of David, until he
had made an end of building
his own house, and the house
of the LORD, and the wall
of Jerusalem round about.

א וַיִּתְחַתֵּן שְׁלֹמֹה אֶת-פַּרְעֹה מֶלֶךְ
מִצְרָיִם: וַיִּקַּח אֶת-בַּת-פַּרְעֹה
וַיְבִיאֶהָ אֶל-עִיר דָּוִד עַד כַּלֹּתוֹ
לִבְנוֹת אֶת-בֵּיתוֹ וְאֶת-בֵּית יְיָ
וְאֶת-חוֹמַת יְרוּשָׁלַם סָבִיב.

When did things start going bad? It's a question you ask when it is clear that a relationship is over. In hindsight, the answer is clear: "The last year was hard. Also, the last five years were a problem. The truth of the matter is, the first year of marriage was very difficult. And to be honest, the wedding night was terrible."

That is the approach of the Book of Kings. The break-up between God and Israel, the Exile, says the Book of Kings, is not about Manasseh. It's not about Jeroboam. It's not about Ahab. The relationship had already soured – at least in hindsight – in that very first verse after the monarchy is established. Really, you can put the book down then, because the relationship is essentially over.

Egypt is the main problem, but Solomon manages to violate all of the other prohibitions outlined in Deuteronomy, too. He keeps too many wives and horses and he hoards too much cash. That, at any rate, is the perspective of the Book of Kings.

Rules of the King

What is Samuel's objection to kingship? He has two main objections. The lesser objection is mentioned first – in the form of Samuel's discourse to the people on *mishpat ha-melekh*, the rules of the king.

I Samuel 8

10 And Samuel told all the words
of the LORD to the people
that asked of him a king.

י וַיֹּאמֶר שְׁמוּאֵל אֵת כָּל-דִּבְרֵי יְיָ:
אֶל-הָעָם הַשֹּׁאֲלִים מֵאִתּוֹ מֶלֶךְ.

11 And he said: 'This will be the manner of the king that shall reign over you: he will **take** your sons, and appoint them to him, for his chariots, and to be his horsemen; and they shall run before his chariots.

יא וַיֹּאמֶר–זֶה יִהְיֶה מִשְׁפַּט הַמֶּלֶךְ אֲשֶׁר יִמְלֹךְ עֲלֵיכֶם: אֶת-בְּנֵיכֶם יִקָּח וְשָׂם לוֹ בְּמֶרְכַּבְתּוֹ וּבְפָרָשָׁיו וְרָצוּ לִפְנֵי מֶרְכַּבְתּוֹ.

12 And he will appoint them to him for captains of thousands, and captains of fifties; and to plow his ground, and to reap his harvest, and to make his instruments of war, and the instruments of his chariots.

יב וְלָשׂוּם לוֹ שָׂרֵי אֲלָפִים וְשָׂרֵי חֲמִשִּׁים: וְלַחֲרֹשׁ חֲרִישׁוֹ וְלִקְצֹר קְצִירוֹ וְלַעֲשׂוֹת כְּלֵי-מִלְחַמְתּוֹ וּכְלֵי רִכְבּוֹ.

13 And he will **take** your daughters to be perfumers, and to be cooks, and to be bakers.

יג וְאֶת-בְּנוֹתֵיכֶם יִקָּח: לְרַקָּחוֹת וּלְטַבָּחוֹת וּלְאֹפוֹת.

14 And he will **take** your fields, and your vineyards, and your oliveyards, even the best of them, and give them to his servants.

יד וְאֶת-שְׂדוֹתֵיכֶם וְאֶת-כַּרְמֵיכֶם וְזֵיתֵיכֶם הַטּוֹבִים יִקָּח: וְנָתַן לַעֲבָדָיו.

15 And he will **take the tenth** of your seed, and of your vineyards, and give to his officers, and to his servants.

טו וְזַרְעֵיכֶם וְכַרְמֵיכֶם יַעְשֹׂר: וְנָתַן לְסָרִיסָיו וְלַעֲבָדָיו.

16 And he will **take** your men-servants, and your maid-servants, and your goodliest young men, and your asses, and put them to his work.

טז וְאֶת-עַבְדֵיכֶם וְאֶת-שִׁפְחוֹתֵיכֶם וְאֶת-בַּחוּרֵיכֶם הַטּוֹבִים וְאֶת-חֲמוֹרֵיכֶם יִקָּח: וְעָשָׂה לִמְלַאכְתּוֹ.

17 He will **take the tenth** of your flocks; and you shall be his servants.

יז צֹאנְכֶם יַעְשֹׂר: וְאַתֶּם תִּהְיוּ-לוֹ לַעֲבָדִים.

18 And you shall cry out in that day because of your king whom you have chosen; and the LORD will not answer you in that day.'

יח וּזְעַקְתֶּם בַּיּוֹם הַהוּא מִלִּפְנֵי מַלְכְּכֶם אֲשֶׁר בְּחַרְתֶּם לָכֶם: וְלֹא-יַעֲנֶה יְיָ אֶתְכֶם בַּיּוֹם הַהוּא.

One word that dominates this passage is "take," *yikach* (יקח). The King, Samuel warns, will take everything. He'll take this, he'll take that. Samuel fears that the king will inevitably become corrupt. Samuel, of course, is sensitive to the potential for corruption of a king because he witnessed the terrible corruption of the priests of Shiloh. The verses about "taking" describe Shiloh too. The priests took inappropriately from the sacrifices; too much, and at the wrong time. Samuel's experience has taught him that people in power take.

But that is Samuel's secondary concern, although, chronologically, it comes first in the book. His main point is described in his valedictory address in chapter 12.

Samuel's Perspective: God in the Center

What was Samuel's speech?

I Samuel 12

1 And Samuel said to all Israel: 'Behold, I have hearkened to your voice in all that you said to me, and have made a king over you.

א וַיֹּאמֶר שְׁמוּאֵל אֶל-כָּל-יִשְׂרָאֵל הִנֵּה שָׁמַעְתִּי בְקֹלְכֶם לְכֹל אֲשֶׁר-אֲמַרְתֶּם לִי: וָאַמְלִיךְ עֲלֵיכֶם מֶלֶךְ.

2 And now, behold, the king walks before you; and I am old and grayheaded; and, behold, my sons are with you; and I have walked before you from my youth to this day.

ב וְעַתָּה הִנֵּה הַמֶּלֶךְ מִתְהַלֵּךְ לִפְנֵיכֶם וַאֲנִי זָקַנְתִּי וָשַׂבְתִּי וּבָנַי הִנָּם אִתְּכֶם: וַאֲנִי הִתְהַלַּכְתִּי לִפְנֵיכֶם מִנְּעֻרַי עַד-הַיּוֹם הַזֶּה.

3 Here I am; witness against me before the LORD, and before His anointed: whose ox have I taken? or whose ass have I taken? or whom have I defrauded? or whom have I oppressed? or of whose hand have I taken a ransom to blind mine eyes therewith? and I will restore it you.'

ג הִנְנִי עֲנוּ בִי נֶגֶד יְיָ וְנֶגֶד מְשִׁיחוֹ אֶת-שׁוֹר מִי לָקַחְתִּי וַחֲמוֹר מִי לָקַחְתִּי וְאֶת-מִי עָשַׁקְתִּי אֶת-מִי רַצּוֹתִי וּמִיַּד-מִי לָקַחְתִּי כֹפֶר וְאַעְלִים עֵינַי בּוֹ: וְאָשִׁיב לָכֶם.

4 And they said: 'You have not defrauded us, nor oppressed us, neither have you taken anything of any man's hand.'

ד וַיֹּאמְרוּ לֹא עֲשַׁקְתָּנוּ וְלֹא רַצּוֹתָנוּ: וְלֹא-לָקַחְתָּ מִיַּד-אִישׁ מְאוּמָה.

5 And he said to them: 'The LORD is witness against you, and His anointed is witness this day, that you have not found anything in my hand.' And they said: 'He is witness.'

ה וַיֹּאמֶר אֲלֵיהֶם עֵד יְיָ בָּכֶם וְעֵד מְשִׁיחוֹ הַיּוֹם הַזֶּה כִּי לֹא מְצָאתֶם בְּיָדִי מְאוּמָה: וַיֹּאמֶר עֵד.

6 And Samuel said to the people: 'It is the LORD that made Moses and Aaron, and that brought your fathers up out of the land of Egypt.

7 Now therefore stand still, that I may plead with you before the LORD concerning all the righteous acts of the LORD, which He did to you and to your fathers.

8 When Jacob came into Egypt, then your fathers cried unto the LORD, and the LORD sent Moses and Aaron, who brought forth your fathers out of Egypt, and they were made to dwell in this place.

9 But they forgot the LORD their God, and He gave them over into the hand of Sisera, captain of the host of Chatzor, and into the hand of the Philistines, and into the hand of the king of Mo'av, and they fought against them

10 And they cried unto the LORD, and said: We have sinned, because we have forsaken the LORD, and have served the Ba'alim and the Ashtaroth; but now deliver us out of the hand of our enemies, and we will serve You.

11 And the LORD sent Jerubba'al, and Bedan, and Jephthah, and Samuel, and delivered you out of the hand of your enemies on every side, and you dwelt in safety.

ו וַיֹּאמֶר שְׁמוּאֵל אֶל־הָעָם: יְיָ אֲשֶׁר עָשָׂה אֶת־מֹשֶׁה וְאֶת־אַהֲרֹן וַאֲשֶׁר הֶעֱלָה אֶת־אֲבֹתֵיכֶם מֵאֶרֶץ מִצְרָיִם.

ז וְעַתָּה הִתְיַצְּבוּ וְאִשָּׁפְטָה אִתְּכֶם–לִפְנֵי יְיָ: אֵת כָּל־צִדְקוֹת יְיָ אֲשֶׁר־עָשָׂה אִתְּכֶם וְאֶת־אֲבוֹתֵיכֶם.

ח כַּאֲשֶׁר־בָּא יַעֲקֹב מִצְרָיִם: וַיִּזְעֲקוּ אֲבוֹתֵיכֶם אֶל־יְיָ וַיִּשְׁלַח יְיָ אֶת־מֹשֶׁה וְאֶת־אַהֲרֹן וַיּוֹצִיאוּ אֶת־אֲבֹתֵיכֶם מִמִּצְרַיִם וַיֹּשִׁבוּם בַּמָּקוֹם הַזֶּה.

ט וַיִּשְׁכְּחוּ אֶת־יְיָ אֱלֹהֵיהֶם: וַיִּמְכֹּר אֹתָם בְּיַד סִיסְרָא שַׂר־צְבָא חָצוֹר וּבְיַד־פְּלִשְׁתִּים וּבְיַד מֶלֶךְ מוֹאָב וַיִּלָּחֲמוּ בָּם.

י וַיִּזְעֲקוּ אֶל־יְיָ וַיֹּאמֶר (וַיֹּאמְרוּ) חָטָאנוּ כִּי עָזַבְנוּ אֶת־יְיָ וַנַּעֲבֹד אֶת־הַבְּעָלִים וְאֶת־הָעַשְׁתָּרוֹת: וְעַתָּה הַצִּילֵנוּ מִיַּד אֹיְבֵינוּ וְנַעַבְדֶךָ.

יא וַיִּשְׁלַח יְיָ אֶת־יְרֻבַּעַל וְאֶת־בְּדָן וְאֶת־יִפְתָּח וְאֶת־שְׁמוּאֵל: וַיַּצֵּל אֶתְכֶם מִיַּד אֹיְבֵיכֶם מִסָּבִיב וַתֵּשְׁבוּ בֶּטַח.

12 And when you saw that Nachash the king of the children of Ammon came against you, you said to me: Nay, but a king shall reign over us; when the LORD your God was your king.

13 Now therefore behold the king whom you have chosen, and whom you have asked for; and, behold, the LORD has set a king over you.

14 If you will fear the LORD, and serve Him, and hearken to His voice, and not rebel against the commandment of the LORD, and both you and also the king that reigns over you be followers of the LORD your God–;

15 but if you will not hearken to the voice of the LORD, but rebel against the commandment of the LORD, then shall the hand of the LORD be against you, and against your fathers.

16 Now therefore stand still and see this great thing, which the LORD will do before your eyes.

17 Is it not wheat harvest to-day? I will call to the LORD, that He may send thunder and rain; and you shall know and see that your wickedness is great, which you have done in the sight of the LORD, in asking you a king.'

18 So Samuel called unto the LORD; and the LORD sent thunder and rain that day; and all the people greatly feared the LORD and Samuel.

יב וַתִּרְאוּ כִּי-נָחָשׁ מֶלֶךְ בְּנֵי-עַמּוֹן בָּא עֲלֵיכֶם וַתֹּאמְרוּ לִי לֹא כִּי-מֶלֶךְ יִמְלֹךְ עָלֵינוּ: וַיי אֱלֹהֵיכֶם מַלְכְּכֶם.

יג וְעַתָּה הִנֵּה הַמֶּלֶךְ אֲשֶׁר בְּחַרְתֶּם אֲשֶׁר שְׁאֶלְתֶּם: וְהִנֵּה נָתַן יי עֲלֵיכֶם מֶלֶךְ.

יד אִם-תִּירְאוּ אֶת-יי וַעֲבַדְתֶּם אֹתוֹ וּשְׁמַעְתֶּם בְּקוֹלוֹ וְלֹא תַמְרוּ אֶת-פִּי יי: וִהְיִתֶם גַּם-אַתֶּם וְגַם-הַמֶּלֶךְ אֲשֶׁר מָלַךְ עֲלֵיכֶם אַחַר יי אֱלֹהֵיכֶם.

טו וְאִם-לֹא תִשְׁמְעוּ בְּקוֹל יי וּמְרִיתֶם אֶת-פִּי יי: וְהָיְתָה יַד-יי בָּכֶם וּבַאֲבֹתֵיכֶם.

טז גַּם-עַתָּה הִתְיַצְּבוּ וּרְאוּ אֶת-הַדָּבָר הַגָּדוֹל הַזֶּה: אֲשֶׁר יי עֹשֶׂה לְעֵינֵיכֶם.

יז הֲלוֹא קְצִיר-חִטִּים הַיּוֹם-אֶקְרָא אֶל-יי וְיִתֵּן קֹלוֹת וּמָטָר: וּדְעוּ וּרְאוּ כִּי-רָעַתְכֶם רַבָּה אֲשֶׁר עֲשִׂיתֶם בְּעֵינֵי יי לִשְׁאוֹל לָכֶם מֶלֶךְ.

יח וַיִּקְרָא שְׁמוּאֵל אֶל-יי וַיִּתֵּן יי קֹלֹת וּמָטָר בַּיּוֹם הַהוּא: וַיִּירָא כָל-הָעָם מְאֹד אֶת-יי וְאֶת-שְׁמוּאֵל.

19 And all the people said to
Samuel: 'Pray for your servants
to the LORD your God,
that we die not; for we have
added unto all our sins this
evil, to ask for us a king.'

20 And Samuel said unto the
people: 'Fear not; you have
indeed done all this evil; yet
turn not aside from following
the LORD, but serve the
LORD with all your heart.'

יט וַיֹּאמְרוּ כָל-הָעָם אֶל-שְׁמוּאֵל
הִתְפַּלֵּל בְּעַד-עֲבָדֶיךָ אֶל-יְיָ אֱלֹהֶיךָ
וְאַל-נָמוּת: כִּי-יָסַפְנוּ עַל-כָּל-
חַטֹּאתֵינוּ רָעָה לִשְׁאֹל לָנוּ מֶלֶךְ.

כ וַיֹּאמֶר שְׁמוּאֵל אֶל-הָעָם אַל-תִּירָאוּ
אַתֶּם עֲשִׂיתֶם אֵת כָּל-הָרָעָה
הַזֹּאת: אַךְ אַל-תָּסוּרוּ מֵאַחֲרֵי יְיָ
וַעֲבַדְתֶּם אֶת-יְיָ בְּכָל-לְבַבְכֶם.

Samuel's bottom line is that God is king. He finds heresy in the request
for a human king. It is an affront to God, not just an issue of corruption.
God is the only true king and God has always sent help in response to the
people's heartfelt prayers.

(There is an important lesson in this chapter for anybody involved
in institutional life or organizing a dinner or otherwise inviting a guest
speaker: Always look at the speech first. Always. Because here, nobody
checked Samuel's speech for Saul's grand inauguration, and – well, we see
what happened.)

You can appreciate Samuel's point if you think back to Exodus. Israel
became a nation by experiencing profound events together in the presence
of God: Passover, the splitting of the Reed Sea, the manna, Revelation,
and the Tabernacle.

From this perspective, Israel's nationhood is already complete.

The culminating event is the building of the Tabernacle, the *mishkan*, a
place for God to dwell amongst the people. The building of the *mishkan* is
funded through the donation of a half-shekel per person. The idea is that
by virtue of being counted into the Covenant, Israel becomes one nation;
bound together and bound to God.

God is at the center of life and all the people are unified through the
Tabernacle. In this vision, the Tabernacle is the unifying institution in
Jewish life.

But now the people request to be unified through a king – which is
something different than a judge.

A king, first of all, is a king of *all* the people. Judges never lose their
tribal status. They remain connected to their tribe.

Judges hold sway for a limited period of time; a king is forever. The
kingship is dynastic, passing on from father to son.

So in requesting a king, the people are asking for someone to rule *all* of the people and to do this *forever*. That's precisely God's role.

Samuel has a good point. It looks as if the people are asking to replace God.

Hannah's Perspective: Fighting Anarchy

Hannah, Samuel's mother, doesn't see the king as replacing God. She sees the king as reflecting God. Hannah prays for kingship:[8]

I Samuel 2

10 They that strive with the LORD shall be broken to pieces; against them will He thunder in heaven; the LORD will judge the ends of the earth; and **He will give strength unto His king, and exalt the horn of His anointed.**

י יְיָ יֵחַתּוּ מְרִיבָו עָלָו בַּשָּׁמַיִם יַרְעֵם־יְיָ יָדִין אַפְסֵי־אָרֶץ: וְיִתֶּן־עֹז לְמַלְכּוֹ וְיָרֵם קֶרֶן מְשִׁיחוֹ.

In Hannah's request for a king, the earthly kingdom ideally functions as a reflection of the heavenly kingdom. This would mark a change from the period described in the Book of Judges, a period whose complete anarchy is exemplified by the stories of Micah,[9] and the Concubine of Give'ah.[10]

This is not the only reason that the Book of Judges is disturbing; the judges themselves are all terribly flawed.[11] The book concludes with the story of civil war and a cry for kingship.

But when you ask Samuel about the period of the judges, he thinks it is wonderful. He says: "What do you need kingship for? What was wrong with the Book of Judges? Whenever you had trouble, God sent you saviors."

For Samuel, the Book of Judges represents a period in Jewish history which worked very well. The people got in trouble, cried out to God and God would send a judge to intervene. Samuel's take on the Book of

8   For a lengthier discussion of this topic, see "The Birth of Samuel and the Birth of Kingship" elsewhere in this volume.

9   Judges 17:1-18:31

10   Judges 19:1-21:25

11   The possible exception is Deborah, who according to the Book of Judges, should not be a leader in the first place – she's a woman – but the general is afraid to fight without her.

Judges is 180 degrees different from the perspective that the book is about anarchy.

As One Man

Right before Samuel's farewell speech, we are told the story of the king of Ammon, whose name is Nachash, who encamps against Yaveish Gile'ad. Yaveish Gile'ad is the one group of people from the Book of Judges who supported the tribe of Benjamin.

I Samuel 11

2 And Nachash the Ammonite said to them: 'On this condition will I make a covenant with you, that all your right eyes be put out; and I will lay it for a reproach upon all Israel.'

3 And the elders of Yaveish said to him: 'Give us seven days' respite, that we may send messengers to all the borders of Israel; and then, if there be none to deliver us, we will come out to you.'

ב וַיֹּאמֶר אֲלֵיהֶם נָחָשׁ הָעַמּוֹנִי
בְּזֹאת אֶכְרֹת לָכֶם בִּנְקוֹר
לָכֶם כָּל-עֵין יָמִין: וְשַׂמְתִּיהָ
חֶרְפָּה עַל-כָּל-יִשְׂרָאֵל.

ג וַיֹּאמְרוּ אֵלָיו זִקְנֵי יָבֵישׁ הֶרֶף לָנוּ
שִׁבְעַת יָמִים וְנִשְׁלְחָה מַלְאָכִים
בְּכֹל גְּבוּל יִשְׂרָאֵל: וְאִם-אֵין
מוֹשִׁיעַ אֹתָנוּ וְיָצָאנוּ אֵלֶיךָ.

Nachash threatens them. So they ask for time, hoping for help. Then the people come crying to Saul:

I Samuel 11

5 And, behold, Saul came following the oxen out of the field; and Saul said: 'What ails the people that they weep?' And they told him the words of the men of Yaveish.

6 And the spirit of God came mightily upon Saul when he heard those words, and his anger was kindled greatly.

ה וְהִנֵּה שָׁאוּל בָּא אַחֲרֵי הַבָּקָר
מִן-הַשָּׂדֶה וַיֹּאמֶר שָׁאוּל
מַה-לָּעָם כִּי יִבְכּוּ: וַיְסַפְּרוּ-
לוֹ-אֶת-דִּבְרֵי אַנְשֵׁי יָבֵישׁ.

ו וַתִּצְלַח רוּחַ-אֱלֹהִים עַל-שָׁאוּל
בשמעו (כְּשָׁמְעוֹ) אֶת-הַדְּבָרִים
הָאֵלֶּה: וַיִּחַר אַפּוֹ מְאֹד.

7 And he took a yoke of oxen,
and cut them in pieces, and
sent them throughout all the
borders of Israel by the hand of
messengers, saying: 'Whoever
comes not forth after Saul and
after Samuel, so shall it be done
to his oxen.' And the dread of
the LORD fell on the people,
and they came out **as one man.**

ז וַיִּקַּח צֶמֶד בָּקָר וַיְנַתְּחֵהוּ
וַיְשַׁלַּח בְּכָל-גְּבוּל יִשְׂרָאֵל בְּיַד
הַמַּלְאָכִים לֵאמֹר אֲשֶׁר אֵינֶנּוּ
יֹצֵא אַחֲרֵי שָׁאוּל וְאַחַר שְׁמוּאֵל
כֹּה יֵעָשֶׂה לִבְקָרוֹ: וַיִּפֹּל פַּחַד-יְיָ
עַל-הָעָם וַיֵּצְאוּ כְּאִישׁ אֶחָד.

Saul takes a yoke of oxen, breaks it into pieces, and sends it throughout Israel. He says: "If you don't follow me, this will happen to you." And all of Israel follows him "as one man."

When you read this story, the first question is: What does Nachash want? His name *nachash* means "snake," so we are very suspicious of him. What does Snake want? He says he wants to gouge out everyone's right eye.

Actually, the true answer is very simple. It lies in his attack of Yaveish Gile'ad.

In the previous chapter, Saul is named king. Chapter 10 concludes by saying, some people support him, some do not. Nachash is concerned about a unified State of Israel: It would wield much more power, because everybody would fight for everyone else. Nachash wants to crush the kingship before it begins. How? Attack the point of greatest vulnerability. And what is that point?

Well, this king of Israel has been appointed from the tribe of Benjamin. Eleven chapters earlier, in the Book of Judges, the tribe of Benjamin was virtually annihilated because of the incident of the concubine of Give'ah. One can make the argument that the king is actually chosen from the tribe of Benjamin in order to make the point that the nation is one. (This would be tantamount to the United States choosing a southerner to be President after the Civil War.) Such a choice underscores the statement, "We are one people."

So Nachash, true to his name, says to himself: They make a lot of good statements; let's see if they'll back it up. What happens if I attack the one tribe that was killed by the other tribes for supporting Benjamin? Not only will I attack this place, which is politically vulnerable, and a supporter of the new "king," but it is also a physically distant territory. When someone is in trouble far away, it is easier to ignore.

Will Israel fight for Yaveish Gile'ad? That is a real test for this nascent kingdom.

Saul's hewing the ox in pieces to send throughout Israel reminds us of the story of the Concubine of Give'ah:

Judges 19

29 And when he was come into his house, he took a knife, and laid hold on his concubine, and divided her, limb by limb, into twelve pieces, and sent her throughout all the borders of Israel.

כט וַיָּבֹא אֶל-בֵּיתוֹ וַיִּקַּח אֶת-הַמַּאֲכֶלֶת וַיַּחֲזֵק בְּפִילַגְשׁוֹ וַיְנַתְּחֶהָ לַעֲצָמֶיהָ לִשְׁנֵים עָשָׂר נְתָחִים: וַיְשַׁלְּחֶהָ בְּכֹל גְּבוּל יִשְׂרָאֵל.

It is very interesting to note that the Tanakh maintains the same language in the battle against Nachash, as in the battle against Benjamin – they gather together as "one man," under one leader, for one purpose:

Judges 20

1 Then all the children of Israel went out, and the congregation was assembled **as one man**, from Dan even to Beer-sheba, with the land of Gile'ad, unto the LORD at Mitzpah.

א וַיֵּצְאוּ כָּל-בְּנֵי יִשְׂרָאֵל וַתִּקָּהֵל הָעֵדָה כְּאִישׁ אֶחָד לְמִדָּן וְעַד-בְּאֵר שֶׁבַע וְאֶרֶץ הַגִּלְעָד: אֶל-יְיָ הַמִּצְפָּה.

This similar phrasing invites us to compare the two stories – the Nach-ash/Saul story is essentially an undoing of the Concubine of Give'ah story – but it's making another point, too.

The story at the end of the Book of Judges is about anarchy, because there is no king. And the Nachash story is probably Saul's finest moment. He doesn't consult Samuel first; he just does what he knows is right.[12] He understands that becoming "one nation" means taking on the responsibil-ity to defend even the weakest and most hated in your midst, which in this case is Yaveish Gile'ad.[13]

---

12   I Samuel 10:10: וַתִּצְלַח עָלָיו רוּחַ אֱלֹהִים "and the spirit of God came mightily upon him"

13   For a lengthier discussion of this topic, see: Gottlieb, Leeor, "The Na-chash Story and the Dead Sea Scrolls" elsewhere in this volume.

In chapter 12 we have Samuel's speech. It was so wonderful in the days of the judges, he says. What do we want a king for?

We are already given the answer in chapter 11, with the battle of Yaveish Gile'ad. The two arguments are placed back to back.

There's no question that the author of the Book of Samuel sides more with Saul than with Samuel, because Saul accomplishes an undoing of the terrible tale of the concubine of Give'ah. Now, there *is* a king in Israel, and that means that now everyone must do what is right in *God's* eyes, not only in his own.

The Nachash Story and the Dead Sea Scrolls

I Samuel 11

Leeor Gottlieb

We're going to look at the first battle fought by newly-inaugurated King Saul: the story of Nachash. First we will read the Tanakh, and then we will examine versions of this story in the Septuagint (the ancient Greek translation of the Bible) and the Dead Sea Scrolls. This chapter will serve as an example of the complexities and the problems that may arise in our understanding of the textual tradition of the Bible.

As we near the end of Chapter 10, Saul has been chosen by God to be the first King of Israel.[1] Samuel introduces Saul to the people of Israel by means of a selection process accomplished by lottery, *goral*.[2] Saul, unaccustomed to the spotlight, hides among the baggage:

I Samuel 10

22 Therefore they asked of the LORD further: 'Is there yet a man come hither?' And the LORD answered: 'Behold, he hid himself among the baggage.'	כב וַיִּשְׁאֲלוּ-עוֹד בַּיי הֲבָא עוֹד הֲלֹם אִישׁ: וַיֹּאמֶר יי הִנֵּה-הוּא נֶחְבָּא אֶל-הַכֵּלִים.
23 And they ran and fetched him from there; and when he stood among the people, he was higher than any of the people from his shoulders and upward.	כג וַיָּרֻצוּ וַיִּקָּחֻהוּ מִשָּׁם וַיִּתְיַצֵּב בְּתוֹךְ הָעָם: וַיִּגְבַּהּ מִכָּל-הָעָם מִשִּׁכְמוֹ וָמָעְלָה.
24 And Samuel said to all the people: 'See him whom the LORD has chosen, that	כד וַיֹּאמֶר שְׁמוּאֵל אֶל-כָּל-הָעָם הַרְאִיתֶם אֲשֶׁר

1   I Samuel 9:15-16
2   I Samuel 10:20-21

there is none like him among all the people?' And all the people shouted, and said: 'Long live the king.'

בָּחַר-בּוֹ יי כִּי אֵין כָּמֹהוּ בְּכָל-הָעָם: וַיָּרִעוּ כָל-הָעָם וַיֹּאמְרוּ יְחִי הַמֶּלֶךְ.

25 Then Samuel told the people the manner of the kingdom, and wrote it in a book, and laid it up before the LORD. And Samuel sent all the people away, every man to his house.

כה וַיְדַבֵּר שְׁמוּאֵל אֶל-הָעָם אֵת מִשְׁפַּט הַמְּלֻכָה וַיִּכְתֹּב בַּסֵּפֶר וַיַּנַּח לִפְנֵי יי וַיְשַׁלַּח שְׁמוּאֵל אֶת-כָּל-הָעָם אִישׁ לְבֵיתוֹ.

26 And Saul also went to his house to Give'ah; and there went with him the men of valor, whose hearts God had touched.

כו וְגַם-שָׁאוּל הָלַךְ לְבֵיתוֹ גִּבְעָתָה: וַיֵּלְכוּ עִמּוֹ-הַחַיִל אֲשֶׁר-נָגַע אֱלֹהִים בְּלִבָּם.

At the end of verse 24, Saul has his formal coronation and the nation hails him king. The constitution is given and everybody is sent home with good feeling. Saul, accompanied by his new entourage, goes on to begin his royal career in Give'ah.

"Like one who remains silent"

We will be examining several verses closely. As we will see, this verse is somewhat problematic.

I Samuel 10

27 But certain base fellows said: 'How shall this man save us?' And they despised him, and brought him no present. But **he was like one who remained silent.**

כז וּבְנֵי בְלִיַּעַל אָמְרוּ מַה-יֹּשִׁעֵנוּ זֶה וַיִּבְזֻהוּ וְלֹא-הֵבִיאוּ לוֹ מִנְחָה: וַיְהִי כְּמַחֲרִישׁ.

Not everyone thinks Saul is fit for the job. What good can *he* do? They scorn him and do not bring him a tribute.

How does Saul react?

The end of the verse reads: "*va-yehi ke-macharish.*"

Le-hacharish means to remain silent. *Le-hiyot cheresh* is to be deaf. *Le-hacharish*, in the *hiphil* declension, is to remain silent; in other words, not to be heard by others. There are some forty examples of this root in the *hiphil* form in Tanakh.

It seems that Saul is a benevolent king. He doesn't go ahead and say, "Behead these evil citizens!" He remains silent. It sounds like a good story and it makes sense.

There is one tiny problem. I explained the word *macharish* as *le-hacharish*, meaning "to remain silent." I would have expected the verse to report his silence in the following indicative form: *va-yacharesh*, "and he remained silent." But it says, *va-yehi ke-macharish*, prefacing the word with the letter *kaf* (כ) that means "like," and denotes analogy. (Hebrew grammarians call it *kaf ha-dimyon*.) In other words, the verse tells us that Saul was "*like* one who remains silent." What does that mean? Did he only feign silence?

In cases like this, we seek out additional, similar usages in the Tanakh. Only, here we have a problem. We can't find another instance of *ke-macharish*. It's a *hapax legomenon*, the only such usage of that verb in the whole Tanakh. So we're left with a puzzle.

Let's continue:

I Samuel 11

1 Then Nachash the Ammonite came up, and encamped against Yaveish-Gileʿad; and all the men of Yaveish said to Nachash: 'Make a covenant with us, and we will serve you.'

א וַיַּעַל נָחָשׁ הָעַמּוֹנִי וַיִּחַן עַל-יָבֵישׁ גִּלְעָד: וַיֹּאמְרוּ כָּל-אַנְשֵׁי יָבֵישׁ אֶל-נָחָשׁ כְּרָת-לָנוּ בְרִית וְנַעַבְדֶךָ.

Nachash the... King?

Who is this Nachash the Ammonite? We are going to assume that Nachash is a king, and not just some private Ammonite hero, although he is not introduced with a regal title.

Is there any indication that he was a king? There *is* a Nachash mentioned at the beginning of II Samuel 10. He is the father of Chanun the Ammonite king who was on very good terms with the House of David. More than once, certain members of the House of David sought refuge with him. So, I would say that Nachash *was* a king, and that he had a dynasty, and his child, Chanun, was king of Ammon after him.

Usually, the Tanakh gives the full title of a character when he is first introduced. That is not always the case, but it is generally true. When we first meet Avimelekh in Genesis,[3] he is referred to as, "*Avimelekh melekh Pelishtim*," "Avimelekh, king of the Philistines." We hear that title from the start.

3   Genesis 26:1

So, here is a second small puzzle: We learn that Nachash is from Ammon, that he leads his people into battle, but we are not immediately told that he is king.

Nachash's Terms

Now, Nachash encamps outside Yaveish Gile'ad, meaning Yaveish *of* Gile'ad. *Gile'ad* is an Israelite faction and *Yaveish* is the name of the city. Camping there is a military maneuver. Nachash is trying to conquer the city. And they don't even put up a fight. The men of Yaveish say, "We will accept your rule even though Yaveish is not part of the kingdom of Ammon – but make a covenant with us and we will serve you."

I Samuel 11

2 And Nachash the Ammonite said to them: 'On this condition will I make it with you, that all your right eyes be put out; and I will lay it for a reproach upon all Israel.'	ב וַיֹּאמֶר אֲלֵיהֶם נָחָשׁ הָעַמּוֹנִי בְּזֹאת אֶכְרֹת לָכֶם בִּנְקוֹר לָכֶם כָּל-עֵין יָמִין: וְשַׂמְתִּיהָ חֶרְפָּה עַל-כָּל-יִשְׂרָאֵל.

Nachash offers his terms for peace: "Poke out your eyes and I'll let you live."

Why does he want to do that? The end of the verse explains: Nachash wants everyone in Israel to know that when he comes to town, nobody can do anything about it. He wishes to humiliate all of Israel.

Josephus[4] explains that gouging out the right eye was intended to reduce the Israelite's abilities in the battlefield. When a soldier holds a shield in his left hand, his left eye is blocked, and he then uses the right eye when attacking. Soldiers without their right eyes would have to choose between being either blind or unshielded in the battlefield.

But there is more to this scenario than making an onerous demand on captives and crippling the enemy.

In the ancient world, maiming was a sign of servitude.[5] Nachash wishes to inflict upon the Israelites not just a functional wound, but a visual

---

4   See later in this essay for historical data on Josephus

5   We can see this practice in the Torah: The slave for life, *eved olam*, is maimed by his master (Exodus 21:6).

We can also see the Torah's response to this practice. Maiming of slaves was accepted in that time and place, but that's not what the God of Israel wants. The Torah does not ask for gouging out an eye or cutting off fingers.

symbol of their inferiority as well. The very faces of the Israelites would bear testimony to Nachash's might.

So what are the people of Yaveish supposed to do now? They can choose between death and maiming. Some choice.

1 Samuel 11

3 And the elders of Yaveish said to him: 'Give us seven days' respite, that we may send messengers unto all the borders of Israel; and then, if there be none to deliver us, we will come out to you.'

ג וַיֹּאמְרוּ אֵלָיו זִקְנֵי יָבֵישׁ הֶרֶף לָנוּ שִׁבְעַת יָמִים וְנִשְׁלְחָה מַלְאָכִים בְּכֹל גְּבוּל יִשְׂרָאֵל: וְאִם-אֵין מוֹשִׁיעַ אֹתָנוּ וְיָצָאנוּ אֵלֶיךָ.

The elders ask for one week, explicitly to seek assistance throughout Israel. Nachash accepts their terms. Why? Because Nachash is perfectly certain that there will be no cavalry riding to the rescue. Since Nachash wants to embarrass the people of Israel, he is perfectly willing to give them time to prove just how impotent Israel really is.

Why is Nachash so sure that no savior will appear? Clearly, he doesn't know about Saul. He must not be aware of the new player on the field. But if he hasn't been paying such close attention to Israelite politics, what makes him so certain that there *isn't* any army to come to the rescue? Another little puzzle.

Saul's Response

1 Samuel 11

4 Then the messengers came to Give'at Sha'ul, and spoke these words in the ears of the people; and all the people lifted up their voice, and wept.

ד וַיָּבֹאוּ הַמַּלְאָכִים גִּבְעַת שָׁאוּל וַיְדַבְּרוּ הַדְּבָרִים בְּאָזְנֵי הָעָם: וַיִּשְׂאוּ כָל-הָעָם אֶת-קוֹלָם וַיִּבְכּוּ.

God permits maiming in two circumstances. In both, the Torah asks for a wound that is not a wound. It may hurt, but it won't leave anyone crippled.

One circumstance is the slave who has had his right ear pierced by his owner, the *eved nirtza* (Exodus 21:6). All of us know people with pierced ears, or have them ourselves: we don't think of pierced ears as a mutilation.

The second type of maiming is circumcision, another kind of symbol that is covenantal. It's a physical sign of that covenant, but again, it's not crippling. That's the Torah's expression of this practice of the ancient world.

The delegates go from place to place. When they get to Give‘at Sha’ul (the *give‘ah*, "hill," where Saul lives) the people react as they do everywhere else. They cry, and they offer no solution.

I Samuel 11

5 And, behold, Saul came following
the oxen out of the field; and Saul
said: 'What ails the people that
they weep?' And they told him
the words of the men of Yaveish.

ה וְהִנֵּה שָׁאוּל בָּא אַחֲרֵי הַבָּקָר
מִן-הַשָּׂדֶה וַיֹּאמֶר שָׁאוּל
מַה-לָּעָם כִּי יִבְכּוּ: וַיְסַפְּרוּ-
לוֹ-אֶת-דִּבְרֵי אַנְשֵׁי יָבֵישׁ.

Saul comes in from the field[6] and says, "What's all the weeping and crying that I hear in the distance?" They bring him up to date.

I Samuel 11

6 And the spirit of God came
mightily upon Saul when he
heard those words, and his
anger was kindled greatly.

ו וַתִּצְלַח רוּחַ-אֱלֹהִים עַל-שָׁאוּל
בשמעו (כְּשָׁמְעוֹ) אֶת-הַדְּבָרִים
הָאֵלֶּה: וַיִּחַר אַפּוֹ מְאֹד.

Immediately upon hearing about the embarrassment that Nachash is heaping upon all of the people of Israel, Saul gains the "spirit of God," *ruach Elohim*. In the time of the Judges, the spirit of God does not necessarily signify the spirit of prophecy – it's *courage*. When you receive courage from God, you prevail – like Samson did, and the other judges before him.

I Samuel 11

7 And he took a yoke of oxen,
and cut them in pieces, and
sent them throughout all the
borders of Israel by the hand of
messengers, saying: 'Whoever
does not sally forth after Saul
and after Samuel, so shall it be
done to his oxen.' And the dread
of the LORD fell on the people,
and they came out as one man.

ז וַיִּקַּח צֶמֶד בָּקָר וַיְנַתְּחֵהוּ
וַיְשַׁלַּח בְּכָל-גְּבוּל יִשְׂרָאֵל בְּיַד
הַמַּלְאָכִים לֵאמֹר אֲשֶׁר אֵינֶנּוּ
יֹצֵא אַחֲרֵי שָׁאוּל וְאַחַר שְׁמוּאֵל
כֹּה יֵעָשֶׂה לִבְקָרוֹ: וַיִּפֹּל פַּחַד-יי
עַל-הָעָם וַיֵּצְאוּ כְּאִישׁ אֶחָד.

6   Why the King of Israel is depicted here as common man – working in the field – is a worthy topic for another lesson.

8 And he numbered them in Bezek;
and the children of Israel were
three hundred thousand, and the
men of Judah thirty thousand.

ח וַיִּפְקְדֵם בְּבָזֶק: וַיִּהְיוּ בְנֵי-
יִשְׂרָאֵל שְׁלֹשׁ מֵאוֹת אֶלֶף
וְאִישׁ יְהוּדָה שְׁלֹשִׁים אָלֶף.

9 And they said to the messengers
that came: 'Thus shall you say
to the men of Yaveish-Gile'ad:
Tomorrow, by the time the
sun is hot, you shall have
deliverance.' And the messengers
came and told the men of
Yaveish; and they were glad.

ט וַיֹּאמְרוּ לַמַּלְאָכִים הַבָּאִים כֹּה
תֹאמְרוּן לְאִישׁ יָבֵישׁ גִּלְעָד
מָחָר תִּהְיֶה-לָכֶם תְּשׁוּעָה בחם
(כְּחֹם) הַשֶּׁמֶשׁ וַיָּבֹאוּ הַמַּלְאָכִים
וַיַּגִּידוּ לְאַנְשֵׁי יָבֵישׁ–וַיִּשְׂמָחוּ.

10 And the men of Yaveish said:
'Tomorrow we will come out to
you, and you shall do with us
all that seems good to you.'

י וַיֹּאמְרוּ אַנְשֵׁי יָבֵישׁ מָחָר
נֵצֵא אֲלֵיכֶם וַעֲשִׂיתֶם לָנוּ
כְּכָל-הַטּוֹב בְּעֵינֵיכֶם.

Saul tells the people: Any cowards who don't show up immediately for my army will lose their cattle. With that feat of determination, Saul musters up a full army from a nation that was helpless only the day before.

I Samuel 11

11 And it was so on the morrow,
that Saul put the people in
three companies; and they came
into the midst of the camp in
the morning watch, and smote
the Ammonites until the heat
of the day; and it came to
pass, that they that remained
were scattered, so that two of
them were not left together.

יא וַיְהִי מִמָּחֳרָת וַיָּשֶׂם שָׁאוּל
אֶת-הָעָם שְׁלֹשָׁה רָאשִׁים
וַיָּבֹאוּ בְתוֹךְ-הַמַּחֲנֶה בְּאַשְׁמֹרֶת
הַבֹּקֶר וַיַּכּוּ אֶת-עַמּוֹן עַד-חֹם
הַיּוֹם: וַיְהִי הַנִּשְׁאָרִים וַיָּפֻצוּ
וְלֹא נִשְׁאֲרוּ-בָם שְׁנַיִם יָחַד.

The next day, Saul launches a surprise attack from the rear and vanquishes Nachash, thus bringing salvation to the people of Yaveish and proving himself to be a charismatic and able king for the people of Israel. That's the end of the story.

We began the story with Saul's coronation, with the people hailing, "Long live the king!" Now, he has the respect of the people. He is now capable of mustering them up for battle duty, and no longer will any foreign king pose such a threat to the people of Israel. Now, Israel has a redeemer. Saul will go before them into war. This is exactly what the people had sought in their request for a king.

The Septuagint Perspective

Now, let us look at parts of it through some other sources, keeping an eye on the portions that we found puzzling.

We'll start with the first known translation of the Tanakh: the Septuagint, or as it is known in Hebrew, *Targum Ha-shevi'im*. The Torah was translated into Greek in the middle of the third century before the Common Era, and Prophets were translated during the next century. So the Greek translation of the Book of Samuel is from around the time of the Maccabbean wars, a bit before or a bit after.

The translation was composed in Alexandria, the largest Jewish community outside the land of Israel. There were more than a million Jews in Egypt, and they all spoke Greek. They couldn't read Tanakh in Hebrew anymore, so they needed a translation.

We are going to look at a piece of the Septuagint from the end of Chapter 10, pretty much where we started the lesson. The Greek has been translated into English. The English very well represents the Greek, which is why we are using this English translation.[7]

SEPTUAGINT: *I Samuel 10*

26 And Saul departed to his house to Gabaa; and there went with Saul mighty men whose hearts God had touched.
27 But evil men said, "Who is this man that shall save us?" And they despised him, and brought him no gifts.

And Saul departed to his house, to Give'ah, and there went with Saul mighty men whose hearts God had touched. We saw that verse before. But evil men said, "Who is this man that shall save us?" (*Mah yoshieinu zeh.*) "And they despised him," (*va-yivzuhu*), "and brought him no gifts," (*ve-lo hevi'u lo minchah*).

Missing here in the Septuagint are the last words from the Hebrew version of this verse: "*va-yehi ke-macharish*," "he was like one who remained silent." These words were not translated into Greek. Why not?

Let's read the next verse:

---

7   Translated from Greek by Sir Lancelot Brenton, London, 1851

SEPTUAGINT: *I Samuel 11*

1 **And it came to pass about a month after this**, that Naas the Ammanite went up, and encamped against Jabis Galaad. and all the men of Jabis said to Naas the Ammanite, "Make a covenant with us, and we will serve you."

Let's compare this to our Hebrew. *"va-ya'al Nachash ha-'Amoni."* What does *"va-ya'al Nachash ha-'Amoni"* correspond to in this English translation of the Greek? That Nachash, the Ammonite, went up. We see that here.

So what do we do about the whole clause in the beginning of the sentence: "And it came to pass about a month after this"?

At the end of verse 26, there is a phrase that is *missing* in the Greek translation: *"va-yehi ke-macharish."* At the start of the next verse, we have an *addition* in Greek that we don't find in the Hebrew text: "And it came to pass about a month after this." How would that phrase translate into biblical Hebrew? "And it came to pass" would be a pretty good translation of *"va-yehi."* So we can definitely agree upon *va-yehi*.

If you know Hebrew, you might suggest *"ke-chodesh"* as a translation for "about a month." And if you start thinking like a scribe – or a teacher at the blackboard – and consider how the words appear in Biblical texts, without any vowels, you'll realize that the difference between *ke-macharish* and *ke-chodesh* is only two letters. The former has a *mem* the latter lacks – and the letter *resh* (ר) in the former is replaced by the letter *dalet* (ד) – two letters that are very similar, differentiated just by a little tail at the end of the top line.

These two very different phrases in English turn out to look practically identical when written in Hebrew.

The Josephus Version

Let's leave the Septuagint momentarily, and continue on to the next source, *Antiquities of the Jews*, a history of the Jewish people written by Flavius Josephus almost 2,000 years ago.

Josephus was the historian who, as an escort of Titus and earlier Vespasian, witnessed the destruction of Jerusalem and the second Temple. Josephus was a Jewish commander until his capture. After that, he became the embedded historian in the Roman camp. Josephus retells the whole Bible, from Creation until his own era.

Antiquities of the Jews, like the Septuagint, was written in Greek; Josephus attended the Romans at the time, but the *lingua franca* of the age was Greek, not Latin. Josephus, as someone who knew Hebrew language, tradition and texts, brings us the Greek History of the Jews in this book.

Let me just emphasize that Josephus is not *translating* the Bible, he is *retelling* it. It is expected, therefore, to sometimes find extra words in a passage from *Antiquities,* unlike with the Septuagint, which purports to be a translation.

Let's look at how Josephus retells the story:

JOSEPHUS: *Antiquities of the Jews 6:67*
So when Samuel had finished this matter, he dismissed the multitude and came himself to the city of Ramah, for it was his own country.

Saul also went away to Give'ah, where he was born, and many good men there were who paid him the respect that was due to him but the greater part were ill men who despised and derided the others, who neither did bring him presents nor did they, in affection or even in words, regard to please him.

This is much longer than the Hebrew, but it corresponds to our text.

JOSEPHUS: *Antiquities of the Jews 6:68*
"After one month, the war which Saul had with Nachash, the king of the Ammonites, obtained him respect from all the people for this Nachash had done a great deal of mischief to the Jews that lived beyond Jordan."

With the use of the phrase, "After one month," it appears that Josephus was translating from a text that agreed with the version that the Septuagint was referencing. Throughout *Antiquities of the Jews*, you'll see that Josephus was using either the Septuagint itself, or something very similar. Josephus was "Israeli;" he could have translated directly from the Hebrew. But because he was writing for the Greeks, he used a Greek-based text.

The art of translation requires that the translator be proficient in two languages. He reads in the original language, and then creates a new text in a second language. The original language here, of course, is Hebrew. So if one translator (and perhaps two, if Josephus was using an original Hebrew text in addition to the Septuagint) wrote: "And it came to be about a month later," he didn't invent that. He must have read it in the original Hebrew. Using the Septuagint and Josephus, we can speculate that, in fact, such a Hebrew text existed in the Second Temple period.

Thanks to the Dead Sea scrolls, we no longer have to speculate. We actually have such a document.

Dead Sea Scrolls

Our ancestors did not have one text called "Tanakh;" they had separate scrolls (*megillot*) for different books – just as Esther is its own scroll which we read from on Purim. This is not just theory, this was discovered in Qumran, right near the Dead Sea, in 1947. By chance, a young Bedouin shepherd stumbled into a hidden cave, and he found some scrolls. Some of these scrolls wound up in St. Marks monastery in Bethlehem and were then purchased by Professor Sukenik of Hebrew University.

This was the beginning of the Qumran findings. Later on, when archaeologists understood that there may be more treasures in these caves, they made further expeditions in the early 1950's and found many, many more scrolls.

Israel had become a State in 1948, but that area was under Jordanian occupation. The Israelis who had been working on the scrolls had no access to the later findings, and some of these scrolls were very, very important.

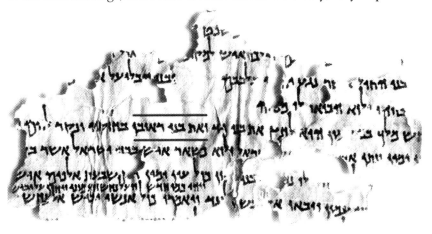

F.M. Cross, "4Q51," Discoveries in the Judaean Desert XVII,
Oxford University Press 2005, 65-66 – Israel Antiquities
Authority. Two horizontal lines added here for orientation.

This is a photo of one of the fragments of a scroll of Samuel found at Qumran, published by Frank Cross. This picture is pretty similar to many hundreds and thousands of fragments found in Qumran. You can see that the fragmentary nature of the Qumran scroll leaves plenty of room for doubt.

There were a total of eleven caves found in Qumran that had scrolls. Cave number four contained the largest deposit. Hundreds of ancient scrolls were found there in various degrees of preservation. Among these scrolls were some fragments of the Book of Samuel. They were far from complete and were very hard to piece together, but they proved to be extremely valuable to our understanding of the text of Samuel.

Having looked through the story in our Tanakh and in the retellings of Josephus and the Septuagint, we will now read a version from one of these scrolls.

What we have here is called 4Q Samuel A (usually marked as 4QSam^a, also known as 4Q 51), denoting cave 4 in Qumran, the Book of Samuel, scroll number 1.

If you can read Hebrew, then you can read this text (or at least parts of it) written thousands of years ago. If this is your first or second time reading parts of the Dead Sea Scrolls, it can be very exciting to find that here we are in the 21st century, and we can read a document written in the 1st century, or earlier. Any problems we have in reading it are due to the fragmentary nature of the scroll – we don't have a problem with the language or with the letters.

It's written in *ketav ashuri*, the Aramaic script that the people of Israel adopted at the beginning of the Second Temple period, as opposed to *ketav ivri*, the earlier, ancient Hebrew script, sometimes called paleo-Hebrew, used throughout the land in the First Temple period.[8]

Can you make out the three words in the center of the document, between the two lines added to the reproduction? It says *"ve'et bnei Reuven,"* meaning "and the Reuvenites."

Wait a minute. We just read the whole Hebrew story and there is no mention of the Reuvenites. Where did that come from?

As we continue, while the more adventurous can read from the photo of the scroll, here is a transcription prepared by Frank Cross,[9] and a translation I've prepared. The words within the brackets in the transcription were not actually found, but are Cross's suggestions as to what might have been found had the scroll remained intact. Large gaps within the manuscript that Cross regards as deliberate (rather than later erasures)

---

8   To some extent, paleo-Hebrew remained; there were some puritans in the Second Temple period who tried to retain that script.

9   "4Q 51," F. M. Cross, *Discoveries in the Judaean Desert XVII*, Oxford 2005, 65,66

are indicated by the Latin word *vacat*, meaning empty. The fragment, as reconstructed, starts in the middle of I Samuel 10:24, which begins "And Samuel said to all the people: 'See him....' "

Dead Sea Scrolls: *4Q Samᵃ X 1-10*

1. [אשר בחר בו יי אין כמוהו בכלכ]ם [ויריעו כול העם ויאמרו יחי המלך]

1 [whom the LORD has chosen, that there is none like him among al]l [the people and all the people shouted, and said long live the king]

2. [וידבר שמואל אל העם את] משפט ה[מלך ויכתב בספר וינח לפני יי *vacat* [

2 [Then Samuel told the people the] manner of the [kingdom, and wrote it in a book, and laid it up before the LORD]

3. [וישלח שמואל את] כו[ל ה]עם וילכו איש למקומ[ו וג]ם [ש]אול ה [לך לביתו גבעתה[

3 [And Samuel sent] al[l the] people away, every man to his hou[se a]nd [S]aul also w[ent to his house to Giveʻah]

4. [וילכו] בני החיל אשר נגע יי בלבבם   *vacat*   ובני הבליעל א]מרו [מ]ה יושיענו[

4 [and there went with him] the men of valor, whose hearts G[o]d had touched. *vacat* but certain base fellows s[aid] h[ow shall this man save us]

5. [ ] זה וי[בזוהו ולוא הביאו מנחה   *vacat*

5 [And they] despised him, and brought him no present.

We see that in line number five, the line is half full. It ends with "*ve-lo heviʼu lo minchah*," "[they] brought him no present," and then there is an empty space till the end of the line. In other words, nothing was erased here. It was left empty because it is the end of the portion – just like in a Torah scroll. This is the end of the story of Saul's coronation according to the Samuel scroll. And now we're starting a new story.

And what is missing from the Dead Sea scrolls at the end of the coronation story? *"Va-yehi ke-macharish,"* "he was like one who remained silent."

The Lost Story of Oppression

Now, let's continue.

Dead Sea Scrolls: *4Q Sam[a] X 1-10*

‎6. [ונ]חש מלך בני עמון הוא לחץ את בני גד ואת בני ראובן בחזקה ונקר להם כ[ול]

6 [And N]achash, king of the Ammonites, oppressed the Gadites and the Reuvenites strongly. He gouged out e[very]

‎7. [ע]ין ימין ונתן אין [מושי]ע ל[י]שראל ולוא נשאר איש בבני ישראל אשר בע[בר] [הירדן]

7 [r]ight eye and no [redeem]er was given to [I]srael and not a man was left of the Israelites of the other side of the Jordan,

Line six. *"Ve-Nachash, melekh bnei Ammon,"* "And Nachash, king of the Ammonites." Here, he is not referred to as *"Nachash ha-'Amoni,"* in the puzzling fashion it is written in our Masoretic Text. Here, he is introduced by his full title, as expected. The word *melekh,* "king," can be discerned quite easily as the second word in the line: Nachash, the king of the Ammonites, oppressed the Gadites and Reuvenites *bichozekah,* "strongly." (In other words, not just *lachatz,* "oppressed," but *lachatz bichozekah,* "oppressed *strongly.*") He gouged out (line 7) the right eyes of the Reuvenites and Gadites.

Remember, in our story, it is the people of Yaveish Gile'ad who are being threatened. Is Gile'ad part of Reuven and Gad?

The answer is no. On the eastern side of the River there lived three tribes, from south to north: Reuven, Gad, and half the tribe of Manasseh. (It is not a stretch to refer to this half tribe as Gile'ad, the name of Manasseh's grandson,[10] as the Tanakh virtually identifies the half of Manasseh that lived East of the Jordan as Gile'ad.[11])

Where is Ammon? Basically it's just about the same territory. For hundreds of years there was a border dispute between the Gile'adites and the

10   cf. Numbers 26:29
11   cf. I Chronicles 27:21

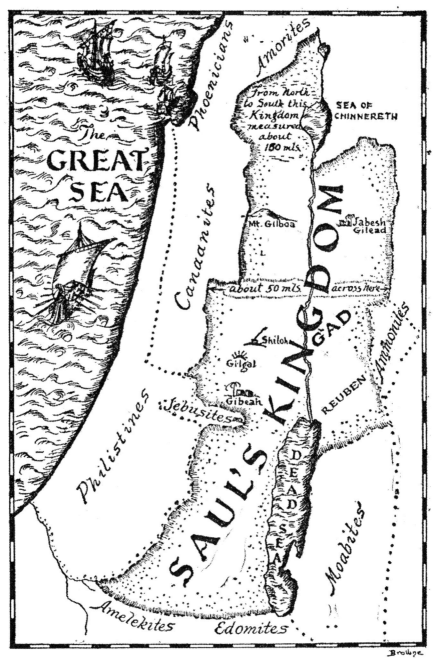

Adapted from
The Graphic Bible by Lewis Browne
Illustration by Marcus Rothkowitz

Ammonites, having to do with the conquest of Sichon and Og in the time of Moses[12] and the story of Jephthah in the time of the Judges.[13] Nothing seems to change. Our story, then, deals with Israelites who lived on the eastern side of the Jordan, and Ammon – who shared something like a confederacy with Moab – was their immediate neighbor.

So, according to the scroll, Ammon had *already* conquered Reuven and Gad. And Nachash, the king of Ammon, had exacted terrible punishment upon the people that he had conquered. Thousands of people from Reuven and Gad were maimed for life. Who remained? Just these people further north, in Gile'ad.

This answers why the Yaveishites didn't even put up a fight. This wasn't the *beginning* of the war. These were the final throes of a terrible defeat of all the Israelite inhabitants east of the Jordan.

Seven Thousand Exceptions

Dead Sea Scrolls: *4Q Sam^a X 1-10*

7. [ע]ין ימין ונתן אין [מושי]ע ל[י]שראל ולוא נשאר איש בבני ישראל אשר בע[בר
[הירדן]

7 [r]ight eye and no [redeem]er was given to [I]srael and not a man was left of the Israelites of the other side of the Jordan,

8. [אש]ר ל[וא נ]קר לו נח[ש מלך] בני [ע]מון כול עין ימין ו[ה]ן שבעת אלפים
[איש

8. whose right eye was not gouged by N[achash, king] of the [A]mmonites. And [**they**] were 7,000 men

Let's continue a little bit. Let's look at the sentence that begins in the middle of line 7 and continues to line 8:

"*ve-lo nish'ar ish be-vnei Yisrael asher be'ever ha-Yarden asher lo niker lo Nachash melekh bnei Ammon kol ayin yemin. Ve-**hen** shiv'at alafim ish*, Not a man was left of the Israelites of the other side of the Jordan, whose right eye was not gouged by Nachash, king of the Ammonites. And **they** were 7,000 men."

---

12   Numbers 21:21-35
13   Judges Chapter 12

Cross reconstructed the word *ve-hen* (והן) "and they." Look at it closely. I suggest the reconstruction using the word *rak* (רק), "only," or "but," or "except." *Rak shiv'at alafim ish.* That would read: "**but** 7,000 men remained."

Many times Tanakh uses the rhetorical device of making a general statement and then offering a clause of exception. A similar example can be found in Kings:

II Kings 17

יח וַיִּתְאַנַּף יְיָ מְאֹד בְּיִשְׂרָאֵל וַיְסִרֵם מֵעַל פָּנָיו: **לֹא נִשְׁאַר רַק שֵׁבֶט יְהוּדָה לְבַדּוֹ.**

18 that the LORD was very angry with Israel, and removed them out of His sight; **there was none left, but the tribe of Judah only**.

That lies within the boundaries of usage for biblical Hebrew. It makes a lot of things much more sensible. Although Cross is a much bigger expert than I, my suggestion might fit the story better.

Let's continue:

Dead Sea Scrolls: *4Q Sam^a X 1-10*

9. [נצלו מיד] בני עמון ויבאו אל [י]בש גלעד   ויאמרו כול אנשי יביש אל נחש
מ[לך]

9 [saved from the hand of] the Ammonites and they came to [Ya]veish Gile'ad and all the men of Yaveish said to Nachash k[ing]

10. [בני עמון כרת] ל[נו ברית ונעבדך ויאמר א]ל[יה]ם נחש [העמוני בזאת אכרת
לכם]

10 [of the Ammonites cut a covenant for] u[s and we will serve you and] Nachash the A[mmonite said to them In this I will cut for you]

"*Nitzlu miyad bnei Amon.*" These are the last seven thousand Gadites and Reuvenites who were able to escape up until now. And what did they do? "*Va-yavo'u el Yaveish Gile'ad,*" "They came to Yaveish Gile'ad." They sought refuge in the closest Israelite city that wasn't conquered up until now, and that was in the Gile'ad.

In other words, *Reuven and Gad were already under Nachash's control*. It was the *escapees* who found shelter in the city of Yaveish – which put the people of Yaveish in great danger for giving shelter to Nachash's enemies.

Va-yavo'u, "and they came," does not refer to Nachash; it refers to the last seven thousand. That's why it is in the plural. These seven thousand people fled to Yaveish Gile'ad.

I'm continuing according to the suggested transcription in line 9, "And all the men of *Yaveish* said to Nachash king of the Ammonites, 'Cut a covenant for us, and we will serve you.' And Nachash the Ammonite said to them, 'In this, I will cut for you.'"

From here on we already know the words. We have them in our story in the Tanakh.

Reading Between the Lines

This is the beginning of Chapter 11 according to our Masoretic Text. Now look back at the picture of the fragment. See the phrase squeezed in between line 8 and line 9 – what Chazal, our Sages of Blessed Memory, call *bein ha-shitin*, "between the lines."

These extra words, according to the Dead Sea Scroll experts (and, again, I'm going to take their word for it) were written by the same exact scribe who originally wrote the rest of the text. It is not a later hand. The first scribe added these words and we'll just try to understand why.

First let's read the words: "*Va-yehi kemo chodesh, va-ya'al Nachash ha-'Amoni va-yichan al Yaveish.*"

Dead Sea Scrolls: *4Q Sam* ^{a} *X 1-10*

8a **And it was about a month** and Nachash the Ammonite went up and camped before Yaveish

ויהי כמו חדש ויעל נחש העמני ויחן על יביש

The formation "*Va-yehi kemo chodesh,*" "About a month" is not very common, but it could work. If we look for a similar example to substantiate the grammar usage of the construct "*va-yehi kemo chodesh,*" we come up with a phrase from the Judah story within the Joseph cycle.[14]

In the story of Yehuda and Tamar, Yehuda wishes to pay his debt to an unknown harlot, but is unable to locate her. The text continues:

---

14   Genesis 38:24

Genesis 38:24

24 And it came to pass **about** three months after, that it was told Judah, saying: 'Tamar your daughter-in-law has played the harlot; and moreover, behold, she is with child by harlotry.' And Judah said: 'Bring her forth, and let her be burnt.'

כד וַיְהִי כְּמִשְׁלֹשׁ חֳדָשִׁים וַיֻּגַּד
לִיהוּדָה לֵאמֹר זָנְתָה תָּמָר
כַּלָּתֶךָ וְגַם הִנֵּה הָרָה
לִזְנוּנִים: וַיֹּאמֶר יְהוּדָה
הוֹצִיאוּהָ וְתִשָּׂרֵף.

"**About** three months," a trimester of pregnancy. The Hebrew word "like" (כמו) is spelled with a *vav* (ו) if it's *ketiv male'* (fully written out), or without a *vav*, if it's *ketiv chaser* (written with letters missing). In this Genesis text, it is written without the *vav* (כמ), *kemi-shlosh chadashim*, while the Samuel scroll uses the full spelling *va-yehi kemo* (כמו) *chodesh*.

This phrase *va-yehi kemo chodesh* takes a significant step closer to *va-yehi ke-mecharish*, the somewhat problematic phrase meaning "and he was like one who was silent" which, you'll notice, is missing from the version here in the scroll. Remember, from the Greek we had hypothesized *va-yehi ke-chodesh*. Now, we seem very clearly to be looking at two different variations of the story, based solely on the very small difference between the *resh* and the *dalet*. One version reads "as one who is silent"; the other, "and it was about a month." The Hebrew phrase from the Dead Sea Scroll fragment explains the wording we found in the Greek versions.

But it is not quite that simple. The Dead Sea Scroll presents its own, different version. These words appear in a different place We have to understand the difficulty of context in our story. Do these words appear in the right place in the story according to the Septuagint or Josephus? No. Where would we expect "*va-yehi kemo chodesh*," "And it was about a month," in our story? After the words "*velo hevi'u lo minchah*," right? "And they brought him no gift." That should be the beginning of the next story. I want to point out the difference of the Samuel scroll from the Septuagint and Josephus.

I'm not giving the author a grade now. I'm not asking if this is a good way to compose a story. I think both ways work.

If we're looking for the exact Hebrew prototype that the Septuagint used, it's not this scroll. Because the Septuagint does not contain the added chapter of the gouging of the tribes of Reuven and Gad – the "*va-yehi kemo chodesh*" in the Septuagint is in the beginning of the story, and not in the middle.

What we *do* have here are the words, *"va-yehi kemo chodesh"* and there must be some kind of correlation between the Hebrew *"va-yehi kemo ch-odesh"* that is written between the lines and the hypothesized Hebrew text underlying the Greek translation of the Septuagint.

What does it mean that it's written between the lines? Probably when the scribe was writing it the first time around, he made a mistake and forgot to include these words. Should they be here, or somewhere else? It may very well be that we have a series of scribal errors in the Dead Sea scroll. Here, it means that the phrase *"va-yehi kemo chodesh"* could have occurred twice in this text, at the beginning of the story and also in the middle.

In other words, we might be talking about a phrase that was repeated, indicating two *different* months that passed. It very well may be.

The Septuagint text has part of the story. The Dead Sea scroll has another part of the story. I mean, the lion's share, but another part of the story, and we have a little bit less than both of those sources.

Puzzles Solved

Let's think about the difficulties that are solved by accessing the versions of this passage offered by the Septuagint and by the Dead Sea Scrolls.

First of all, *"va-yehi ke-macharish,"* with the peculiar *kaf ha-dimyon* before the verb *macharish*, becomes *"va-yehi kemo chodesh,"* which reflects clearer syntax. Nachash is appropriately introduced by his regal title, which solves yet another one of our puzzles from the beginning. It solves another problem, too: Nachash's certainty that there would be no savior. In the Dead Sea Scroll version, Nachash has *already* ripped through the Reuvenites and Gadites... and been met with no reprisal whatsoever.

Why are there these differences, these discrepancies, between the different textual traditions? What purpose does it serve? If we're talking about a *girsah*, a "version" serving a purpose, that means that we assume that it is purposeful. But what if a whole passage was deleted, not on purpose, but by an innocent mistake? That can happen. In other words, I'm not so sure that there really *is* a purpose here.

A scribe can skip a line or two; one of the easiest ways to lose a text is when there are similar words that recur, and you read the first one and skip to the next one. Everything in the middle gets left out. And then all you're left with is: va-yehi ke, followed by this word, which contains either a *resh* (ר) or a *dalet* (ד). A scribe may not be sure what it is, and the letter becomes a *resh*. Forever. *Va-yehi ke-macharish*. It may just be the result of an accident, a scribal error.

Masoretes Preserved One Text

Our text, the Masoretic text, is quite different from the Samuel scroll. Could one posit, then, that the *ba'alei ha-masorah*, the "Masoretes," changed the Hebrew text of our story? Absolutely not! They merely recorded the sacred text that had been handed down to them over the generations. But how can one be sure that what had been passed down during the Second Temple period and the Talmudic period was necessarily the original text written by the author of Samuel? If, for any reason, part of the text was lost – through scribal or other error – this corrupted text would have reached the *ba'alei ha-masorah* and would ultimately be permanently recorded in their monumental project of preserving and unifying the text of the Hebrew Bible. The evidence that we have seen here suggests that both *"va-yehi kimo chodesh,"* and, *"va-yehi ke-macharish,"* existed at the same time – around the end of the Second Temple period. But after the destruction of the second Temple, only one version survived, the predecessor of what is known as the Masoretic text.

The claim I am making here opens up a much larger topic that demands more attention – what do we do with discrepancies in the Biblical textual tradition? Not just here but also in other places. This much larger issue must be dealt with elsewhere.[15] For now it will suffice to appreciate the historical opportunity afforded to our generation in the unveiling of this very interesting version of the Nachash story, a version that was lost for two millennia, sealed in a cave in the slopes overlooking the Dead Sea.[16]

---

15   On this, see B. Barry Levy, *Fixing God's Torah* (Oxford, 2001), and Marc Shapiro, *The Limits of Orthodox Theology*, (Oxford, 2004) pp.91-103 –Ed.

16   The author wishes to stress that although only minimal bibliography is cited throughout the article (as it is the written form of an oral presentation), the reader would benefit in knowing that the present unit has generated much scholarly discussion and more than one opinion has been voiced about the significance of the various textual data discussed here. The inquisitive reader is encouraged to consult the bibliography cited by F. M. Cross *(loc. cit.)* as well as another view voiced by A. Rofé, "4QMidrash Samuel? Observations Concerning the Character of 4QSam^a," *Textus* 19 (1998) pp. 63-74.

YCT Tanakh Companion

Amalek: Ethics, Values and
Halakhic Development

Rabbi Nathaniel Helfgot

As religious Jews, we try to orient our lives according to God's will. Even so, we are not always comfortable with all of the commandments.

There are those commandments that may be inconvenient or expensive to follow — eating only kosher food, for example — and those that are downright challenging, such as refraining from evil speech.

There are even those commandments which make us question: How can this be what God really wants from us?

In Samuel, we see one such commandment: the directive to destroy the tribe of Amalek. God demands absolute fealty to the dictates of His command.

I Samuel 15

2 Thus says the LORD of hosts: I remember that which Amalek did to Israel, how he set himself against him in the way, when he came up out of Egypt.

ב כֹּה אָמַר יְיָ צְבָאוֹת פָּקַדְתִּי אֵת אֲשֶׁר-עָשָׂה עֲמָלֵק לְיִשְׂרָאֵל: אֲשֶׁר-שָׂם לוֹ בַּדֶּרֶךְ בַּעֲלֹתוֹ מִמִּצְרָיִם.

3 Now go and smite Amalek, and utterly destroy all that they have, and spare them not; but slay both man and woman, infant and suckling, ox and sheep, camel and ass.

ג עַתָּה לֵךְ וְהִכִּיתָה אֶת-עֲמָלֵק וְהַחֲרַמְתֶּם אֶת-כָּל-אֲשֶׁר-לוֹ וְלֹא תַחְמֹל עָלָיו: וְהֵמַתָּה מֵאִישׁ עַד-אִשָּׁה מֵעֹלֵל וְעַד-יוֹנֵק מִשּׁוֹר וְעַד-שֶׂה מִגָּמָל וְעַד-חֲמוֹר.

In fact, when Saul spares the animals and the king of Amalek, it costs him his throne.

The divine command to Saul follows two earlier Biblical references to Amalek. The first, in Exodus, follows the infamous battle in which Amalek attacked the Israelites immediately after their departure from Egypt. After the battle, God decrees:

Exodus 17

16 He said: 'The hand upon the throne of the LORD: the LORD will have war with Amalek from generation to generation.'

טז וַיֹּאמֶר כִּי-יָד עַל-כֵּס יָ-הּ מִלְחָמָה לַיי בַּעֲמָלֵק: מִדֹּר דֹּר.

Later, in Deuteronomy, God commands:

Deuteronomy 25

19 Therefore it shall be, when the LORD your God has given your rest from all your enemies round about, in the land which the LORD your God gives you for an inheritance to possess it, that you shall destroy the remembrance of Amalek from under heaven; you shall not forget.

יט וְהָיָה בְּהָנִיחַ יְיָ אֱלֹהֶיךָ לְךָ מִכָּל-אֹיְבֶיךָ מִסָּבִיב בָּאָרֶץ אֲשֶׁר-יְיָ אֱלֹהֶיךָ נֹתֵן לְךָ נַחֲלָה לְרִשְׁתָּהּ תִּמְחֶה אֶת-זֵכֶר עֲמָלֵק מִתַּחַת הַשָּׁמָיִם: לֹא תִּשְׁכָּח.

Saul's botched war on Amalek seems a coda to the Torah's earlier decrees.

In fact, one of the most famous accountings of the Torah's 613 commandments, *Sefer Ha-Chinukh*, states explicitly that each individual Jew is commanded to kill each individual Amalekite, man, woman and child:

"The Israelites were charged with three precepts at the time of their entry into the land of Israel: to appoint a king for themselves, to build the chosen Temple, and to eradicate the descendants of Amalek. In truth, though, on every *individual* among the Israelite males there lies also the duty to kill them and make them perish from the world, if the power lies in their hand, in every place and every time, if perhaps one out of all their descendants will be found." (Mitzvah #604; emphasis added.)

How are we to conceptualize this difficult commandment for ourselves? How should we approach the question of Amalek when we teach Samuel, or Exodus, or Deuteronomy?

The *Sefer Ha-Chinukh* prescribes the killing of Amlekite children without raising any moral qualms, possibly in part because it is impossible to actually fulfill the commandment. The Talmud ruled that the invasions and exiles of Sancherib, king of Assyria and destroyer of Samaria, "mixed up the nations"¹ more than 2,500 years ago and it is impossible to trace individuals back to specific Biblical nations. Biblical laws of how to treat any of the Canaanite and neighboring nations are therefore effectively irrelevant. In other words, there are no Amalekites walking around today.

There is a strand within the Jewish community, and even within Jewish thought, that sees this as a purely technical issue. "Of course we should destroy the Amalekite. We have to follow the Torah and must resist the terrible lure of the alien Kantian ethics of the West. Whatever God says is *ipso facto* the right thing to do."

From this perspective, eliminating Amalek is one of those commandments we can't perform — such as the Temple worship — but it reflects a fully moral commandment that is not abberational in any way, nor should give us any ethical qualms.

The God of Morality or the Morality of God

This debate over whether a Divine command is by definition moral is an old one. Plato's dialogue *Euthyphro* phrases the question like this: "Do the gods command that which is holy because it is holy, or is it holy because the gods command it?"

For our monotheistic purposes this can be rephrased as: Is moral behavior commanded by God because it *is* moral, or is it moral because it's willed by God?

Without going into a lengthy excursus, let me just state what I believe to be eminently clear from the sources.

The majority position in Judaism is that there is indeed such a thing as free-standing morality which can be intuited and understood, and which is separate from any specific Divine commandment.²

The very fact that Abraham can challenge God regarding Sodom and say, "will not the Judge of all the earth act justly?"³ implies that God must live up to the demands of justice, and that justice is accessible to man.

Notice what God *doesn't* say to Abraham.

God doesn't tell Abraham: "Silence, you puny little human. Who are you to tell Me what is right? Whatever I say is right." God doesn't pull rank on Abraham. He never tells Abraham, "You don't see the whole picture. *I* have the whole picture."

---

1   Talmud Bavli, Berakhot 28a

2   For a sustained and vigorous presentation of the case for this assertion in the Jewish tradition see A. Sagi, *Yahadut: Bein Dat le-Mussar* (Tel-Aviv, 1998) pp. 10-102

3   Genesis 18:25

What God says is, "You have a point, Abraham, you are asking a legitimate question, but I will show you in terms accessible to the human intelligence that I have a *moral* answer for you." God justifies His plans within a moral compass and Abraham accepts it. Are there fifty righteous people, are there forty, are there ten? In the end, there are no redeeming qualities in Sodom.

Abraham is convinced that God operates with justice. In fact, when God decides to speak to Abraham about Sodom, He identifies Himself with justice:

Genesis 18

19 For I (God) have known him
(Abraham), to the end that he
may command his children and
his household after him, that they
may keep the way of the LORD,
to do righteousness and justice;
to the end that the LORD
may bring upon Abraham that
which He has spoken of him.

יט כִּי יְדַעְתִּיו לְמַעַן אֲשֶׁר יְצַוֶּה
אֶת-בָּנָיו וְאֶת-בֵּיתוֹ אַחֲרָיו
וְשָׁמְרוּ דֶּרֶךְ יְיָ לַעֲשׂוֹת צְדָקָה
וּמִשְׁפָּט: לְמַעַן הָבִיא יְיָ עַל-
אַבְרָהָם אֵת אֲשֶׁר-דִּבֶּר עָלָיו.

Since God's aim in destroying Sodom is justice, He is invested in sharing His motives with Abraham.

Moses describes God in similar terms:

Deuteronomy 32

4 The Rock, His work is perfect;
for all His ways are justice; a
God of faithfulness and without
iniquity, just and right is He.

ד הַצּוּר תָּמִים פָּעֳלוֹ כִּי כָל-
דְּרָכָיו מִשְׁפָּט: אֵל אֱמוּנָה
וְאֵין עָוֶל צַדִּיק וְיָשָׁר הוּא.

Judaism, and certainly Tanakh, does not assume an arbitrary, capricious, or demonic God. The Bible assumes that God is a good God — omnipotent, omniscient and good. This assumption of goodness is what allows Abraham to challenge God. It is what allows Jeremiah to challenge God. It is what allows Job to challenge God.

Most medieval Jewish thinkers agree with this assumption of God's goodness. So when we are morally offended by the notion of killing Amalekite babies, when we question the apparent commandment, we are in fact affirming a very traditional Jewish view of God and morality.

As Jews confronting these texts, and even more so as parents and teachers, we have to pay attention to several different levels of discussion of Amalek.

There are the Biblical texts.

There is *halachah*, Jewish law: We don't know who Amalekites are, so the commandment is functionally null and void. (Of course that position avoids the moral questions, but at least it also avoids actual bloodshed.)

And then there are the various rabbinic interpretations and commentaries, who have dealt with the texts, the law, and perhaps the moral issues.

We have already seen the position of the *Sefer Ha-Chinukh*, who maintains God has commanded every Jew to kill every individual Amalekite in any and all situations. We will now look carefully at the basic texts, the sources in Exodus, Deuteronomy and Samuel. We will then turn to Maimonides, who as we know tends to be a definitive guide to Jewish law, and who, as we will see, has a reading of all the Amalekite passages that is consistent but at odds with that of the *Sefer Ha-Chinukh*. We will then turn to some modern permutations, before finally concluding with some general principles on how to approach morally troubling texts.

Reading Closely

First, what does the Torah itself say? When we isolate the Torah passages on this subject, and read them without referencing material from the Book of Samuel and other sources, we discover that the Torah itself never commands a genocidal war against Amalek.

(The Torah *does* command such a war against the seven Canaanite nations[4], which is a separate, albeit related, issue. That war, it is important to note, is mitigated by the "call to peace"[5] which the Torah explicitly says must be offered the nations before fighting them. If they are willing to accept the conquest of the Israelites, then there is no war, genocidal or otherwise.)

Let's look again at Exodus 17:16:

"...The hand upon the throne of the LORD: the LORD will have war with Amalek from generation to generation."

---

4   Deuteronomy 7:1-2. "The Hittite, and the Girgashite, and the Amorite, and the Canaanite, and the Perizzite, and the Hivite, and the Jebusite, seven nations greater and mightier than you." These are the nations that the Israelites are commanded to subdue upon entering the promised land.

5   Deuteronomy 20:10-11 and Ramban's commentary to the verse.

That is not a war here on earth. It is a war which takes place in the Divine realm rather than in our own.

Deuteronomy 25:19 is also not a clear call to genocide:

> "Therefore it shall be, when the LORD thy God has given you rest from all your enemies round about, in the land which the LORD your God gives you for an inheritance to possess it, that you **shall destroy the remembrance of Amalek** from under heaven; you shall not forget."

What does it mean to destroy the *remembrance* of Amalek?

Does it mean to destroy all Amalek in a war? If so, then there is no individual requirement to hunt and find every single Amalekite and kill him or her. (It might mean that within the context of warfare, though, the war against Amalek must be a total war. We must not negotiate peace with them.)

What about *after* the war? After they surrender, is there an obligation to go from house to house and kill every single Amalekite?

Looking honestly in Deuteronomy for the plain meaning of the text, this is not clear at all. The truth is,[6] even when it comes to the command (regarding the seven nations) to "save nothing alive that breathes,"[7] if you carefully study the Tanakh, including Joshua and Judges, one can certainly argue that there was no call for genocidal war in the modern sense. No one went from house to house after a war, trying to kill every individual from the seven Canaanite nations, so that, too, is far from the simple textual reading there.

"Save nothing alive that breathes" is a call for total war. Don't fool around; just go in and bomb. In almost every war, that is the reality.

But after the surrender, the war is over. That is the evidence from Tanakh, and that is what Maimonides codifies as the normative ruling.

The notion that the destruction of Amalek requires genocide, then, doesn't come from the Torah. It appears, rather, in the Book of Samuel:

I Samuel 15

2 Thus says the LORD of hosts: I remember that which Amalek did to Israel, how he set himself against him in the way, when he came up out of Egypt.

ב כֹּה אָמַר יְיָ צְבָאוֹת פָּקַדְתִּי אֵת
אֲשֶׁר-עָשָׂה עֲמָלֵק לְיִשְׂרָאֵל: אֲשֶׁר-
שָׂם לוֹ בַּדֶּרֶךְ בַּעֲלֹתוֹ מִמִּצְרָיִם.

---

6   See R. Yaaqov Medan and R. Yoel Bin Nun's essays in the compendium *Musar Ve-Kibush Be-Milchama* (Alon Shvut, 1993)

7   Deuteronomy 20:16

3 Now go and smite Amalek, and utterly destroy all that they have, and spare them not; but slay both man and woman, infant and suckling, ox and sheep, camel and ass.	ג עַתָּה לֵךְ וְהִכִּיתָה אֶת-עֲמָלֵק וְהַחֲרַמְתֶּם אֶת-כָּל-אֲשֶׁר-לוֹ וְלֹא תַחְמֹל עָלָיו: וְהֵמַתָּה מֵאִישׁ עַד-אִשָּׁה מֵעֹלֵל וְעַד-יוֹנֵק מִשּׁוֹר וְעַד-שֶׂה מִגָּמָל וְעַד-חֲמוֹר.

The command seems clear: Everyone must be killed.

This, however, is certainly not what happened. Amalekites reappear 15 chapters later,[8] when David is commanded to destroy them — and even there it doesn't sound like a war of annihilation.

Rabbi Yaaqov Medan, in a seminal essay on the topic of Amalek,[9] proves cogently that even the phrase "infant and suckling" does not mean genocide in the sense of killing every single Amalekite you meet on the street. If you lived at the time of Samuel, and discovered that your shoe-maker happened to be from Amalek, you would not have been obligated to kill him.

Rabbi Medan suggests that we should understand this phrase as only being applicable in the context of war. When at war with Amalek, we must be willing to make no compromises — even when it comes to bombing civilian locales. That's what happens under certain circumstances. That's what the United States did in World War II. Sometimes success-fully, sometimes unsuccessfully. This is part of the reality of war.

Rabbinic authorities (though not *Sefer Ha-Chinukh*) apply another meaning to "infant and suckling." They interpret it to mean that war with Amalek should be waged as a *national* initiative.[10] This is not an injunc-tion to be taken on by private individuals. When Israel has a properly functioning government, a Sanhedrin and a king and prophets, then it is up to the leadership to launch such a war. God has not commanded each and every Israelite to become an assassin, waging private wars against Amalek. War is a national effort.

There are two different issues here. One has to do with timing; is this a time of war, or a time of peace? The other has to do with the participants; is this binding only upon the Israelite nation, or upon each individual? Both approaches read the command to destroy Amalek as something less than genocidal.

---

8   I Samuel 30:1

9   "Amalek" in *Al Derekh ha-Avot* (Alon Shvut, 2001), pp. 317-391, espe-cially 372-380.

10   See Maimonides in Hilkhot Melakhim, chapter 6

Private Affair

We have however seen that there are those who maintain that the war against Amalek is a war for all time, and one which is incumbent upon each individual personally. This has become the assumption on the street: that every Jew has an obligation to kill every Amalekite.

In fact, this assumption seems to emerge from the Mekhilta:[11] "Rabbi Eliezer says that if anyone from the nations of the world comes to convert to Judaism, he should be accepted. If he is Amalek, he should *not* be accepted."

Clearly, this is not describing a wartime conversion. Rabbi Eliezer states that if a nice Amalekite boy would discover that he loves Judaism and wants to become a Jew — the answer would be no.

The Mekhilta tells us not to accept Amalekite converts, and the *Sefer Ha-Chinukh* extends this teaching: not only do we turn away converts, but we have to kill each and every individual Amalekite in every situation.

What is the basic source for turning away Amalekite converts? It rests in the story of David and the young Amalekite from the Book of Samuel:

II Samuel 1

5 And David said to the young man that told him: "How do you know that Saul and Jonathan his son are dead?"

6 And the young man that told him said: "As I happened by chance upon Mount Gilbo'a, behold, Saul leaned upon his spear; and, lo, the chariots and the horsemen pressed hard upon him.

7 "And when he looked behind him, he saw me, and called to me. And I answered: 'Here am I.'

8 "And he said to me: 'Who are you?' And I answered him: 'I am an Amalekite.'

ה וַיֹּאמֶר דָּוִד אֶל-הַנַּעַר הַמַּגִּיד
לוֹ: אֵיךְ יָדַעְתָּ כִּי-מֵת
שָׁאוּל וִיהוֹנָתָן בְּנוֹ?

ו וַיֹּאמֶר הַנַּעַר הַמַּגִּיד לוֹ נִקְרֹא
נִקְרֵיתִי בְּהַר הַגִּלְבֹּעַ וְהִנֵּה שָׁאוּל
נִשְׁעָן עַל-חֲנִיתוֹ: וְהִנֵּה הָרֶכֶב
וּבַעֲלֵי הַפָּרָשִׁים הִדְבִּקֻהוּ.

ז וַיִּפֶן אַחֲרָיו וַיִּרְאֵנִי: וַיִּקְרָא
אֵלַי וָאֹמַר הִנֵּנִי.

ח וַיֹּאמֶר לִי מִי-אָתָּה: וָאֹמַר
(וָאֹמַר) אֵלָיו עֲמָלֵקִי אָנֹכִי.

---

9 "And he said to me: 'Stand, I pray
you, beside me, and slay me, for
the agony has taken hold of me;
because my life is just yet in me.'

ט וַיֹּאמֶר אֵלַי עֲמָד-נָא עָלַי
וּמֹתְתֵנִי כִּי אֲחָזַנִי הַשָּׁבָץ:
כִּי-כָל-עוֹד נַפְשִׁי בִּי.

10 "So I stood beside him, and slew
him, because I was sure that he
could not live after he fell; and
I took the crown that was upon
his head, and the bracelet that
was on his arm, and have brought
them hither unto my lord."

י וָאֶעֱמֹד עָלָיו וַאֲמֹתְתֵהוּ כִּי יָדַעְתִּי כִּי
לֹא יִחְיֶה אַחֲרֵי נִפְלוֹ: וָאֶקַּח הַנֵּזֶר
אֲשֶׁר עַל-רֹאשׁוֹ וְאֶצְעָדָה אֲשֶׁר
עַל-זְרֹעוֹ וָאֲבִיאֵם אֶל-אֲדֹנִי הֵנָּה.

11 Then David took hold on
his clothes, and rent them;
and likewise all the men
that were with him.

יא וַיַּחֲזֵק דָּוִד בִּבְגָדָו וַיִּקְרָעֵם:
וְגַם כָּל-הָאֲנָשִׁים אֲשֶׁר אִתּוֹ.

12 And they wailed, and wept, and
fasted until even, for Saul, and
for Jonathan his son, and for
the people of the LORD, and
for the house of Israel; because
they were fallen by the sword.

יב וַיִּסְפְּדוּ וַיִּבְכּוּ וַיָּצֻמוּ עַד-הָעָרֶב:
עַל-שָׁאוּל וְעַל-יְהוֹנָתָן בְּנוֹ וְעַל-עַם
יְיָ וְעַל-בֵּית יִשְׂרָאֵל-כִּי נָפְלוּ בֶּחָרֶב.

13 And David said to the young
man that told him: "Whence are
you?" And he answered: 'I am the
son of an Amalekite stranger.'

יג וַיֹּאמֶר דָּוִד אֶל-הַנַּעַר הַמַּגִּיד
לוֹ אֵי מִזֶּה אָתָּה: וַיֹּאמֶר
בֶּן-אִישׁ גֵּר עֲמָלֵקִי אָנֹכִי.

14 And David said to him: 'How
were you not afraid to put
forth your hand to destroy
the LORD'S anointed?'

יד וַיֹּאמֶר אֵלָיו דָּוִד: אֵיךְ לֹא יָרֵאתָ
לִשְׁלֹחַ יָדְךָ לְשַׁחֵת אֶת-מְשִׁיחַ יְיָ.

15 And David called one of the
young men, and said: 'Go
near, and fall upon him.' And
he smote him that he died.

טו וַיִּקְרָא דָוִד לְאַחַד מֵהַנְּעָרִים
וַיֹּאמֶר גַּשׁ פְּגַע-בּוֹ: וַיַּכֵּהוּ וַיָּמֹת.

16 And David said to him: 'Your
blood be upon your head; for
your mouth testified against
you, saying: I have slain
the LORD'S anointed.'

טז וַיֹּאמֶר אֵלָיו דָּוִד דמיך (דָּמְךָ)
עַל-רֹאשֶׁךָ: כִּי פִיךָ עָנָה בְךָ לֵאמֹר
אָנֹכִי מֹתַתִּי אֶת-מְשִׁיחַ יְיָ.

The Mekhiltah says:

> "At the same moment that the lad identified himself as an Amalekite, David remembered what was said to Moses, our teacher "If one comes from the nations of the world to convert, accept him, but if he comes from Amalek, do not accept him." Immediately David said to him: "Your blood be upon your head, for your mouth testified against you."[12]

According to the Mekhilta's reading, David kills the Amalekite lad not because he has killed Saul, the anointed of God, but because he is an Amalekite. This is the basis for the approach of the *Sefer Ha-Chinukh*.

Maimonides, however, disagrees. He disagrees with the *Sefer Ha-Chinukh* on the general conception of eliminating Amalek. And he disagrees with the Mekhilta on the specific case of David and the Amalekite.

The case arises in Maimonides' discussion of the laws of legal procedure.[13] The law is that a court cannot punish anyone based solely on self-confession. Confession is not enough in Judaism: there must be two witnesses to establish a criminal act and punish the criminal. Given this, how do we understand David's execution of the Amalekite, and Joshua's earlier execution of Akhan?[14] How could they be executed when there were no witnesses against them?

Maimonides says that the lad was not killed because he was an Amalekite. Maimonides says it was simply a unique instance, a *"hora'at sha'ah,"* or a special prerogative of the royal throne — presumably because of the dishonor to Saul. Maimonides does not accept the notion that being an Amalekite is an automatic capital offense.

In fact, when Maimonides talks about converts, he states: "We accept converts from *all* the nations of the world."[15] There are no exceptions to this. Maimonides believes that you *can* accept converts from Amalek.[16]

Maimonides is actually on very firm ground here, because according to a famous Talmudic passage,[17] there were descendants of Haman who were Jews. How did they become Jews? The assumption is that they somehow joined the Jewish people through conversion. And that's the Maimonidian position: You *can* have converts from Amalek.

How can there be Jewish converts from Amalek? Because Maimonides

---

12   Ibid.

13   Mishneh Torah, Hilchot Sanhedrin, 18:6

14   Joshua 7:19-26

15   Hilchot Isurei Biyah, 12:17

16   This is the traditional understanding of Maimonides' position as cited by later commentators.

17   Talmud Bavli Gitin, 52b מבני בניו של המן למדו תורה בבני ברק

believes that there is no commandment for genocide in an absolute racial sense, in the Nazi manner, where it was of little consequence whether one was actually a practicing Jew or not. For Maimonides, wiping out the memory of Amalek is not about exterminating a blood line; it is about something else.

We see this most explicitly in Maimonides when he discusses the laws of warfare. Maimonides says the Jewish body politic can never launch a war without first offering "a call to peace." And Maimonides says this applies to fighting "anybody."[18] And "anybody" means everybody; the seven Canaanite nations, Amalek, anyone.

If they accept the Noachide laws[19] and make peace on that basis, then war should no longer be required.

What happens if they don't accept the seven commandments? What if they want to maintain their autonomy as idolators, living in the land of Israel?

Maimonides says:[20] "If they do not accept upon themselves the seven Noachide commandments, then you shall kill all the males and take the rest as booty. You should not kill women or children."

This law, though, says Maimonides, does not apply to "the seven Canaanite nations, and Amalek, who have *not* made peace." For them, says Maimonides, not a soul should be left alive if they do not accept the terms.

It is striking to note what is included in Maimonides' discussion in the laws of making peace or not making peace.

In effect, Maimonides is saying: "Do not make war with anyone in the world without first offering them peace"[21] (Amalek here is considered in the same category as every other nation, in terms of war.) "But the Seven Nations and Amalek, who have *not* made peace, do not spare a soul from among them, as it says, 'thus shall you do to all...', only from those nations (who have not made peace) do you not leave a soul. And so it says concerning Amalek, 'extirpate the memory of Amalek.'"

Notice carefully Maimonides' amazing act of exegesis. The Torah says

---

18   Hilchot Melakhim, 6:1

19   Talmud Bavli, Sanhedrin 56a: "Our Rabbis taught: seven precepts were the sons of Noah commanded: to establish courts, to refrain from: blasphemy, idolatry; adultery; bloodshed; robbery; and eating flesh from a living animal." To follow these laws would be all that would be required of a non-Israelite in order for him to show acknowledgment of the God of the Israelites.

20   Maimonidies, Hilchot Melakhim 6:4

21   Deuteronomy 20:10

of the Seven Nations, "do not leave alive a soul."[22] The Torah also says of the Seven Nations, "sue for peace and if they take peace, good. Let them live. And they will have to accept the seven commandments."

Maimonides creates an equation between "do not leave a soul alive" and "extirpate the memory of Amalek." Maimonides continues the equation and argues that if both the Seven Nations and Amalek are under one roof for destruction, the conditions for that mandate must be identical. Thus, Maimonides claims that Amalek too must first be approached with an offer of peace. If they accept, surrender, and accept the Noahide code, they are spared and are allowed safe dwelling in the land. He applies the same rubric to both Amalek and the seven nations.

What is his basis? How does he know that?

Because he read through the Book of Samuel, and because the Jewish tradition starting with the Sages seemed to have understood the command to "destroy the remembrance of Amalek" as a national activity, not an individual obligation.

Maimonides has done a couple of things here.

He has interpreted the killing of Amalekite women and children as the normative approach in the context of war, rather than as a commandment in all situations. And he has brought the command to call for peace as a normative approach in all wars, even that against Amalek.

And the consequence is plain. If Amalek makes peace, they are not killed. For Maimonides, there is no absolute extirpation of Amalek.

This is a second reading of the sources, a very different reading than that of the *Sefer Ha-Chinukh*, and one much less familiar to the average Jew. It is an approach that emerges from Maimonides' reading of the sources.

Maimonides seems to have been limiting the ramifications of our understanding of Amalek — downgrading the obligation from genocide, to having application only during war. What might be the motivation for this exegetical and legal move?

Recent Responses

There is a fascinating responsum from the great religious authority from the late 19th century, R. Avraham Sachatchover. He writes:[23]

> Maimonides' position is that both the Seven Nations and Amalek are accepted and allowed to live if they make peace, that is that they accept the Noahide commandments, taxation, and servitude.

---

22   Deuteronomy 20:16
23   Responsa Avnei Nezer, Orat Hayyim, Vol. 2: #508.

And the need for the Give'onites to engage in subterfuge was because they wanted Joshua to make a covenant with them.

And it is difficult to understand, that while making peace is valid with regards to the seven nations, how do we know that this applies to Amalek as well?

And it appears to me that... the descendants of Amalek are punished because of the sins of their forefathers, and at first blush (this is problematic) for it states in the Torah that "Parents shall not die on account of their father's (sins) nor children for the sins of the fathers?"

However, it is known before God that their hate is rooted in their hearts... and if they continue to act in the ways of their forefathers (they are punished). **However, if they repent from their ways and accept the Noahide commandments, they no longer continue in the path of their forefathers, and are no longer held responsible for the sins of their forefathers."**

R. Sachatchover has incorporated the classic rabbinic approach to the following two Biblical verses:

Deuteronomy 24

16 The fathers shall not be put to death for the children, neither shall the children be put to death for the fathers; **every man shall be put to death for his own sin.**

טז לֹא-יוּמְתוּ אָבוֹת עַל-בָּנִים
וּבָנִים לֹא-יוּמְתוּ עַל-אָבוֹת:
אִישׁ בְּחֶטְאוֹ יוּמָתוּ.

Exodus 20

5 you shall not bow down to them, nor serve them; for I the LORD your God am a jealous God, **visiting the iniquity of the fathers upon the children** unto the third and fourth generation of them that hate Me.

ה לֹא-תִשְׁתַּחֲוֶה לָהֶם וְלֹא
תָעָבְדֵם: כִּי אָנֹכִי יְיָ אֱלֹהֶיךָ אֵל
קַנָּא פֹּקֵד עֲוֹן אָבֹת עַל-בָּנִים
עַל-שִׁלֵּשִׁים וְעַל-רִבֵּעִים לְשֹׂנְאָי.

How do you jibe those two? What is the Rabbinic solution? If they continue in the footsteps of their fathers, then they receive a type of double punishment. But if they don't, history is not destiny. Genetics is not destiny (the Sages and R. Sachatchover agree upon this). The amazing thing is that this rabbinic solution, generally understood to apply to Jews, is now taken by the R. Sachatchover to include non-Jews and even Amalek! If our Amalekite has decided to abandon his evil ways and his identification with the evil ideology that Amalek represents, and if that's what he wants, of course you accept him. Just like you accept the nation if they decide to surrender and take upon themselves the seven Noachide commandments.

In a different responsum, R. Eliezer Waldenberg[24] quotes the Chazon Ish, Rabbi Avraham Yeshayahu Karelitz, one of the great Talmudic scholars of the early part of the mid-twentieth century.

He attempts to explain the Mekhilta we cited by pointing to the Talmud's claim[25] that the descendants of Haman studied Torah in Bnei Brak. It seems that Hamanites *did* come into the Jewish fold and the assumption is that it was as converts.

It appears that one does accept Amalekite converts but once they go to war, all bets are off. In a total war, converts are treated like any other Amalekite.

The Chazon Ish says that as soon as the converted Amalekite went to war against Israel, there can no longer be any assupmtion of higher sensitivity on his part; he should have not been accepted and, therefore, the conversion is not real. He also cites the Netziv who says something similar: It is in the context of war that the unmitigated battle against Amalek takes place.

So here we have two relatively recent rabbinic figures, from the 19th and 20th centuries, who basically follow the Maimonidean approach, not that of the *Sefer Ha-Chinukh*. The Chazon Ish and the Avnei Nezer state that faced with a harmless person of undeniable Amalekite descent – the operative law is not genocide. Jews are not commanded to kill the would-be convert, or an Amalekite baby for that matter.

Avi Sagi's trenchant summary of the positions we have explored in appreciating Maimonides' rulings serve as a fitting coda to this section of the essay:

> The author of Avnei Nezer posits that Maimonides' approach is based upon two assumptions:
>
> 1) The punishment of Amalek relates to the actual events that occurred in the past, and the punishment is not simply vengeance; the punishment has a purpose: the total eradication of acts such as those committed by Amalek.
>
> 2) The Torah, which includes in his eyes the rabbinic exegesis, reflects a comprehensive unified legal system. If there exists a general directive that parents do not bear responsibility for the sins of the fathers, this must apply to Amalek as well.
>
> From these two assumptions he concludes that if Amalek does not act as "Amalek" ...it is forbidden to kill him. Such an interpre-

---

24   Responsa *Tzitz Eliezer* Vol 13:71

25   Gittin 57b

tation which is repeated in the works of a number of contemporary halakhic authorities has a solid foundation in Maimonides writings in Mishneh Torah and The Guide for the Perplexed. In The Guide (3:41), Maimonides adopts the position that punishing Amalek is an instrumental, purposeful act and not spurred by ethnic hatred for the Amalek race. The purpose is to deter Amalek-like behavior... Maimonides also adopts the general position that "The Laws of the Torah are not to bring vengeance to the world, but rather reflections of mercy, loving-kindness and peace in the world" (Hil. Shabbat Ch. 2:3)

This general principle illuminates the Maimonidean exegesis regarding the punishment put upon Amalek; as the Torah does not engage in vengeance for vengeance sake, there must be a purpose for the punishment. Thus if they make peace there is no need for their eradication. In other words, Maimonides' exegesis fits with the general spirit of the Torah, its basic assumptions regarding fairness and justice that must be meted out to every human being.[26]

In the real world, where no Amalekite DNA test is possible, there is no practical difference between the Maimonidian approach and the *Sefer Ha-Chinukh* approach. But the moral difference is profound. For *Sefer Ha-Chinukh*, God has commanded genocide to be performed by each individual Jew, but the conditions are lacking due to forces beyond our control. For Maimonides, and subsequently for the Chazon Ish and the Sachatchover, however, there is no such far-reaching demand. God has not commanded genocide after all. And, to answer Euthyphro's question, what God wants is indeed what is moral.

Conclusion

I want to conclude by stepping back again, and looking at one particular response to the Euthyphro question, that of my revered teacher, Rabbi Aharon Lichtenstein. Rav Lichtenstein has a beautiful Hebrew essay[27] about the tension between ethics and religion. It serves as a fitting summary of the approach that we need to inculcate more fully in our religious community today:

The parameters of ethics and morality and its truths have an important role to play in understanding Halakha and defining its boundaries. Of course, a Jew must be ready to answer the call "I am here" if the command "to offer him up as an offering" is thrust upon him. However, prior to unsheathing the sword, he is per-

26   (Sagi, pg. 223-4, my translation)

27   "Halakha Va-Halakhim" in *Arachim Be-Mivchan Milchamah*, (Jerusalem, 1986) pp. 13-24.

mitted, and even obligated to clarify, to the best of his ability, if indeed this is what he actually has been commanded. Is the command indeed so clear-cut and is the collision of values indeed so frontal and unavoidable.

To the extent that there is a need and room for halachic exegesis-and this must be clarified—a **sensitive and insightful conscience** is one of the factors that shape the decision making process.

Just as Maimonides in his day, consciously, was assisted by a particular metaphysical approach to the world in order to plumb the depths of the meaning of Biblical verses, so too one can make use of an ethical perspective in order to understand the content of Halakha and to outline, at time, its parameters.

Clearly this process requires extreme care and responsibility. It must be assured that—and this is rooted in deep connection to authentic Torah and religious piety—one is attempting to understand the Halakha and not judge it, or God forbid to distort it.[28]

Indeed, this passage should serve as a clarion call of the direction that our great thinkers and rabbinic decisors must constantly consider in approaching their teaching and guidance. The moral intuitions, implanted into us by the grace of God, should not be discounted out of hand, but judiciously used to understand, interpret and enhance the Torah that has been revealed to us by that same God who is the source of all being.[29]

---

28   Ibid., pp. 20-21 (my translation, NH).

29   An important essay touching on many of the issues addressed in this chapter was published after this book was already in galleys: Eugene Korn, "Moralization in Jewish Law: Genocide, Divine Commands, and Rabbinic Reasoning," *The Edah Journal* 5, no.2 (*Sivan* 5766).

David and Saul: A comparison
I Samuel 15-17

Rabbi Nathaniel Helfgot

When reading the Book of Samuel, one is struck by the contrast between the careers of King Saul and King David. For all his great promise, Saul flames out very quickly. Conversely, King David takes longer to come to power, but possesses an enviable ability to maintain his grasp on the kingship.

David enters the story with very little introduction, whereas Saul is furnished with a distinguished background. Saul's genealogy is presented to us directly in the Book of Samuel. Not only are we told that Saul is handsome, but he is tall; head and shoulders above everyone else.[1] The text romances the reader with Saul's wonderful qualities. Conversely, in chapter 16, after God has rejected Saul, David steps out of relative obscurity to make his own appearance.

Saul's golden period is tragically short. Anointed in chapter 10, within two chapters Saul is already ignoring the directives of the prophet Samuel. By chapter 13, he has been stripped of the promise of a continuing dynasty.

God punishes Saul for two infractions, first rejecting his dynasty, and then wresting from Saul his personal kingship. First and foremost, Saul's dynasty is discontinued as a result of ignoring God's instructions, and offering sacrifices without waiting for Samuel the prophet.[2] Secondly, Saul loses his personal grasp on the kingship[3] for failing to heed Samuel's admonition regarding the disposal of the Amalekites and their belongings.[4] (It is important to recognize both stages in the rejection of Saul, since the

---

1   I Samuel 9:2
2   I Samuel 13:14
3   I Samuel 15:23
4   I Samuel 15:18-19

separate but related questions of kingship and dynasty are central to the Book of Samuel.[5])

Roots

David begins the process of establishing a secure grasp on the reins of power and on the transmission of that power, without his having the benefit of a proper background. There is no mention of his mother. There is no detailed description of his family, beyond the family name and the names of some of his siblings. We are not informed if the House of Jesse is a well-connected family.[6]

In this way, David is much like the seminal patriarchal figure of Genesis: Abraham.

Abraham pops up on the stage of Biblical history as a mature adult. There is no account of his early years. Instead, there is a large lacunae in his personal history.

So, too, with King David.

The presentation also parallels the introduction of another great leader, Moses our teacher.

In Exodus, Moses appears and is chosen by God as the leader, not because of family connections, or other extraneous factors, but because of his personality and his deeds.[7] From his origins, he is presented as an ordinary person:

Exodus 2

1 And there went a man of the house of Levi, and took to wife a daughter of Levi.

א וַיֵּלֶךְ אִישׁ מִבֵּית לֵוִי: וַיִּקַּח אֶת-בַּת-לֵוִי.

Two anonymous people get married. Who are they? We don't know. Are they rich? We don't know. Are they poor? We don't know. Are they important? We don't know. Are they old? We don't know. Are they young? We don't know. We know practically nothing about them.

---

5   See Berman, Joshua, "David's Request to Build the Temple," in the present volume.

6   In fact, a number of traditional, as well as modern sources argue that one of the agendas of the author of the Book of Ruth may be to highlight the esteemed genealogical roots of King David. The Book of Ruth ends with a family tree that culminates with David (Ruth 4:22).

7   The various Midrashic portrayals of Moses, which depict Moses as a miraculously "chosen" baby from the outset, only serve to highlight the plain text's refusal to depict the child as anything other than ordinary.

We are not told if Moses has brothers. His brother and sister simply appear later on out of thin air. We are not informed about their births because at this juncture the text is not interested in the genealogy and connections of Moses' family. Not until chapter six of Exodus (*Parshat Va'eira*) are we given Moses' genealogy, and introduced to his father Amram, and mother Yokheved. But at the early stages of the narrative, when we first encounter baby Moses, we are interested in him alone. He's first chosen not because of his family, but because of his actions, he is sensitive to injustice. He responds when the Egyptian hits the Hebrew.[8] He sees the shepherds taking advantage of Yitro's daughters, and goes to help them.[9]

As with Moses, David is chosen to enter God's service because of his deeds and his character.

David does not at first appear to be from an important family. Moreover, he is not presented as particularly tall or handsome. In contrast, Saul is presented as *andrish*, as they say in Yiddish, somebody totally different from everybody else.

Perhaps we are not presented with David's pedigree at this time because we don't want to interrupt the flow of the Saul-David story. We meet David in his early adulthood because we are not interested in him until then.

Another important theme running through this story is that ultimately it is one's actions that are definitive – not one's family, or looks. For the rest of this book, we watch the actions of Saul and David very closely, as the legitimacy of their kingships are at stake.

For King and Country!

When the people ask for a king, we should take note of the terminology that the Tanakh uses:

I Samuel 8

7 And the LORD said to Samuel: 'Hearken to the voice of the people in all that they say to you; for they have not **rejected** you, but they have **rejected** Me, that I should not be king over them.

ז וַיֹּאמֶר יי אֶל-שְׁמוּאֵל שְׁמַע בְּקוֹל הָעָם לְכֹל אֲשֶׁר-יֹאמְרוּ אֵלֶיךָ: כִּי לֹא אֹתְךָ מָאָסוּ כִּי-אֹתִי מָאֲסוּ מִמְּלֹךְ עֲלֵיהֶם.

---

8   Exodus 2:11-12
9   Exodus 2:16-17

8 According to all the works which
they have done since the day that
I brought them up out of Egypt
even to this day, in that **they have
forsaken Me**, and served other
gods, so do they also to you.

ח כְּכָל-הַמַּעֲשִׂים אֲשֶׁר-עָשׂוּ מִיּוֹם
הַעֲלֹתִי אוֹתָם מִמִּצְרַיִם וְעַד-הַיּוֹם
הַזֶּה וַיַּעַזְבֻנִי וַיַּעַבְדוּ אֱלֹהִים
אֲחֵרִים: כֵּן הֵמָּה עֹשִׂים גַּם-לָךְ.

The very act of asking for an earthly king is a rejection of God's kingship – so the theme of this request is rejection.

Remember, God uses the very same term when Saul is ultimately rejected:

I Samuel 15

24 And Saul said to Samuel:
'I have sinned; for I have
transgressed the commandment
of the LORD, and your words;
because I feared the people,
and hearkened to their voice.

כד וַיֹּאמֶר שָׁאוּל אֶל-שְׁמוּאֵל
חָטָאתִי כִּי-עָבַרְתִּי אֶת-פִּי-יְיָ
וְאֶת-דְּבָרֶיךָ: כִּי יָרֵאתִי
אֶת-הָעָם וָאֶשְׁמַע בְּקוֹלָם.

25 Now therefore, I pray
you, pardon my sin, and
return with me, that I may
worship the LORD.'

כה וְעַתָּה שָׂא נָא אֶת-חַטָּאתִי:
וְשׁוּב עִמִּי וְאֶשְׁתַּחֲוֶה לַייָ.

26 And Samuel said to Saul: 'I will
not return with you; for you have
rejected the word of the LORD,
and the LORD has **rejected** you
from being king over Israel.'

כו וַיֹּאמֶר שְׁמוּאֵל אֶל-שָׁאוּל
לֹא אָשׁוּב עִמָּךְ: כִּי מָאַסְתָּה
אֶת-דְּבַר יְיָ וַיִּמְאָסְךָ יְיָ
מִהְיוֹת מֶלֶךְ עַל-יִשְׂרָאֵל.

There is a kind of irony here. The people had rejected God by asking for a king, but God conceded and gave them one. It was considered
that the king, at least, would act within the limits of divine leadership. It
was imperative that the Israelite king accept God's prophet as a superior
authority.

Saul is rejected for more than simply not honoring Samuel's request
to wait for him before sacrificing. His is a greater crime. Saul's error was
that he saw himself as being fundamentally superior to the prophet. That
is the wrong perspective.

I Samuel 15

17 And Samuel said: 'Though you be little in your own sight, are you not head of the tribes of Israel? And the LORD anointed you king over Israel;

18 and the LORD sent you on a journey, and said: Go and utterly destroy the sinners the Amalekites, and fight against them until they are consumed.

19 Why then did you not hearken to the voice of the LORD, but flew upon the spoil, and did that which was evil in the sight of the LORD?'

20 And Saul said unto Samuel: 'Yea, I have hearkened to the voice of the LORD, and have gone the way which the LORD sent me, and have brought Agag the king of Amalek, and have utterly destroyed the Amalekites.

21 But the people took of the spoil, sheep and oxen, the chief of the devoted things, to sacrifice to the LORD your God in Gilgal.'

22 And Samuel said: 'Has the LORD as great delight in burnt-offerings and sacrifices, as in hearkening to the voice of the LORD? Behold, **to obey is better than sacrifice, and to hearken than the fat of rams.**

23 **For rebellion is as the sin of witchcraft, and stubbornness is as idolatry and terafim.** Because you have rejected the word of the LORD, He has also rejected you from being king.'

יז וַיֹּאמֶר שְׁמוּאֵל הֲלוֹא אִם־קָטֹן אַתָּה בְּעֵינֶיךָ רֹאשׁ שִׁבְטֵי יִשְׂרָאֵל אָתָּה: וַיִּמְשָׁחֲךָ יְיָ לְמֶלֶךְ עַל־יִשְׂרָאֵל.

יח וַיִּשְׁלָחֲךָ יְיָ בְּדָרֶךְ: וַיֹּאמֶר לֵךְ וְהַחֲרַמְתָּה אֶת־הַחַטָּאִים אֶת־עֲמָלֵק וְנִלְחַמְתָּ בּוֹ עַד כַּלּוֹתָם אֹתָם.

יט וְלָמָּה לֹא־שָׁמַעְתָּ בְּקוֹל יְיָ: וַתַּעַט אֶל־הַשָּׁלָל וַתַּעַשׂ הָרַע בְּעֵינֵי יְיָ?

כ וַיֹּאמֶר שָׁאוּל אֶל־שְׁמוּאֵל אֲשֶׁר שָׁמַעְתִּי בְּקוֹל יְיָ וָאֵלֵךְ בַּדֶּרֶךְ אֲשֶׁר־שְׁלָחַנִי יְיָ: וָאָבִיא אֶת־אֲגַג מֶלֶךְ עֲמָלֵק וְאֶת־עֲמָלֵק הֶחֱרַמְתִּי.

כא וַיִּקַּח הָעָם מֵהַשָּׁלָל צֹאן וּבָקָר רֵאשִׁית הַחֵרֶם: לִזְבֹּחַ לַיְיָ אֱלֹהֶיךָ בַּגִּלְגָּל.

כב וַיֹּאמֶר שְׁמוּאֵל הַחֵפֶץ לַיְיָ בְּעֹלוֹת וּזְבָחִים כִּשְׁמֹעַ בְּקוֹל יְיָ: הִנֵּה שְׁמֹעַ מִזֶּבַח טוֹב לְהַקְשִׁיב מֵחֵלֶב אֵילִים.

כג כִּי חַטַּאת־קֶסֶם מֶרִי וְאָוֶן וּתְרָפִים הַפְצַר: יַעַן מָאַסְתָּ אֶת־דְּבַר יְיָ וַיִּמְאָסְךָ מִמֶּלֶךְ.

The ideal authority structure for Israel is a pyramid. God occupies the pinnacle, followed by the prophet who brings His word, and last is the king – who follows God's word. Saul is rejected for jumping the hierarchy.

Suddenly, a new king must be sought, and God already has one in mind.

Seeing is Choosing

I Samuel 16

1 And the LORD said to Samuel: 'How long will you mourn for Saul, as I have rejected him from being king over Israel? fill your horn with oil, and go, I will send you to Jesse of Bethlehem; for I have **seen** among his sons a king for Me.'

א וַיֹּאמֶר יי אֶל-שְׁמוּאֵל עַד-מָתַי אַתָּה מִתְאַבֵּל אֶל-שָׁאוּל וַאֲנִי מְאַסְתִּיו מִמְּלֹךְ עַל-יִשְׂרָאֵל: מַלֵּא קַרְנְךָ שֶׁמֶן וְלֵךְ אֶשְׁלָחֲךָ אֶל-יִשַׁי בֵּית-הַלַּחְמִי–כִּי-רָאִיתִי בְּבָנָיו לִי מֶלֶךְ.

The term here is *re'iyah*, sight. In Biblical Hebrew, *re'iyah* has a dual meaning. Not only does it mean "to see," it also, in certain instances, means "to choose." That's why in Deuteronomy, when discussing the whereabouts of the ultimate home of the Temple in Jerusalem, the reference is:"*ha-makom asher* **yivchar** *Hashem*,"[10] "the place which God will *choose*." Earlier, in Genesis, the phrase is used when God chooses the place for the binding of Isaac (which later becomes the site of the Holy Temple).[11] God tells Abraham to go "*el ha-'aretz asher* **ar'eka**"[12] – "to the land where I (God) will *show* you." After the binding, this same place is named by Abraham: "*Be-har Hashem* **yera'eh**": "In the mount the Lord will be seen."[13] It's the place which God *sees* and then is *seen*.

This place, *Har Ha-Moriah* (the mount upon which the Lord will be seen), is the same place where:

Deuteronomy 16

16 Three times in a year shall all your males **be seen before the face of the LORD** your God in

טז שָׁלוֹשׁ פְּעָמִים בַּשָּׁנָה יֵרָאֶה כָל-זְכוּרְךָ אֶת-פְּנֵי יי אֱלֹהֶיךָ

---

10 Deuteronomy 12:5,11,18,26; 14:26; 15:7; 17:8 ; 18:6 etc.
11 See II Chronicles 3:1
12 Genesis 12:1
13 Genesis 22:14

בַּמָּקוֹם אֲשֶׁר יִבְחָר בְּחַג הַמַּצּוֹת
וּבְחַג הַשָּׁבֻעוֹת וּבְחַג הַסֻּכּוֹת:
וְלֹא יֵרָאֶה אֶת-פְּנֵי יְיָ רֵיקָם.

the place which He shall **choose**;
on the feast of unleavened bread,
and on the feast of weeks, and on
the feast of tabernacles; and they
shall not **be seen before the face
of the LORD** empty (handed).

Seeing and choosing are intricately and profoundly connected.[14]

The David story continues with Samuel going to Bethlehem at God's request, to the house of Jesse.

I Samuel 16

ו וַיְהִי בְּבוֹאָם וַיַּרְא אֶת-אֱלִיאָב:
וַיֹּאמֶר אַךְ נֶגֶד יְיָ מְשִׁיחוֹ.

ז וַיֹּאמֶר יְיָ אֶל-שְׁמוּאֵל אַל-תַּבֵּט
אֶל-מַרְאֵהוּ וְאֶל-גְּבֹהַּ קוֹמָתוֹ
כִּי מְאַסְתִּיהוּ: כִּי לֹא אֲשֶׁר
יִרְאֶה הָאָדָם כִּי הָאָדָם יִרְאֶה
לַעֵינַיִם וַיְיָ יִרְאֶה לַלֵּבָב.

6 And it came to pass, when they
were come, that he **saw** Eliav,
and said: 'Surely the LORD'S
anointed is before Him.'

7 But the LORD said to Samuel:
'Look not on his looks, or on
the height of his stature; because
I have rejected him; for it is
not as man may **see**: for man
sees the outward appearance
(*lit:* "to the eyes"), but the
LORD **sees** to the heart.'

This last verse is both beautiful and sad. Samuel has chosen "another Saul" – and has based his decision on outward appearance, not inner deeds.

What does the text tell us about Eliav, David's older brother?

It speaks of "his looks, and his height."

What does the Bible say about Saul the first time we meet him?

I Samuel 9

א וַיְהִי-אִישׁ מבן ימין
(מִבִּנְיָמִין) וּשְׁמוֹ קִישׁ

1 Now there was a man of
Benjamin, whose name was Kish,

---

14   The theme of *re'iyah*, of being seen, seeing, of choosing, also occurs in the Moses story. Moses is told by his father-in-las Jethro to "go and *see*" if there are people that he can choose to be Judges in his stead. ["You shall *envision* from amongst the people"] (Exodus 18:21). It is the same idea, to see. The *chozeh*, the *ro'eh.* The "visionary," the "seer." And then the text says: *va-yivchar Moshe anshei chayil*, (Exodus 18:25) he then **"chooses** capable men." This is another example of the interplay between the verbs "choose" and "see."

the son of Abiel, the son of Zeror, the son of Becorath, the son of Aphiah, the son of a Benjamite, a mighty man of valour.

בֶּן-אֲבִיאֵל בֶּן-צְרוֹר בֶּן-בְּכוֹרַת בֶּן-אֲפִיחַ בֶּן-אִישׁ יְמִינִי: גִּבּוֹר חָיִל.

2 And he had a son, whose name was Saul, **chosen** and goodly, and there was not among the children of Israel a goodlier person than he: from his shoulders and upward he was higher than any of the people.

ב וְלוֹ-הָיָה בֵן וּשְׁמוֹ שָׁאוּל בָּחוּר וָטוֹב וְאֵין אִישׁ מִבְּנֵי יִשְׂרָאֵל טוֹב מִמֶּנּוּ: מִשִּׁכְמוֹ וָמַעְלָה גָּבֹהַּ מִכָּל-הָעָם.

This presentation focuses on all the external elements. Saul's family is well-connected. Plus, he's personally brave and mighty; he is tall, exceptional, and he stands out.

Eliav is every inch as tall and as handsome as Saul. And so it makes a lot of sense that Samuel is drawn to Eliav.

Remember the very beginning of the book of Samuel, where we learn why the young prophet is named Samuel:

I Samuel 1

27 'For this child I prayed; and the LORD has granted me my petition which I asked of Him;

כז אֶל-הַנַּעַר הַזֶּה הִתְפַּלָּלְתִּי: וַיִּתֵּן יְיָ לִי אֶת-שְׁאֵלָתִי אֲשֶׁר שָׁאַלְתִּי מֵעִמּוֹ.

28 therefore I also have lent him to the LORD; as long as he liveth he is **lent to (sha'ul)** the LORD.' And he (Samuel) worshiped the LORD there.

כח וְגַם אָנֹכִי הִשְׁאִלְתִּהוּ לַיָי כָּל-הַיָּמִים אֲשֶׁר הָיָה הוּא שָׁאוּל לַיָי: וַיִּשְׁתַּחוּ שָׁם לַיָי.

"He is lent (*sha'ul*) to God." The connection between Samuel and *Sha'ul*, as Saul is known in the original Hebrew, is so intense because their names, as well as their destinies, are linked in this way from the very birth of Samuel.

God now instructs Samuel not to attend to those feelings of connection regarding Eliav, for God has rejected him, just as He rejected Saul because of what he represented: the idea of wielding power, rather than yielding to the prophet and to God.

Samuel then calls Avinadav.

Threes and Fours

I would call your attention now to a literary phenomenon often used in the Tanakh: groupings of items by threes and fours.[15] There are many occurrences where a list of three is followed by a fourth which is (generally) an exception to the set of three.

Amos 1

3 For thus says the LORD: For **three** transgressions of Damascus, yea, for **four**, I will not reverse it: because they have threshed Gile‘ad with sledges of iron.

ג כֹּה אָמַר יְיָ עַל-שְׁלֹשָׁה פִּשְׁעֵי דַמֶּשֶׂק וְעַל-אַרְבָּעָה לֹא אֲשִׁיבֶנּוּ: עַל-דּוּשָׁם בַּחֲרֻצוֹת הַבַּרְזֶל אֶת-הַגִּלְעָד.

This is a theme that repeats itself often in the David narratives. We see an example of this here, too: Eliav is one. Avinadav is two. Shammah is the third one to be rejected.

I Samuel 16

8 Then Jesse called Avinadav, and made him pass before Samuel. And he said: 'Neither has the LORD chosen this.'

9 Then Jesse made Shammah pass by. And he said: 'Neither has the LORD chosen this.'

ח וַיִּקְרָא יִשַׁי אֶל-אֲבִינָדָב וַיַּעֲבִרֵהוּ לִפְנֵי שְׁמוּאֵל: וַיֹּאמֶר גַּם-בָּזֶה לֹא-בָחַר יְיָ.

ט וַיַּעֲבֵר יִשַׁי שַׁמָּה: וַיֹּאמֶר גַּם-בָּזֶה לֹא-בָחַר יְיָ.

Then he brings the other seven children for review. Their names are not recorded. Three children are identified and then the rest are lumped together. The fourth child named in the text is David – the chosen one.

And then we meet him:

I Samuel 16

12 And he sent, and brought him in. Now he was ruddy, with **beautiful eyes**, and **goodly to look upon**. And the LORD said: 'Arise, anoint him; for this is he.'

יב וַיִּשְׁלַח וַיְבִיאֵהוּ וְהוּא אַדְמוֹנִי עִם-יְפֵה עֵינַיִם וְטוֹב רֹאִי: וַיֹּאמֶר יְיָ קוּם מְשָׁחֵהוּ כִּי-זֶה הוּא.

---

15   Professor Yair Zakovitch has written about this at great length: Y. Zakovitch, "The Literary Model of Three and Four in the Bible," Doctoral Dissertation (Hebrew), Jerusalem, 1978

David, in contrast to these other tall, good-looking men, is *admoni*, "ruddy." *Admoni* in Biblical Hebrew does not mean "redhead," but probably refers to skin tone.

Further, he is described as "of beautiful eyes, and goodly to look upon" which, of course, is a play on "God sees the heart, while Man sees externals" (I Samuel 16:7, as above).

And, of course, it is David who is chosen.

Touched with Spirit

We meet in David a political leader who is imbued with the spirit of God for his entire career. This is unique in the annals of Judges/Samuel.

I Samuel 16

13 Then Samuel took the horn of oil, and anointed him in the midst of his brethren; and **the spirit of the LORD came mightily upon David from that day forward**. So Samuel rose up, and went to Ramah.

יג וַיִּקַּח שְׁמוּאֵל אֶת-קֶרֶן הַשֶּׁמֶן וַיִּמְשַׁח אֹתוֹ בְּקֶרֶב אֶחָיו וַתִּצְלַח רוּחַ-יי אֶל-דָּוִד מֵהַיּוֹם הַהוּא וָמָעְלָה: וַיָּקָם שְׁמוּאֵל וַיֵּלֶךְ הָרָמָתָה.

Up until this time, the current judge might receive the spirit of God for a discrete period of time in order to fulfill his mission. The prophetic vision of any given judge was not constant. Many judges are not even described as having "the spirit of God" rest upon them at all. David is the first political leader in this period to to be gifted in this way, clearly indicating a move to a new stage in Biblical history.

Although the text states that Saul had prophetic vision, Saul's divine inspiration was temporary:

I Samuel 10

11 And it came to pass, when all who knew him before saw that, behold, he prophesied with the prophets, then the people said to one another: 'What has happened to the son of Kish? Is Saul also among the prophets?'

יא וַיְהִי כָּל-יוֹדְעוֹ מֵאִתְּמוֹל שִׁלְשֹׁם וַיִּרְאוּ וְהִנֵּה עִם-נְבִאִים נִבָּא: וַיֹּאמֶר הָעָם אִישׁ אֶל-רֵעֵהוּ מַה-זֶּה הָיָה לְבֶן-קִישׁ הֲגַם שָׁאוּל בַּנְּבִיאִים?

Saul enjoyed this status for a fraction of his tenure as king. In short order, he lost his ability to communicate with God and soon found the avenues to God's word shut off to him. The first distancing blow suffered by Saul is Samuel's retirement into seclusion at Ramah. By the end, Saul turns to necromancy in an attempt to receive guidance.

The 151st Psalm

In the course of the archaeological explorations at the Qumran caves in the Judean Desert, a number of scrolls containing texts of *Tehillim*, Psalms, were discovered. While we have 150 psalms in our standard text, a number of extra psalms have been found in the Qumran text. (This is similar to the Septuagint, the Greek translation of the Tanakh, where there are also more than 150 psalms.)

The following text, discovered in the eleventh cave in Qumran,[16] is similar to that denoted as Psalm 151 in the Septuagint. This is a very beautiful psalm which we do not have in our Book of Psalms, but in imagery and tone it sounds as if it is from David's hand. This seems to be one of those original psalms that our sages decided not to include in our canon.

This poem provides a window into David's heart; the place into which typically only God can "see."

Hallelujah! Of David the son of Jesse. I was younger than my brothers, the sons of my father, and he made made me a shepherd for his sheep and a leader of his goats.	הללויה! לדויר בן ישי. קטן הייתי מן אחי וצעיר מבני אבי וישמני רועה לצונו ומושל בגדיותיו.

This is anticipatory and foreshadows that David will eventually become the leader of the flock of Israel. The theme of the shepherd, of leading the flock, echoes Moses' career as a shepherd.

In contrast to the Biblical text of the Book of Samuel, the Qumran passage offers us some fascinating details:

My hands made rejoicing and my fingers a harp and I made glory to God.	ידי עשו עונג ואצבעותי כנור ואשימה ליי כבוד

---

16   For further information on the Dead Sea Scrolls, including an illustration of a scroll fragment, see Gottlieb, Leeor, "The Nachash Story and the Dead Sea Scrolls," in the present volume.

David is presented as having a musical background. What is the motivating force behind David's love of music?

I said in my soul: The hills don't testify to Him and the valleys don't proclaim. Trees raise up my words and the flocks my deeds. Who will declare and who will speak and who will tell the deeds of the Master of all?	ואמרתי אני בנפשי ההרים לוא יעידו לו והגבעות לוא יגדו עלו העצים את דברי והצואן את מעשי כי מי יגיד ומי ידבר ומי יספר את מעשי אדון הכל?

This psalm is wonderful because it gives us a portrait of David from his youth as a very religious, spiritual individual.

God sees everything – he listens and hears.	ראה אלוה הכול-הוא שמע והוא האזין.

Why did God choose David? Because, argues this Qumranic psalm, God heard and saw David's inner fire. David's spirituality rendered David worthy of the monarchy.

He sent his prophet to anoint me, Samuel to **raise me up.**	שלח נביאו למושחני את שמואל לגדלני.

This wonderful phrase, "raise me up," reminds us of Samuel himself who was "raised up"[17] in the House of God. In effect, David becomes a Samuel-like figure.

My brothers went out to see him. Fine of form, fine of appearance, tall in stature	יצאו אחי לקראתו יפי התור ויפי המראה הגבהים בקומתם

Eliav is not the only brother of David's who is tall. David's brothers all look like Saul – handsome, tall and broad.

Fine of hair.	היפים בשערם

The text of the Bible, of course, never mentions this fact. It may be that here the text has projected elements of the portrait of Absalom, David's

---

17   I Samuel 2:21, 26

son, as well as Joseph – using long, beautiful hair to paint the picture of David's siblings, none of whom, ironically, will reach the pinnacle of leadership.

LORD God did not choose them. He sent and picked me from behind their flocks. He anointed me with the holy oil And set me as a prince for His people and ruler of the children of His covenant.

לוא בחר יי אלוהים בם
וישלח ויקחני מאחר הצואן
וימשחני בשמן הקודש
וישימני נגיד לעמו
ומושל בבני בריתו.

In the Qumran text David is chosen because he is a religious and spiritual individual.

That is not the reason given in our version of the Book of Samuel. Our canonical text gives us no explicit reason why David is chosen, other than that God knows David to be inherently greater than his brothers.[18]

We will see, however, that this psalm ultimately reflects the plain textual reading, because the next chapter of Samuel will give a very clear picture of David's fitness for the job.

God's instrument

The story of David and Goliath is no mere story about the battle to slay a giant. Embedded in the story is a metaphor about Saul and David, and the struggle for the kingship of Israel. Saul is described by the text in terms reminiscent of the language used to describe the "giant," and like Goliath, ultimately fails to fulfill his promise of greatness.

David, by contrast, the youngest and smallest, is ultimately victorious against both giants in his life: Goliath and Saul. What David expresses in the Goliath story surely validates God's choice of David as his champion.

Before he faces Goliath, David is brought in to the house of Saul to help the king withstand a new affliction:

---

18   There are many parallels between the story of Samuel choosing David, and the story of Abraham's binding of Isaac. For example, when God sends the prophet in I Samuel 16:1, He says, " *ve-lekh eschlachakha... ki ra'iti be-vanav li me-lekh,*" "I will send you because I have seen for myself a king." Samuel is supposed to go and choose one of the children, but he is not told in advance which one. The mother plays no role in either story. There is a sacrifice in both stories. Both stories have the phrase "that I will show you" (I Samuel 16:3, and Genesis 22:2). There are other parallels that can be explored but this is beyond the scope of our discussion.

I Samuel 16

14 Now the spirit of the LORD
had departed from Saul,
and an evil spirit from the
LORD terrified him.

יד וְרוּחַ יְיָ סָרָה מֵעִם שָׁאוּל:
וּבִעֲתַתּוּ רוּחַ-רָעָה מֵאֵת יְיָ.

God's spirit rests on David forever and ever. On the other hand, when
it departs Saul, David is brought in to play soothing music for him.

I Samuel 16

16 Let our lord now command
your servants, that are before
you, to seek out a man who is
a skillful player on the harp;
and it shall be, when the evil
spirit from God comes upon
you, that he shall play with his
hand, and you shalt be well.'

טז יֹאמַר-נָא אֲדֹנֵנוּ עֲבָדֶיךָ לְפָנֶיךָ
יְבַקְשׁוּ אִישׁ יֹדֵעַ מְנַגֵּן בַּכִּנּוֹר:
וְהָיָה בִּהְיוֹת עָלֶיךָ רוּחַ-אֱלֹהִים
רָעָה וְנִגֵּן בְּיָדוֹ וְטוֹב לָךְ.

17 And Saul said unto his servants:
'**See for me** now a man that can
play well, and bring him to me.'

יז וַיֹּאמֶר שָׁאוּל אֶל-עֲבָדָיו: רְאוּ-נָא
לִי אִישׁ מֵיטִיב לְנַגֵּן וַהֲבִיאוֹתֶם אֵלָי.

Notice the exact same language that God had used in looking for his
chosen king: "...for I have **seen** among his sons a king for Me."[19] It does
not say *bechar*, "choose." It uses the same term, "**see**." It is almost as if Saul
is another instrument in the hand of God.

I Samuel 16

18 Then answered one of the young
men, and said: 'Behold, **I have
seen a son of Jesse of Bethlehem**,
that is skillful in playing, and
a mighty man of valor, and a
man of war, and prudent in
affairs, and a comely person,
and the LORD is with him.'

יח וַיַּעַן אֶחָד מֵהַנְּעָרִים וַיֹּאמֶר הִנֵּה
רָאִיתִי בֶּן לְיִשַׁי בֵּית הַלַּחְמִי יֹדֵעַ
נַגֵּן וְגִבּוֹר חַיִל וְאִישׁ מִלְחָמָה
וּנְבוֹן דָּבָר וְאִישׁ תֹּאַר: וַייָ עִמּוֹ.

David has all the outer qualities that Saul has, but that's not why he
is God's choice. Then David goes to Saul and is able to comfort him and
become a member of his entourage.

19   I Samuel 16:1

David's Delivery Service

David is sent to his brothers at the war front. There is a tremendous amount of language here which reminds us of the stories of Joseph and his brothers and the conflict that arises when sending the younger son to find out about the older brothers.[20] There are many similarities.

I Samuel 17

18 And bring these ten cheeses to the captain of their thousand, and to your brethren **bring greetings** (*peace*), and take their pledge.

יח וְאֵת עֲשֶׂרֶת חֲרִצֵי הֶחָלָב הָאֵלֶּה תָּבִיא לְשַׂר הָאָלֶף: וְאֶת-אַחֶיךָ תִּפְקֹד לְשָׁלוֹם וְאֶת-עֲרֻבָּתָם תִּקָּח.

This is very reminiscent of Joseph's task set by Jacob:

Genesis 37

14 And he said to him: 'Go now, **see whether it is peaceful with your brethren**, and **peaceful with the flock**; and bring me back word.' So he sent him out of the vale of Hebron, and he came to Shechem.

יד וַיֹּאמֶר לוֹ לֶךְ-נָא רְאֵה אֶת-שְׁלוֹם אַחֶיךָ וְאֶת-שְׁלוֹם הַצֹּאן וַהֲשִׁבֵנִי דָּבָר: וַיִּשְׁלָחֵהוּ מֵעֵמֶק חֶבְרוֹן וַיָּבֹא שְׁכֶמָה.

If we look carefully at the story, we notice once again the emergence of a pattern of three and four.

I Samuel 17

13 And the **three** eldest sons of Jesse had gone after Saul to the battle; and the names of his **three** sons that went to the battle were Eliav the first-born, and next unto him Avinadav, and the third Shammah.

יג וַיֵּלְכוּ שְׁלֹשֶׁת בְּנֵי-יִשַׁי הַגְּדֹלִים הָלְכוּ אַחֲרֵי-שָׁאוּל לַמִּלְחָמָה: וְשֵׁם שְׁלֹשֶׁת בָּנָיו אֲשֶׁר הָלְכוּ בַמִּלְחָמָה אֱלִיאָב הַבְּכוֹר וּמִשְׁנֵהוּ אֲבִינָדָב וְהַשְּׁלִשִׁי שַׁמָּה.

There are seven children but only the three big ones are mentioned. They were probably the tall ones, the beautiful ones, the ones who Samuel would have chosen, the most Saul-like. And, of course, David is the fourth mentioned – the exception – he *hadn't* followed Saul into battle:

20   Genesis 37

I Samuel 17

14 And David was the youngest; and
the three eldest followed Saul.

יד וְדָוִד הוּא הַקָּטָן וּשְׁלֹשָׁה
הַגְּדֹלִים הָלְכוּ אַחֲרֵי שָׁאוּל.

It is very interesting that David was sent with a couple of things into
battle for his brothers.

I Samuel 17

17 And Jesse said to David his son:
'Take now for your brethren
an *ephah* of this parched corn,
and these ten loaves, and
carry them quickly to the
camp to your brethren.'

יז וַיֹּאמֶר יִשַׁי לְדָוִד בְּנוֹ קַח-נָא לְאַחֶיךָ
אֵיפַת הַקָּלִיא הַזֶּה וַעֲשָׂרָה לֶחֶם
הַזֶּה וְהָרֵץ הַמַּחֲנֶה לְאַחֶיךָ.

He is supposed to bring bread.

In the previous chapter, David goes to bring tribute to Saul and this is
what he brings:

I Samuel 16

19 Wherefore Saul sent messengers
to Jesse, and said: 'Send me David
your son, who is with the sheep.'

20 And Jesse took a donkey laden
with **bread**, and a bottle of
wine, and a **kid**, and sent them
by David his son to Saul.

יט וַיִּשְׁלַח שָׁאוּל מַלְאָכִים
אֶל-יִשָׁי: וַיֹּאמֶר שִׁלְחָה אֵלַי
אֶת-דָּוִד בִּנְךָ אֲשֶׁר בַּצֹּאן.

כ וַיִּקַּח יִשַׁי חֲמוֹר לֶחֶם וְנֹאד
יַיִן וּגְדִי עִזִּים אֶחָד: וַיִּשְׁלַח
בְּיַד-דָּוִד בְּנוֹ אֶל-שָׁאוּל.

A number of people have pointed out this interesting detail: David
brings three things, bread, wine and a goat, and he brings it on top of a
donkey.

This should remind us of the story of Saul's coronation:

I Samuel 10

1 Then Samuel took the vial of oil,
and poured it upon his head, and
kissed him, and said: 'Is it not
that the LORD has anointed you
to be prince over His inheritance?

א וַיִּקַּח שְׁמוּאֵל אֶת-פַּךְ הַשֶּׁמֶן וַיִּצֹק

עַל-רֹאשׁוֹ-וַיִּשָּׁקֵהוּ: וַיֹּאמֶר-הֲלוֹא
כִּי-מְשָׁחֲךָ יְיָ עַל-נַחֲלָתוֹ לְנָגִיד.

2 When you are departed from me to-day, then you shall find two men by the tomb of Rachel, in the border of Benjamin at Zelzah; and they will say to you: The donkeys which you went to seek are found; and, lo, your father has left off caring for the donkeyes, and is anxious concerning you, saying: What shall I do for my son?

ב בְּלֶכְתְּךָ הַיּוֹם מֵעִמָּדִי וּמָצָאתָ שְׁנֵי אֲנָשִׁים עִם-קְבֻרַת רָחֵל בִּגְבוּל בִּנְיָמִן בְּצֶלְצַח: וְאָמְרוּ אֵלֶיךָ נִמְצְאוּ הָאֲתֹנוֹת אֲשֶׁר הָלַכְתָּ לְבַקֵּשׁ וְהִנֵּה נָטַשׁ אָבִיךָ אֶת-דִּבְרֵי הָאֲתֹנוֹת וְדָאַג לָכֶם לֵאמֹר מָה אֶעֱשֶׂה לִבְנִי?

3 Then shall you go on forward from therce, and you shall come to the terebinth of Tabor, and there you shall meet three men going up to God to Beth-el, one carrying **three kids**, and another carrying **three loaves of bread**, and another carrying **a bottle of wine**.

ג וְחָלַפְתָּ מִשָּׁם וָהָלְאָה וּבָאתָ עַד-אֵלוֹן תָּבוֹר וּמְצָאוּךָ שָּׁם שְׁלֹשָׁה אֲנָשִׁים עֹלִים אֶל-הָאֱלֹהִים בֵּית-אֵל: אֶחָד נֹשֵׂא שְׁלֹשָׁה גְדָיִים וְאֶחָד נֹשֵׂא שְׁלֹשֶׁת כִּכְּרוֹת לֶחֶם וְאֶחָד נֹשֵׂא נֵבֶל-יָיִן.

4 And they will salute you, and give you two cakes of bread; which you shall receive of their hand.

ד וְשָׁאֲלוּ לְךָ לְשָׁלוֹם: וְנָתְנוּ לְךָ שְׁתֵּי-לֶחֶם וְלָקַחְתָּ מִיָּדָם.

5 After that you shall come to the hill of God, where is the garrison of the Philistines; and it shall come to pass, when you are come there to the city, that you shall meet a band of prophets coming down from the high place with a psaltery, and a timbrel, and a pipe, and a **harp**, before them; and they will be prophesying.

ה אַחַר כֵּן תָּבוֹא גִּבְעַת הָאֱלֹהִים אֲשֶׁר-שָׁם נְצִבֵי פְלִשְׁתִּים: וִיהִי כְבֹאֲךָ שָׁם הָעִיר וּפָגַעְתָּ חֶבֶל נְבִאִים יֹרְדִים מֵהַבָּמָה וְלִפְנֵיהֶם נֵבֶל וְתֹף וְחָלִיל וְכִנּוֹר וְהֵמָּה מִתְנַבְּאִים.

6 And the spirit of the LORD will come mightily upon you, and you shall prophesy with them, and shall be turned into another man.'

ו וְצָלְחָה עָלֶיךָ רוּחַ יי וְהִתְנַבִּיתָ עִמָּם: וְנֶהְפַּכְתָּ לְאִישׁ אַחֵר.

David takes up where Saul leaves off: in effect taking Saul's place. David is busied with gifts of food, "God's spirit rests on him," and he is, in effect, "a new man."[21] Not only is David sent by his father with goats, with

---

21   I Samuel 16:13

bread, and with wine on top of a donkey, but he becomes the harpist of Saul – he becomes the prophesying player of the harp from Saul's story.[22]

David is clearly coming to replace Saul.

This theme is continued in the story of David and Goliath. In the story of David and Goliath, David is presented as different than his three brothers who are warriors. David is not sent as a warrior. He's sent as a messenger boy, probably because he's scrawny. People have trouble envisioning him as a soldier. In fact, later on, Goliath is going to laugh at him because he is not outfitted as a soldier, and he is "fair."[23]

He certainly does not look the part of a warrior. But God sees past what the eyes see, and into the heart.[24]

Dressed to Kill

It is very striking how many verses the text devotes to the armaments and the battle fatigues of Goliath. It tells us, of course, how big he was. And it also tells us exactly what he carried.

I Samuel 17

4 And there went out a champion from the camp of the Philistines, named Goliath, of Gath, whose height was six cubits and a span.

ד וַיֵּצֵא אִישׁ-הַבֵּנַיִם מִמַּחֲנוֹת פְּלִשְׁתִּים גָּלְיָת שְׁמוֹ מִגַּת: גָּבְהוֹ שֵׁשׁ אַמּוֹת וָזָרֶת.

5 And he had a helmet of brass upon his head, and he was clad with a coat of mail; and the weight of the coat was five thousand shekels of brass.

ה וְכוֹבַע נְחֹשֶׁת עַל-רֹאשׁוֹ וְשִׁרְיוֹן קַשְׂקַשִּׂים הוּא לָבוּשׁ: וּמִשְׁקַל הַשִּׁרְיוֹן חֲמֵשֶׁת-אֲלָפִים שְׁקָלִים נְחֹשֶׁת.

It reads like *Jane's Defence Weekly* magazine; everything Goliath wears underscores his height and strength.

I Samuel 17

6 And he had greaves of brass upon his legs, and a javelin of brass between his shoulders.

ו וּמִצְחַת נְחֹשֶׁת עַל-רַגְלָיו: וְכִידוֹן נְחֹשֶׁת בֵּין כְּתֵפָיו.

---

22   I Samuel 10:5
23   I Samuel 17:42
24   I Samuel 16:7

7 And the shaft of his spear
was like a weaver's beam; and
his spear's head weighed six
hundred shekels of iron; and his
shield-bearer went before him.

ז וחץ (וְעֵץ) חֲנִיתוֹ כִּמְנוֹר אֹרְגִים
וְלַהֶבֶת חֲנִיתוֹ שֵׁשׁ-מֵאוֹת שְׁקָלִים
בַּרְזֶל: וְנֹשֵׂא הַצִּנָּה הֹלֵךְ לְפָנָיו.

Goliath seems to have everything. Note, however, what is not mentioned here in this original presentation of his armaments. In a wonderful
literary technique for suspense, the key armament is omitted: his *sword*.
David, in contrast, enters into the battle unarmed. Conspicuously absent
is a sword for David.

I Samuel 17

34 And David said unto Saul:
'Your servant kept his father's
sheep; and when there came
a lion, or a bear, and took
a lamb out of the flock,

לד וַיֹּאמֶר דָּוִד אֶל-שָׁאוּל רֹעֶה הָיָה
עַבְדְּךָ לְאָבִיו בַּצֹּאן: וּבָא הָאֲרִי
וְאֶת-הַדּוֹב וְנָשָׂא שֶׂה מֵהָעֵדֶר.

35 I went out after him, and smote
him, and delivered it out of his
mouth; and when he arose against
me, I caught him by his beard,
and smote him, and slew him.

לה וְיָצָאתִי אַחֲרָיו וְהִכִּתִיו וְהִצַּלְתִּי
מִפִּיו: וַיָּקָם עָלַי וְהֶחֱזַקְתִּי
בִּזְקָנוֹ וְהִכִּתִיו וַהֲמִיתִיו.

36 Your servant smote both the
lion and the bear; and this
uncircumcised Philistine
shall be as one of them,
seeing he has taunted the
armies of the living God.'

לו גַּם אֶת-הָאֲרִי גַּם-הַדּוֹב הִכָּה עַבְדֶּךָ:
וְהָיָה הַפְּלִשְׁתִּי הֶעָרֵל הַזֶּה כְּאַחַד
מֵהֶם כִּי חֵרֵף מַעַרְכֹת אֱלֹהִים חַיִּים.

37 And David said: 'The LORD
that delivered me out of the paw
of the lion, and out of the paw of
the bear, He will deliver me out
of the hand of this Philistine.'
And Saul said to David: 'Go, and
the LORD shall be with you.'

לז וַיֹּאמֶר דָּוִד יי אֲשֶׁר הִצִּלַנִי מִיַּד
הָאֲרִי וּמִיַּד הַדֹּב הוּא יַצִּילֵנִי מִיַּד
הַפְּלִשְׁתִּי הַזֶּה: וַיֹּאמֶר שָׁאוּל
אֶל-דָּוִד לֵךְ וַיי יִהְיֶה עִמָּךְ.

38 And Saul clad David with his
apparel, and he put a helmet
of brass upon his head, and he
clad him with a coat of mail.

לח וַיַּלְבֵּשׁ שָׁאוּל אֶת-דָּוִד מַדָּיו
וְנָתַן קוֹבַע נְחֹשֶׁת עַל-רֹאשׁוֹ:
וַיַּלְבֵּשׁ אֹתוֹ שִׁרְיוֹן.

39 And David girded his sword upon his apparel, and he essayed to go, but could not; for he had not tried it. And David said unto Saul: 'I cannot go with these; for I have not tried them.' And David took them off him.

לט וַיַּחְגֹּר דָּוִד אֶת־חַרְבּוֹ מֵעַל לְמַדָּיו וַיֹּאֶל לָלֶכֶת כִּי לֹא־נִסָּה וַיֹּאמֶר דָּוִד אֶל־שָׁאוּל לֹא אוּכַל לָלֶכֶת בָּאֵלֶּה כִּי לֹא נִסִּיתִי וַיְסִרֵם דָּוִד מֵעָלָיו׃

40 And he took his staff in his hand, and chose him five smooth stones out of the brook, and put them in the shepherd's bag which he had, even in his scrip; and his sling was in his hand; and he drew near to the Philistine.

מ וַיִּקַּח מַקְלוֹ בְּיָדוֹ וַיִּבְחַר־לוֹ חֲמִשָּׁה חַלֻּקֵי־אֲבָנִים מִן־הַנַּחַל וַיָּשֶׂם אֹתָם בִּכְלִי הָרֹעִים אֲשֶׁר־לוֹ וּבַיַּלְקוּט וְקַלְעוֹ בְיָדוֹ וַיִּגַּשׁ אֶל־הַפְּלִשְׁתִּי׃

41 And the Philistine came nearer and nearer to David; and the man that bore the shield went before him.

מא וַיֵּלֶךְ הַפְּלִשְׁתִּי הֹלֵךְ וְקָרֵב אֶל־דָּוִד וְהָאִישׁ נֹשֵׂא הַצִּנָּה לְפָנָיו׃

42 And when the Philistine looked about, and saw David, he disdained him; for he was but a youth, and ruddy, and of a fair countenance.

מב וַיַּבֵּט הַפְּלִשְׁתִּי וַיִּרְאֶה אֶת־דָּוִד וַיִּבְזֵהוּ כִּי־הָיָה נַעַר וְאַדְמֹנִי עִם־יְפֵה מַרְאֶה׃

43 And the Philistine said to David: 'Am I a dog, that you come to me with staves?' And the Philistine cursed David by his god.

מג וַיֹּאמֶר הַפְּלִשְׁתִּי אֶל־דָּוִד הֲכֶלֶב אָנֹכִי כִּי־אַתָּה בָא־אֵלַי בַּמַּקְלוֹת וַיְקַלֵּל הַפְּלִשְׁתִּי אֶת־דָּוִד בֵּאלֹהָיו׃

44 And the Philistine said to David: 'Come to me, and I will give your flesh to the fowls of the air, and to the beasts of the field.'

מד וַיֹּאמֶר הַפְּלִשְׁתִּי אֶל־דָּוִד לְכָה אֵלַי וְאֶתְּנָה אֶת־בְּשָׂרְךָ לְעוֹף הַשָּׁמַיִם וּלְבֶהֱמַת הַשָּׂדֶה׃

45 Then said David to the Philistine: '**You come to me with a sword**, and with a spear, and with a javelin; but **I come to you in the name of the LORD of hosts**, the God of the armies of Israel, whom you have taunted.'

מה וַיֹּאמֶר דָּוִד אֶל־הַפְּלִשְׁתִּי אַתָּה בָּא אֵלַי בְּחֶרֶב וּבַחֲנִית וּבְכִידוֹן וְאָנֹכִי בָא־אֵלֶיךָ בְּשֵׁם יְיָ צְבָאוֹת אֱלֹהֵי מַעַרְכוֹת יִשְׂרָאֵל אֲשֶׁר חֵרַפְתָּ׃

Only as the battle is joined does the sword of Goliath appear.

The first time the sword of Goliath is mentioned, it is David who is doing the mentioning. In contrast to the sword, David comes in God's name. His faith is the reason David is chosen.

David recognizes that his strength comes from God's name alone. This recognition is the hallmark of a theologically legitimate king. If a king does not recognize that, then he will not prevail.

That is part of Saul's trouble. Saul gets upset when the women say, "Saul has slain his thousands, and David his tens of thousands."[25] If Saul recognized fully that everything exists for the glory of God, then these vain words would not disturb him. It is only because Saul is concerned about the aggrandizement of power that this bothers him. In Saul's nightmare scenario, he, as Chief of Staff, is being eclipsed by some whippersnapper who gets all the glory.

David, who speaks in God's name, kills the Philistine:

I Samuel 17

50 So David prevailed over the Philistine with a sling and with a stone, and smote the Philistine, **and slew him**; but **there was no sword in the hand of David**.

נ וַיֶּחֱזַק דָּוִד מִן-הַפְּלִשְׁתִּי בַּקֶּלַע וּבָאֶבֶן וַיַּךְ אֶת-הַפְּלִשְׁתִּי וַיְמִתֵהוּ וְחֶרֶב אֵין בְּיַד-דָּוִד.

51 And David ran, and **stood over the Philistine, and took his sword**, and drew it out of the sheath thereof, **and slew him**, and cut off his head therewith. And when the Philistines saw that their mighty man was dead, they fled.

נא וַיָּרָץ דָּוִד וַיַּעֲמֹד אֶל-הַפְּלִשְׁתִּי וַיִּקַּח אֶת-חַרְבּוֹ וַיִּשְׁלְפָהּ מִתַּעְרָהּ וַיְמֹתְתֵהוּ וַיִּכְרָת-בָּהּ אֶת-רֹאשׁוֹ: וַיִּרְאוּ הַפְּלִשְׁתִּים כִּי-מֵת גִּבּוֹרָם וַיָּנֻסוּ.

The sword is one of the key elements here in the whole story. There's the sword of Saul which David doesn't take,[26] and there's the sword of Goliath which is turned against its owner.

David ultimately succeeds by using his own weapon, the river stones. Accomplishing such a heroic feat with such a humble weapon shows that David's true weapon is his faith in God. It is only once the might of God has assured David's success, that David takes Goliath's sword.

This doubled death language in the story of Goliath foreshadows the doubled narrative of Saul's death.

---

25   I Samuel 18:7
26   I Samuel 17:39

The double deaths of King Saul and Goliath

Saul's death is confusing due to contradictions between the two versions of the story.

Did Saul kill himself?

I Samuel 31

4 Then said Saul to his armour-bearer: 'Draw your sword, and thrust me through therewith; lest these uncircumcised come and thrust me through, and make a mock of me.' But his armour-bearer would not; for he was sore afraid. Therefore **Saul took his sword, and fell upon it**.

ד וַיֹּאמֶר שָׁאוּל לְנֹשֵׂא כֵלָיו שְׁלֹף חַרְבְּךָ וְדָקְרֵנִי בָהּ פֶּן-יָבוֹאוּ הָעֲרֵלִים הָאֵלֶּה וּדְקָרֻנִי וְהִתְעַלְּלוּ-בִי וְלֹא אָבָה נֹשֵׂא כֵלָיו כִּי יָרֵא מְאֹד וַיִּקַּח שָׁאוּל אֶת-הַחֶרֶב וַיִּפֹּל עָלֶיהָ.

Or did the Amalekite lad kill him?

II Samuel 1

5 And David said to the young man that told him: 'How did you know that Saul and Jonathan his son are dead?'

ה וַיֹּאמֶר דָּוִד אֶל-הַנַּעַר הַמַּגִּיד לוֹ: אֵיךְ יָדַעְתָּ כִּי-מֵת שָׁאוּל וִיהוֹנָתָן בְּנוֹ.

6 And the young man that told him said: 'As I happened by chance upon mount Gilbo'a, behold, Saul leaned upon his spear; and, lo, the chariots and the horsemen pressed hard upon him.

ו וַיֹּאמֶר הַנַּעַר הַמַּגִּיד לוֹ נִקְרֹא נִקְרֵיתִי בְּהַר הַגִּלְבֹּעַ וְהִנֵּה שָׁאוּל נִשְׁעָן עַל-חֲנִיתוֹ: וְהִנֵּה הָרֶכֶב וּבַעֲלֵי הַפָּרָשִׁים הִדְבִּקֻהוּ.

7 And when he looked behind him, he saw me, and called to me. And I answered: Here am I.

ז וַיִּפֶן אַחֲרָיו וַיִּרְאֵנִי: וַיִּקְרָא אֵלַי וָאֹמַר הִנֵּנִי.

8 And he said to me: Who are you? And I answered him: I am an Amalekite.

ח וַיֹּאמֶר לִי מִי-אָתָּה: וָיֹאמַר (וָאֹמַר) אֵלָיו עֲמָלֵקִי אָנֹכִי.

9 And he said to me: Stand, I pray you, beside me, and slay me, for the agony has taken hold of me; because my life is yet in me.

ט וַיֹּאמֶר אֵלַי עֲמָד-נָא עָלַי וּמֹתְתֵנִי–כִּי אֲחָזַנִי הַשָּׁבָץ: כִּי-כָל-עוֹד נַפְשִׁי בִּי.

10 So **I stood beside him, and slew him**, because I was sure that he could not live after he fell; and I took the crown that was upon his head, and the bracelet that was on his arm, and have brought them here to my lord.'

י וָאֶעֱמֹד עָלָיו וַאֲמֹתְתֵהוּ כִּי יָדַעְתִּי כִּי
לֹא יִחְיֶה אַחֲרֵי נִפְלוֹ: וָאֶקַּח הַנֵּזֶר
אֲשֶׁר עַל־רֹאשׁוֹ וְאֶצְעָדָה אֲשֶׁר
עַל־זְרֹעוֹ וָאֲבִיאֵם אֶל־אֲדֹנִי הֵנָּה.

In the Goliath story, it seems as if we have the same problem, because if one examines the text superficially, it appears that David kills the Philistine twice.

It says, "So David prevailed over the Philistine with a sling and with a stone, and smote the Philistine, and slew *(va-yimtehu)* him."[27] David kills Goliath and he's dead. And then in the next verse, we read: "And David ran, and stood over the Philistine, and took his sword, and drew it out of the sheath thereof, and slew *(va-yemotetehu)* him."[28] How do you kill someone who's dead? Often in Biblical Hebrew, there may be a difference between two similar words, especially when they are in close proximity to one another.

Le-hamit means to "kill." *Va-yemotetehu* means to "finish someone off." Goliath is dying, then David deals the final blow.

As a child reading Shakespeare, I remember having trouble with the phrase, "I am slain." I didn't understand. What did *that* mean? If you're slain, how can you be talking?

What it meant was: "I have been mortally wounded."

That's what this says. With *"Va-yemotetehu,"* David mortally wounds Goliath and then finishes him off with his own sword. David, having come in God's name, goes forth to conquer Goliath, the hearts of the people, and his other enemies.

David and Saul: Mirror Images

The reason why David is chosen, according to the text, is because he is willing to recognize that everything is about God. It is when David loses sight of this that everything goes wrong.

Ultimately, David makes all the same mistakes that Saul does.

I recently taught the story of David and Batsheva. Learning it again, I gained new insight.

---

27   I Samuel 17:50
28   I Samuel 17:51

One way to read the David and Batsheva story is that roles have switched: David acts the part of Saul and Uriah acts the part of David. The themes played out between Saul and David are being replayed with David and Uriah.

Themes of the pursuer and the pursued are mirrored, and that of a king trying to kill off a loyal soldier. In fact, remember that Saul sent David out to the Philistines to die right after killing Goliath.[29] David does the same by sending Uriah back to the worst part of the battle.

Uriah uses David language when he says:

II Samuel 11

11 And Uriah said to David: 'The Ark, and Israel, and Judah, abide in booths; and my lord Yo'av, and the servants of my lord, are encamped in the open field; shall I then go into my house, to eat and to drink, and to lie with my wife? as you live, and as your soul lives, I will not do this thing.'

יא וַיֹּאמֶר אוּרִיָּה אֶל־דָּוִד הָאָרוֹן
וְיִשְׂרָאֵל וִיהוּדָה יֹשְׁבִים בַּסֻּכּוֹת
וַאדֹנִי יוֹאָב וְעַבְדֵי אֲדֹנִי עַל־פְּנֵי
הַשָּׂדֶה חֹנִים וַאֲנִי אָבוֹא אֶל־
בֵּיתִי לֶאֱכֹל וְלִשְׁתּוֹת וְלִשְׁכַּב
עִם־אִשְׁתִּי חַיֶּךָ וְחֵי נַפְשֶׁךָ
אִם־אֶעֱשֶׂה אֶת־הַדָּבָר הַזֶּה׃

Is this not similar to what David had said?

II Samuel 7

2 The king said to Nathan the prophet: 'See now, I dwell in a house of cedar, but the Ark of God dwells within curtains.'

ב וַיֹּאמֶר הַמֶּלֶךְ אֶל־נָתָן הַנָּבִיא רְאֵה
נָא אָנֹכִי יוֹשֵׁב בְּבֵית אֲרָזִים׃ וַאֲרוֹן
הָאֱלֹהִים יֹשֵׁב בְּתוֹךְ הַיְרִיעָה׃

David becomes like Saul; concerned about power and the kingship, rather than about his role as the chosen servant of God.

David becomes a Saul-like figure, which is part of the tragedy of David's decline at the end of the Book of Samuel. He ultimately emerges from it, but it is part of the pathos of the David and Batsheva story.

The Anti-Saul

We have explored briefly in this essay the fact that there is no background supplied for David in the Book of Samuel. David, just like Moses before him, shows up on the scene in the middle of the story. This hap-

---

29   I Samuel 18:25

pens in order that we not be sidetracked. David just shows up and takes over.

He is chosen by God because of his actions rather than because of some special family connection. He emerges as the anti-Saul. He emerges in stark contrast to Saul and to his own brothers, who are like Saul – tall and concerned with battle accouterments.

(If weapons are your strength, you are in trouble, because the Philistines have better ones. One big strength of the Philistines was the production and use of weapons. Remember, there were no weapons in Israel because the Philistines controlled the weapons industry.)[30]

There were two reasons the people gave for requesting a king: to judge the people fairly, and to fight wars.

If there is one duty to fulfill as a king in the Book of Judges or in the Book of Samuel, it is this: You must get rid of the Philistines. If not, you have not succeeded. The war with the Philistines was the most important battle. A secondary opponent was, of course, Amalek.

Saul failed in both attempts. The king who ultimately destroys the Philistines in the Book of Samuel is David. After David there are no more problems from the Philistines. Or Amalek. From Chapter 29 of I Samuel after Amalek flees Ziklag and David pursues and defeats them, Amalek is no longer a threat in the book of Samuel. That is the end of Amalek's arc of power. So David fulfills his mission as the one who fights the wars of God.

Will David also fulfill the second part of his mission as the just and righteous king? At the end of Samuel I, he is a tremendous proponent of fairness and justice: He follows the law, twice he doesn't kill Saul, he refrains from murdering Naval. (Not only does he restrain himself, but he recognizes that God has given him the opportunity to do so – and he is grateful.)

The real question is, will David ever regain the right to claim that he comes in the name of God?

---

30   I Samuel 13:19-22

YCT Tanakh Companion

The Theological Significance of the Urim Ve-Thummim

Rabbi Hayyim Angel

From the period of the Judges until the middle of King David's reign, the Israelites used various physical objects as oracles to ascertain the will of God. Most mysterious were the *Urim Ve-Thummim*[1] (UT), which the high priest carried inside[2] his breastplate. Additionally, Israelites used the lottery (*goral*), and possibly replicas of the high priest's *ephod* (see discussion below).

Actual information pertaining to the use of these oracles is scarce. Although Israelite leaders frequently "inquired of God" (לשאול בה'),[3] there

---

1   Ibn Ezra, Ramban, and Abarbanel (on Exodus 28:30) aver that the *Urim* and *Thummim* were different objects. Ibn Ezra quotes Nehemiah 7:65 ("until a priest with Urim and Thummim…") in support of this position. Targum Pseudo-Jonathan and Rashi (on Exodus 28:30), in contrast, maintain that the UT was one object, perhaps an engraving of one of God's Names. We will follow the view of Ibn Ezra, et al, and refer to the UT in the plural. For fuller linguistic discussions, see Cornelis Van Dam, *The Urim and Thummim: A Means of Revelation in Ancient Israel* (Winona Lake, IN: Eisenbrauns, 1997), pp. 132-139. A full review of recent literature will be found in this essay's final note.

2   Following the simplest reading of Exodus 28:30 and Leviticus 8:8, that Moses installed the UT *"el ha-choshen."* This reading is adopted by Rashi, Ibn Ezra, Ramban, Ritva (*Yoma* 73b), and Abarbanel, *contra* Ralbag, R. Sherira, and R. Hai Ga'on (quoted in *Torah Shelemah* Exodus 28:85), who believe that the gemstones on the breastplate themselves were the UT. See Van Dam, pp. 16-21, 154-160, for discussions of early Jewish sources such as the DSS, Philo, and Josephus, all of whom may have associated the UT with the gemstones of the breastplate. See also Robert Hayward, "Pseudo-Philo and the Priestly Oracle," *JJS* 46 (1995), pp. 43-54.

3   See Judges 1:1-2; 20:18-27; I Samuel 10:19-22; 14:17-19, 36-43; 22:9-16; 23:1-6; 28:6; 30:1-8; II Samuel 2:1; 5:17-23. Van Dam (pp. 109-112, 182-190) maintains that לשאול בה' should be viewed as a technical term for oracular inquiry of God.

are only seven explicit references to the UT in the entire Bible.[4]

Ironically, much of our inability to understand the nature of the UT derives from the fact that the ancient Israelites were so completely familiar with them.

Ramban observes[5] that in contrast to the intricate descriptions and directives pertaining to nearly all other utensils of the Tabernacle, the UT receive none whatsoever. God simply instructed Moses to put *the* (definite article) UT into the breastplate, indicating that Moses and the ancient Israelites were fully aware of the UT's identity.

Ramban further observes that God never commanded Bezalel to manufacture the UT, and the Torah does not mention the creation of the UT in Exodus 35-40. Perhaps God Himself gave them to Moses. Alternatively, one could argue that Moses and the Israelites had the UT in their possession from an earlier period, perhaps passed down from the patriarchs.

Moreover, a search for articles on the theological significance of the UT also yields little; most scholars who write about the UT are interested primarily in comparisons with ancient Near Eastern parallels. In this essay, we will consider traditional Jewish interpretations of the theological role of oracles in the period from Joshua until David. We then will examine the apparent discontinuation of oracular consultation during the reign of David. While the biblical evidence is scant, it appears that a composite picture can be drawn that points to the UT's playing a central role in the spiritual evolution of Israel.

Urim Ve-Thummim

> Although the decree of a prophet could be revoked, the decree of the UT could not be revoked, as it is said: By the judgment of the *Urim* (Yoma 73b).[6]

While the high priest bearing the UT served as a mouthpiece of God's

---

4   See Exodus 28:30; Leviticus 8:7-8 (command and installation of the UT); Numbers 27:21 (instructions that Joshua should inquire of God); Deuteronomy 33:8 (the UT were entrusted to Levites); I Samuel 28:6 (King Saul inquired of the UT, but was not answered); Ezra 2:63~Nehemiah 7:65 (priests without documentation of pedigree were not accepted to the priesthood, pending a verdict from the UT, which were no longer available).

5   Exodus 28:30

6   Translations of talmudic passages are taken from the Soncino translation, with minor modifications.

direct message, the prophet had an element of human input, not necessarily expressing God's precise words.[7] In this regard, the UT's transmission of actual words approached the word-for-word reliability of Moses' superior prophecy.[8]

Faith in the Oracle

The verdicts of the UT were considered infallible to the point that, during the episode of "the concubine at Give'ah," the Israelites suffered precisely because they had such belief in the veracity of the UT's messages.[9] Although the UT had ruled that the tribe of Judah should lead the assault against the sinful Benjaminites, the tribal confederation suffered two horrific losses. Yet, the Israelites persisted with the UT, eventually learning that they would be victorious in the third battle.

Technically, the UT were not mistaken; they simply informed the tribal confederation that Judah should lead, and that they should continue the battle. The UT did not indicate that the confederation would be *victorious* until the third battle.

However, God obviously understood what the tribes wanted to know: would they *defeat* the Benjaminites? Did their imprecise formulation prompt God to offer an incomplete answer?

Ralbag and Abarbanel fault the people for not asking the critical follow-up question—whether they would win the war with Judah leading. Only in their third inquiry, by asking if they should continue, did the people provide sufficient information to warrant a complete response. As a result of their imprecise questioning, the tribal confederation suffered unnecessary losses.[10]

---

7   Rambam (*Guide* II:45) argues that the UT worked on the level of divine inspiration, which he considers lower than prophecy. Abarbanel (on Exodus 28:30) explains that the priest himself did not need to attain the loftier level of prophecy, but the accuracy of the UT's messages themselves were regarded as higher than that of prophecy. For further discussion of the differences between inquiries of the UT and prophecy, see Norman M. Bronswick. "The Prophetic and the Priestly Oracle in the Rabbinic View," in the *Rabbi Joseph H. Lookstein Memorial Volume*, ed. Leo Landman (New York: Ktav, 1980), pp. 67-83.

8   See Exodus 33:9-11; Numbers 12:6-8. *Zohar* (Pekudei 230b) states that the high priest's face would shine as he received a message from the UT. This is reminiscent of Moses, whose face also glowed after receiving his prophecies (Exodus 34:29-35). Cf. *Leviticus Rabbah* 21:12.

9   Judges 20:18-28

10   Cf. *Sifrei Zuta* Numbers 27:21

Several others maintain that God deliberately misled the people in this episode: God wanted to punish the eleven tribes for not having been equally zealous against the idolatrous shrine of Micah in Judges 17-18.[11] According to this opinion, the manner in which the Israelites formulated their questions had no bearing on the outcome.

Similarly, the Jerusalem Talmud[12] understands the words *"Urim Ve-Thummim"* in this manner: they "light" (*Urim*) the path Israel should follow when Israel is "pure" (*tamim*).

This talmudic passage goes on to suggest that since the people of that generation were not pure, God did not light up the proper path for them to follow.[13]

Silent Oracle

There are two biblical accounts of oracular inquiry, however, in which the UT did not respond at all. In I Samuel 14, Saul battled the Philistines, unaware that his son Jonathan had violated an earlier ban against eating:[14]

I Samuel 14

36 Saul said, 'Let us go down after the Philistines by night and plunder among them until the light of morning; and let us not leave a single survivor among them.' 'Do whatever you please,' they replied. But the priest said, 'Let us approach God here.'

37 So Saul inquired of God, 'Shall I go down after the Philistines? Will You deliver them into the hands of Israel?' But this time He did not respond to him.

לו וַיֹּאמֶר שָׁאוּל נֵרְדָה אַחֲרֵי פְלִשְׁתִּים לַיְלָה וְנָבֹזָה בָהֶם עַד-אוֹר הַבֹּקֶר וְלֹא-נַשְׁאֵר בָּהֶם אִישׁ וַיֹּאמְרוּ

כָּל-הַטּוֹב בְּעֵינֶיךָ עֲשֵׂה: וַיֹּאמֶר הַכֹּהֵן נִקְרְבָה הֲלֹם אֶל-הָאֱלֹהִים.

לז וַיִּשְׁאַל שָׁאוּל בֵּאלֹהִים הַאֵרֵד אַחֲרֵי פְלִשְׁתִּים הֲתִתְּנֵם בְּיַד יִשְׂרָאֵל וְלֹא עָנָהוּ בַּיּוֹם הַהוּא.

---

11   See *Yoma* 73b, *Sanhedrin* 103b, followed by Rashi, Kara, Radak.

12   *Yoma* 7:3

13   See Van Dam, pp. 131-139, for discussion of possible etymologies of the term UT. Cf. Van Dam pp. 31-32 for further sources indicating that the UT actually lit up.

14   Translations of biblical verses are taken from the NJPS, with minor modifications.

Distressed by the lack of response, Saul concluded that someone must have sinned. They subsequently cast lots,[15] and Jonathan was discovered. From the flow of the narrative, it appears that God did not answer Saul because of Jonathan's violation of the ban. Alternatively, one might argue that Saul was punished for his own sin — preventing Achiyah from receiving an oracular message earlier in the same battle:[16]

God again withheld response from Saul at the end of the king's life:

I Samuel 28

5 When Saul saw the Philistine force, his heart trembled with fear.

ה וַיַּרְא שָׁאוּל אֶת-מַחֲנֵה פְלִשְׁתִּים: וַיִּרָא וַיֶּחֱרַד לִבּוֹ מְאֹד.

6 And Saul inquired of the LORD, but the LORD did not answer him, either by dreams or by Urim or by prophets.

ו וַיִּשְׁאַל שָׁאוּל בַּיי וְלֹא עָנָהוּ יְיָ: גַּם בַּחֲלֹמוֹת גַּם בָּאוּרִים גַּם בַּנְּבִיאִם.

In this instance,[17] several commentators aver that God refused to answer Saul as a punishment for having ordered the massacre of the priestly city of Nob (I Samuel 22:7-19). Thus, in both cases where God withheld response, commentators generally assume that the lack of response indicates blameworthiness of the inquirer himself.[18] It is noteworthy that Saul was the victim on both occasions, and these were his only two recorded oracular inquiries of God.

Inquiry on behalf of the people

All biblical inquiries of the UT related to matters of national significance.[19] A majority of inquiries of God pertained to military decisions.[20]

---

15   Rashi, Radak, Abarbanel ad loc.

16   I Samuel 14:17-19

17   Here and in Numbers 27:21, only "*Urim*" is mentioned; presumably, the UT are meant. Cf. Van Dam, pp. 177-182.

18   See *Berakhot* 12b; Rashi, Kara, Radak, Ralbag in both instances.

19   Mishnah *Yoma* 71b: And one inquired (of the UT) only for a king. Whence do we know these things? R. Abbahu said: Scripture said, "But he shall present himself to Eleazar the priest, who shall on his behalf seek the decision of the Urim" (Numbers 27:21); 'he' i.e., the king, 'and all the children of Israel with him', i.e., the [Priest] Anointed for Battle, 'even all the congregation', that is the Sanhedrin (*Yoma* 73b).

20   Judges 1:1; 18:5; 20:18-27; I Samuel 14:17-19, 37-41; 23:1-6; 28:6; 30:1-8; II Samuel 5:19-23.

Additionally, David chose his first capital at Hebron after inquiring of God,[21] and Samuel located Saul at the latter's coronation through an inquiry.[22] The elders of Joshua's time were criticized for not having inquired of God before making a treaty with the deceitful Give'onites,[23] implying that it would have been proper to have done so. Were they available, the UT would have been consulted to determine the ancestry of priests at the beginning of the Second Temple period.[24] Finally, David is reported by Doeg as having made unspecified inquiries of God while fleeing Saul.[25] All inquiries on record were from leaders, and all concerned matters of national consequence.

The Ephod

In addition to the high priest's UT, the ancient Israelites seem to have replicated the *ephod* of the high priest as an alternate means of inquiring of God.

After Saul's massacre of Nob, Achimelekh's son Evyatar escaped to David's camp, bringing with him an *ephod*.[26] The priests in Nob wore *ephod*s made of *linen*,[27] clearly a different garment from the golden *ephod*[28] (with *tekhelet* and *argaman*) of the high priest. Based on this verse, Radak and Ralbag conclude that spiritual leaders in that period made linen replicas of the high priest's *ephod*, as a sign of spiritual distinction.[29]

I Samuel 22

18 Thereupon the king said to Doeg, 'You, Doeg, go and strike down the priests.' And Doeg the Edomite went and struck down the priests himself; that day, he killed eighty-five men who wore the linen *ephod*.

יח וַיֹּאמֶר הַמֶּלֶךְ לדויג (לְדוֹאֵג) סֹב אַתָּה וּפְגַע בַּכֹּהֲנִים: וַיִּסֹּב דויג (דּוֹאֵג) הָאֲדֹמִי וַיִּפְגַּע-הוּא בַּכֹּהֲנִים וַיָּמֶת בַּיּוֹם הַהוּא שְׁמֹנִים וַחֲמִשָּׁה אִישׁ נֹשֵׂא אֵפוֹד בָּד.

21   II Samuel 2:1

22   I Samuel 10:22

23   Joshua 9:14-15

24   Ezra 2:61-63; Nehemiah 7:63-65

25   I Samuel 22:10-16

26   I Samuel 23:6

27   I Samuel 22:18

28   Exodus 28:2-6

29   Cf. I Samuel 2:18; II Samuel 6:14; I Chronicles 15:27. See also Rambam *Hil. Kelei HaMikdash* 10:13; Ramban on Exodus 2:18; R. Isaiah D'Trani and Metzudat David on I Samuel 22:18.

19 He put Nob, the town of the priests, to the sword: men and women, children and infants, oxen, asses, and sheep—[all] to the sword.

יט וְאֵת נֹב עִיר־הַכֹּהֲנִים הִכָּה לְפִי־ חֶרֶב מֵאִישׁ וְעַד־אִשָּׁה מֵעוֹלֵל וְעַד־ יוֹנֵק וְשׁוֹר וַחֲמוֹר וָשֶׂה לְפִי־חָרֶב.

20 But one son of Achimelekh son of Achitub escaped—his name was Evyatar—and he fled to David.

כ וַיִּמָּלֵט בֶּן־אֶחָד לַאֲחִימֶלֶךְ בֶּן־אֲחִטוּב וּשְׁמוֹ אֶבְיָתָר וַיִּבְרַח אַחֲרֵי דָוִד.

However, it appears that these *ephod*s were used as alternative oracles to the UT. This opinion is supported by the two final recorded instances of inquiry of God during Saul's lifetime.

I Samuel 23

1 David was told: 'The Philistines are raiding Ke'ilah and plundering the threshing floors.'

א וַיַּגִּדוּ לְדָוִד לֵאמֹר: הִנֵּה פְלִשְׁתִּים נִלְחָמִים בִּקְעִילָה וְהֵמָּה שֹׁסִים אֶת־הַגֳּרָנוֹת.

2 **David consulted the LORD**, 'Shall I go and attack those Philistines?' And the LORD said to David, 'Go; attack the Philistines and you will save Ke'ilah.'

ב וַיִּשְׁאַל דָּוִד בַּיי לֵאמֹר הַאֵלֵךְ וְהִכֵּיתִי בַּפְּלִשְׁתִּים הָאֵלֶּה: וַיֹּאמֶר יי אֶל־דָּוִד לֵךְ וְהִכִּיתָ בַפְּלִשְׁתִּים וְהוֹשַׁעְתָּ אֶת־קְעִילָה.

3 But David's men said to him, 'Look, we are afraid here in Judah, how much more if we go to Ke'ilah against the forces of the Philistines!'

ג וַיֹּאמְרוּ אַנְשֵׁי דָוִד אֵלָיו הִנֵּה אֲנַחְנוּ פֹה בִיהוּדָה יְרֵאִים וְאַף כִּי־נֵלֵךְ קְעִלָה אֶל־מַעַרְכוֹת פְּלִשְׁתִּים.

4 **So David consulted the LORD again**, and the LORD answered him, 'March down at once to Ke'ilah, for I am going to deliver the Philistines into your hands.'

ד וַיּוֹסֶף עוֹד דָּוִד לִשְׁאוֹל בַּיי וַיַּעֲנֵהוּ יי וַיֹּאמֶר קוּם רֵד קְעִילָה כִּי־אֲנִי נֹתֵן אֶת־פְּלִשְׁתִּים בְּיָדֶךָ.

5 David and his men went to Ke'ilah and fought against the Philistines; he drove off their cattle and inflicted a severe defeat on them. Thus David saved the inhabitants of Ke'ilah.

ה וַיֵּלֶךְ דָּוִד וַאֲנָשָׁיו קְעִילָה וַיִּלָּחֶם בַּפְּלִשְׁתִּים וַיִּנְהַג אֶת־מִקְנֵיהֶם וַיַּךְ בָּהֶם מַכָּה גְדוֹלָה וַיֹּשַׁע דָּוִד אֵת יֹשְׁבֵי קְעִילָה.

6 **When Evyatar son of Achimelekh fled to David at Keʻilah, he brought down an *ephod* with him.**	ו וַיְהִי בִּבְרֹחַ אֶבְיָתָר בֶּן-אֲחִימֶלֶךְ אֶל-דָּוִד קְעִילָה: אֵפוֹד יָרַד בְּיָדוֹ.

David still was in possession of Evyatar's *ephod* after the Amalekite raid on Ziklag.[30] David specifically asked for the *ephod*, at which point he inquired of God in the same manner as one would use for inquiring of the UT. God responded, as He did when David consulted him about the Philistines attacking Keiʻlah.

I Samuel 30

7 David said to the priest Evyatar son of Achimelekh, 'Bring the *ephod* up to me.' When Evyatar brought up the *ephod* to David,	ז וַיֹּאמֶר דָּוִד אֶל-אֶבְיָתָר הַכֹּהֵן בֶּן-אֲחִימֶלֶךְ הַגִּישָׁה-נָּא לִי הָאֵפוֹד וַיַּגֵּשׁ אֶבְיָתָר אֶת-הָאֵפוֹד אֶל-דָּוִד.
8 David inquired of the LORD, 'Shall I pursue those raiders? Will I overtake them?' And He answered him, 'Pursue, for you shall overtake and you shall rescue.'	ח וַיִּשְׁאַל דָּוִד בַּיי לֵאמֹר אֶרְדֹּף אַחֲרֵי הַגְּדוּד-הַזֶּה הַאַשִּׂגֶנּוּ וַיֹּאמֶר לוֹ רְדֹף כִּי-הַשֵּׂג תַּשִּׂיג וְהַצֵּל תַּצִּיל.

Only two chapters earlier,[31] Saul had inquired of the UT to no avail. But if the UT were continuously in the possession of Evyatar and David, how could Saul have inquired at all?

Radak and Abarbanel, who believe that the *ephod* of Evyatar was that of the high priest, are forced to argue that Saul must have sent messengers to David and Evyatar.

However, Ibn Ezra[32] and Ramban[33] maintain that Saul had the *real* UT with the high priest's *ephod*, whereas Evyatar inquired of God using his linen *ephod*. This latter opinion is preferable, especially in light of the repeated emphasis on the *ephod*,[34] while the UT were with Saul.

Thus, it appears that in the time of Samuel, spiritual leaders made replicas of the high priest's *ephod*, and sometimes inquired of God through

---

30	I Samuel 30
31	I Samuel 28:6
32	On Exodus 28:6
33	On Exodus 28:30
34	I Samuel 23:6; and I Samuel 30:7-8

them.[35] From the language of the text in both cases, the method of inquiry of an *ephod* was identical to that of an inquiry of the UT.

Inquiring of God

The Israelites viewed the responses of the UT (and its *ephod* substitute) as prophetic, providing specific and accurate responses to the questioner. Although one had the right to initiate inquiry through the UT, God could refuse an answer,[36] or offer partial answers, either because of the inquirer's lowered spiritual state, or because of an insufficiently specific question.[37]

The word-for-word prophetic accuracy of the UT resembled the lofty prophecies of Moses; indeed, the UT appears to have "replaced" Moses. This point is highlighted by Ibn Ezra's explanation of Moses' superior prophecy: "Not so with My servant Moses; he is trusted throughout My household."[38] Moses could inquire of God directly, whereas all other prophets had to wait until God would reveal prophecy to them. Of course, Israelites were allowed to initiate inquiry of the UT, but later prophets could not initiate dialogue with God.

In all cases of inquiry of God through prophetic oracles (UT and *ephod*), leaders of the nation inquired of God, and God responded directly. All inquiries of the UT pertained to matters of national significance.

What emerges from these discussions is that these oracles were viewed as divinely inspired and always accurate. Therefore, it would stand to reason that oracles would enjoy widespread use for the remainder of the biblical period. Yet, David is the last person reported to have inquired of God through oracles. Why was this practice apparently discontinued?

The (Apparent) Discontinuation of the UT

By the beginning of the Second Temple period, the UT were unavailable, according to Ezra and Nehemiah.[39] Midrashim and later commen-

35   However, they never replicated the UT, which remained exclusively in the breastplate of the high priest. It appears that in illegitimate oracular cults in Israel, people substituted *teraphim* for the UT. See Judges 17:5 (and Rashi, Malbim on Judges 18:5); Hosea 3:3-4. Cf. Rashbam on Exodus 28:30, who specifically contrasts *teraphim*, which work through the spirit of impurity, and the UT—the epitome of holiness. See also *Numbers Rabbah* 20:20.

36   I Samuel 14:36-37; 28:6

37   Judges 20:18-28

38   Numbers 12:7

39   "Of the sons of the priests, the sons of Habaiah, the sons of Hakkoz, the sons of Barzillai who had married a daughter of Barzillai and had taken

tators debate whether the returning exiles did not have the UT at all,[40] or whether they physically had the objects — but divine inspiration had ceased.[41]

According to the Talmud,[42] the UT fell into disuse after the period of the "former prophets." However, that teaching debates what this term means: one opinion considers Samuel, David, and Solomon the early prophets, implying that everyone after them are "latter prophets." According to the second opinion, all prophets preceding Haggai, Zechariah, and Malachi are considered "former prophets." The biblical evidence supports both positions: David is the last leader on record who inquired of the UT, but there is no evidence that they were *not* used until the beginning of the Second Temple period. We simply do not know what happened between David and Zerubbabel from the biblical text.

Transfer of Oracular Authority to Prophets

Nevertheless, it appears that the absence of biblical evidence regarding the consultation of prophetic oracles *after* the time of David is significant, an indication that David began a permanent movement away from employing prophetic oracles. The first instance in which David, uncharacteristically, did *not* inquire of an oracle is when he asked Nathan the prophet about his desire to build a Temple to house the Ark.[43] Interestingly, Nathan was *mistaken* in his initial judgment — his first answer is made without benefit of prophecy. He is later corrected by God.

In later biblical history, kings regularly consulted prophets before going to war. The kings Ahab and Jehoshaphat[44] inquired of prophets for military advice, and Jehoram[45] followed suit.[46] In these and many related

---

his name—these searched for their genealogical records, but they could not be found, so they were disqualified for the priesthood. The Tirshatha ordered them not to eat of the most holy things until a priest with Urim and Thummim should appear." – Ezra 2:61-63; Nehemiah 7:63-65

40   See *Shevuot* 16a; *Song Rabbah* 8:9; Rashi on *Yoma* 21b; Ritva on *Yoma* 73b, Ra'avad *Hil. Bet HaBehirah* 4:1.

41   See *Yoma* 21b; *Kiddushin* 31a; Rambam, *Hil. Kelei HaMikdash* 10:10-11.

42   *Sotah* 48b

43   II Samuel 7:1-2

44   I Kings 22:5-8

45   II Kings 3:9-1

46   Note the strikingly similar formulations between Ahab's inquiry of his prophets and the Israelites' inquiry of the UT in the Concubine of Give'ah episode:

cases, it is clear that the increased influence of prophecy had supplanted the earlier practice of oracular inquiry.[47]

The ascendancy of prophecy over oracles also can be deduced from Joshua's leadership. Although the Torah commands Joshua to consult the UT,[48] there is no recorded instance of his doing so. Instead, God spoke directly to Joshua as a prophet. Abarbanel and Malbim[49] conclude that the people of Israel did not consult the UT in Joshua's lifetime precisely because Joshua had attained prophecy.[50]

However, this answer alone is insufficient: after all, there were prophets during the period of the Judges,[51] and Samuel, Nathan, and Gad prophesied during the reigns of Saul and David — all while national leaders still consulted oracles. Therefore, the ascendancy of prophecy alone cannot fully explain the discontinuation of the use of oracles.

Increased Role of Wisdom

In a second striking instance of David ending his reliance on the oracle, the king returned his priests Evyatar and Zadok back to Jerusalem as he fled Absalom;[52] certainly, this was a break from the past, when a leader would have kept his priests and the Ark with him at wartime in order to inquire of God.

David did not bring the priests with him during Absalom's rebellion because of the increased respect he had developed for wise advisors. The text compares the reliability of Achitofel to that of oracles:

I Kings 22:6: So the king of Israel gathered the prophets, about four hundred men, and asked them, "Shall I march upon Ramoth-Gilead for battle, or shall I not?" "March," they said, "and the Lord will deliver [it] into Your Majesty's hands."

Judges 20:28: "Shall we again take the field against our kinsmen the Benjaminites, or shall we not?" The Lord answered, "Go up, for tomorrow I will deliver them into your hands."

47   See also Jeremiah 21:1-2; II Kings 19:1-7 (~Isaiah 37:1-7); Jeremiah 37:3-21; 38:14-18. For a fuller survey, see Van Dam, pp. 242-247.

48   Numbers 27:21

49   On Judges 1:1

50   Cf. *Numbers Rabbah* 12:9, Netziv on Numbers 27:21, who aver that the commandment for Joshua to inquire of the UT applies only if he needs it, and not if he becomes a prophet. In contrast, Ralbag (on Judges 1:1) presumes that Joshua did consult the UT in his lifetime (even though the Book of Joshua does not indicate that he did), since he was instructed by the Torah to do so.

51   See for example, Judges 2:1-5; 4:4; 6:7-10; 10:11-15.

52   II Samuel 15:24-29

II Samuel 16
23 Now the counsel of Achitofel, which he counselled in those days, was as if a man inquired of the word of God; so was all the counsel of Achitofel both with David and with Absalom.

כג וַעֲצַת אֲחִיתֹפֶל אֲשֶׁר יָעַץ בַּיָּמִים
הָהֵם כַּאֲשֶׁר יִשְׁאַל- (אִישׁ)
בִּדְבַר הָאֱלֹהִים: כֵּן כָּל-עֲצַת
אֲחִיתֹפֶל גַּם-לְדָוִד גַּם לְאַבְשָׁלֹם.

The prominent roles of Achitofel and Hushai in this narrative demonstrate the immense respect commanded by wise officers.

Obstacles to Divine Inspiration

According to a few rabbinic sources, David stopped inquiring of the UT because of his concern that the high priest Evyatar had lost his divine inspiration.[53] Perhaps David feared that the UT might not always be a reliable source of information, since the priest bearing them could be unworthy. As a result, David discontinued his own use of oracles, and his successors followed suit.

Also, we learned that sin might cause God to refrain from responding to an inquiry. This was the lesson of Saul's failed inquiries of God.[54] Perhaps David, plagued by the recent episode with Batsheva, deliberately returned the priests to Jerusalem during Absalom's rebellion because he feared that God would not respond to him.[55]

To summarize: increased dependence on prophecy and wisdom moved David and his successors away from oracular advice; fear of the priesthood's corruptibility and/or personal sin also may have been factors in David's decision.

Presence of the Ark

An additional reason why Israel discontinued its inquiries of the UT lies in the possibility that the physical presence and accessibility of the Ark may have been necessary for oracular consultation.

---

53   *Sotah* 48b; cf. *Seder Olam Rabbah* 14
54   I Samuel 14:36-37; 28:6
55   See *Sanhedrin* 107a, which states that the *Shekhinah*, the Divine presence, temporarily left David after this episode.

Earlier, we discussed two horrific losses sustained by the Israelite alliance despite their strict adherence to the UT's instructions to proceed in the battle against the Benjaminites.[56] As mentioned above, several commentators explain that during the first two inquiries, God deliberately misled the nation as a punishment for other sins, or else the UT did not provide a full response because the nation formulated their message imprecisely. However, the text suggests a different reason for the faulty response during the first two inquiries:

Judges 20

27 The Israelites inquired
   of the LORD (for the Ark
   of God's Covenant was
   there in those days),

כז וַיִּשְׁאֲלוּ בְנֵי-יִשְׂרָאֵל בַּיי: וְשָׁם אֲרוֹן בְּרִית הָאֱלֹהִים בַּיָּמִים הָהֵם.

28 and Pinchas son of Eleazar son
   of Aaron the priest ministered
   before Him in those days,
   'Shall we again take the field
   against our kinsmen the
   Benjaminites, or shall we
   not?' The LORD answered,
   'Go up, for tomorrow I will
   deliver them into your hands.'

כח וּפִינְחָס בֶּן-אֶלְעָזָר בֶּן-אַהֲרֹן עֹמֵד לְפָנָיו בַּיָּמִים הָהֵם לֵאמֹר הַאוֹסִף עוֹד לָצֵאת לַמִּלְחָמָה עִם-בְּנֵי-בִנְיָמִן אָחִי אִם-אֶחְדָּל: וַיֹּאמֶר יי עֲלוּ כִּי מָחָר אֶתְּנֶנּוּ בְיָדֶךָ.

Abarbanel and Malbim believe that this detail unlocks the narrative: Given that Pinchas and the Ark are not mentioned until the final inquiry of the UT, it is possible that the first two inquiries were made of a different priest, and not in the presence of the Ark. Abarbanel and Malbim posit that unconventional inquiry may have warranted the incomplete response from the UT. From this vantage point, the Ark is seen as a necessary part of the inquiry.

I Samuel 14

17 And Saul said to the troops with
   him, 'Take a count and see who
   has left us.' They took a count
   and found that Jonathan and
   his arms-bearer were missing.

יז וַיֹּאמֶר שָׁאוּל לָעָם אֲשֶׁר אִתּוֹ פִּקְדוּ-נָא וּרְאוּ מִי הָלַךְ מֵעִמָּנוּ: וַיִּפְקְדוּ וְהִנֵּה אֵין יוֹנָתָן וְנֹשֵׂא כֵלָיו.

---

56   Judges 20:18-28

18 Thereupon Saul said to Achiyah, 'Bring the Ark of God here'; for the Ark of God was at the time among the Israelites.	יח וַיֹּאמֶר שָׁאוּל לַאֲחִיָּה הַגִּישָׁה אֲרוֹן הָאֱלֹהִים: כִּי-הָיָה אֲרוֹן הָאֱלֹהִים בַּיּוֹם הַהוּא וּבְנֵי יִשְׂרָאֵל.
19 But while Saul was speaking to the priest, the confusion in the Philistine camp kept increasing; and Saul said to the priest, 'Withdraw your hand.'	יט וַיְהִי עַד דִּבֶּר שָׁאוּל אֶל-הַכֹּהֵן וְהֶהָמוֹן אֲשֶׁר בְּמַחֲנֵה פְלִשְׁתִּים וַיֵּלֶךְ הָלוֹךְ וָרָב: וַיֹּאמֶר שָׁאוּל אֶל-הַכֹּהֵן אֱסֹף יָדֶךָ.

Once again, the Ark's presence is noted in the context of Divine inquiry. In this instance, commentators are troubled by Saul's command for the priest to "withdraw his hand" — did Achiyah touch the Ark? Presumably not. Either the "Ark" in this passage is synonymous with the UT,[57] or the priest inquired of the UT in the presence of the Ark,[58] or the UT were in the Ark.[59] According to all three interpretations, the Ark and UT play cooperative roles in the process of inquiry.

Ironically, David's request of Nathan the prophet regarding building the Temple is remarkable as the first clear instance when David did not inquire of the UT.

II Samuel 7

1 When the king was settled in his palace and the Lord had granted him safety from all the enemies around him.	א וַיְהִי כִּי-יָשַׁב הַמֶּלֶךְ בְּבֵיתוֹ: וַיי הֵנִיחַ-לוֹ מִסָּבִיב מִכָּל-אֹיְבָיו.
2 The king said to the prophet Nathan: 'Here I am dwelling in a house of cedar, while the Ark of the Lord abides in a tent!'	ב וַיֹּאמֶר הַמֶּלֶךְ אֶל-נָתָן הַנָּבִיא רְאֵה נָא אָנֹכִי יוֹשֵׁב בְּבֵית אֲרָזִים וַאֲרוֹן הָאֱלֹהִים יֹשֵׁב בְּתוֹךְ הַיְרִיעָה.

David's attempt to build a permanent home for the Ark, also necessitated a transition from the UT to other means of guidance. If inquiry of the UT required the physical presence and accessibility of the Ark, then the days of oracular inquiries were numbered.

At the beginning of the Second Temple period, the Ark was no longer present,[60] having been hidden, or taken into captivity.[61] And therefore,

57   As according to Rashi on I Samuel 14:18.
58   Radak, ibid
59   Ralbag, ibid
60   *Yoma* 21b
61   *Yoma* 52b-54a

the UT either were no longer physically present, or they could not function absent the Ark.

It appears, then, that the functionality of the UT depended on the physical presence and accessibility of the Ark. So long as the Ark was without a permanent home, it accompanied the Israelites in their travels and wars — and the Israelites were able to inquire freely of the UT. However, once David began a plan to ensconce the Ark in a permanent home, he abruptly stopped inquiring of the UT, turning instead for guidance to prophets and wise men.

The Divine-Human Continuum in Biblical Israel

In 1985, Professor Yaakov Elman published two articles analyzing the position of R. Zadok HaKohen of Lublin in reference to the transition from the age of prophecy to the age of Oral Law. According to R. Zadok, the end of the age of prophecy facilitated a flourishing of the development of the Oral Law, a step impossible so long as people could turn to the prophets for certain religious guidance. Therefore, the first Mishnah in *Avot* includes the prophets as a vital link in the spiritual leadership of Israel:[62]

> *Moses received the Torah at Sinai and transmitted it to Joshua,*
> *Joshua to the elders, the elders to the prophets, and the prophets*
> *to the men of the Great Assembly.* (Mishnah *Avot* 1:1).

In light of our analysis of the UT, we may elaborate on R. Zadok's understanding of the transition between direct revelation and human interpretation.

Moses himself epitomized direct revelation. He had no need to use the UT—God spoke to him with word for word accuracy, and Moses was able to initiate dialogue with God.

It is with Joshua that we first find tension over the role of the UT.

Numbers 27

18 And the LORD said to Moses:
'Take Joshua the son of Nun,

יח וַיֹּאמֶר יְיָ אֶל-מֹשֶׁה קַח-לְךָ
אֶת-יְהוֹשֻׁעַ בֶּן-נוּן אִישׁ אֲשֶׁר-רוּחַ

---

62   See his articles, "R. Zadok HaKohen on the History of Halakha," *Tradition* 21:4 (Fall 1985), pp. 1-26; and "Reb Zadok HaKohen of Lublin on Prophecy in the Halakhic Process," in *Jewish Law Association Studies I: Touro Conference Volume*, ed. B.S. Jackson. (Chico, CA: Scholars Press, 1985), pp. 1-16.

a man in whom is spirit, and
lay your hand upon him;

19 and set him before Eleazar
the priest, and before all the
congregation; and give him
a charge in their sight.

20 And you shall put of your
honor upon him, that all the
congregation of the children
of Israel may hearken.

21 And he shall stand before Eleazar
the priest, who shall inquire for
him by the judgment of the Urim
before the LORD; at his word
shall they go out, and at his word
they shall come in, both he, and
all the children of Israel with
him, and all the congregation.'

בוֹ: וְסָמַכְתָּ אֶת-יָדְךָ עָלָיו.

יט וְהַעֲמַדְתָּ אֹתוֹ לִפְנֵי אֶלְעָזָר
הַכֹּהֵן וְלִפְנֵי כָּל-הָעֵדָה
וְצִוִּיתָה אֹתוֹ לְעֵינֵיהֶם.

כ וְנָתַתָּה מֵהוֹדְךָ עָלָיו לְמַעַן
יִשְׁמְעוּ כָּל-עֲדַת בְּנֵי יִשְׂרָאֵל.

כא וְלִפְנֵי אֶלְעָזָר הַכֹּהֵן יַעֲמֹד וְשָׁאַל
לוֹ בְּמִשְׁפַּט הָאוּרִים לִפְנֵי יְיָ:
עַל-פִּיו יֵצְאוּ וְעַל-פִּיו יָבֹאוּ הוּא
וְכָל-בְּנֵי-יִשְׂרָאֵל אִתּוֹ וְכָל-הָעֵדָה.

On the one hand, the death of Moses appeared to signal the dawn of an age where God would communicate primarily through the UT — Joshua was instructed to consult the UT for matters of national concern. On the other hand, Joshua was Moses' disciple, who had conferred upon him some of Moses' prophetic honor. This tension between Joshua's own prophecy and his instructions to inquire of the UT is manifested in the Book of Joshua. In that book, Joshua never inquires of the UT; communicating instead with God exclusively through prophecy. The predominant explanation of this phenomenon is that Joshua did not need to inquire of the UT, precisely because he had attained prophetic revelation.[63] The only reference to inquiry of God in the Book of Joshua occurs when Joshua and the elders *failed* to use the UT before making peace with the deceitful Give'onites.[64] This narrative exposes the limitations of prophetic revelation and the possible advantage of the oracle.

Thus, Joshua represents a crossroads in the transition between Moses and later generations. He was a prophetic disciple of Moses, and therefore did not consult the UT as a general rule; however, he still was limited

---

63   See, for example, *Numbers Rabbah* 12:9; Abarbanel, Malbim on Judges
1:1; Netziv on Numbers 27:21.

64   Joshua 9:14-15

at those times when he did not receive prophecy. The Torah presents an inherent tension in his role as Moses' successor, captured in the moment of his appointment.

After Joshua's death, the nation immediately turns to the UT:

Judges 1

1 And it came to pass after the death of Joshua, that the children of Israel asked the LORD, saying: 'Who shall go up for us first against the Canaanites, to fight against them?'	א וַיְהִי אַחֲרֵי מוֹת יְהוֹשֻׁעַ וַיִּשְׁאֲלוּ בְּנֵי יִשְׂרָאֵל בַּיי לֵאמֹר: מִי יַעֲלֶה-לָּנוּ אֶל-הַכְּנַעֲנִי בַּתְּחִלָּה לְהִלָּחֶם בּוֹ.
2 And LORD said: 'Judah shall go up; behold, I have delivered the land into his hand.'	ב וַיֹּאמֶר יי יְהוּדָה יַעֲלֶה: הִנֵּה נָתַתִּי אֶת-הָאָרֶץ בְּיָדוֹ.

The first act after Joshua's death signals the beginning of the next period: the UT would now serve as the primary means of receiving divine communiqués. Judges and prophets were available for guidance as well, but the UT was a significant channel for divine decisions. This period became the golden age of oracular revelation in Israel, to the point where priests appear to have made replicas of the *ephod* so they also could ascertain God's will via oracular inquiry.

Once David began preparations for building a Temple, the next transition was effected: he no longer consulted the UT, but instead turned to prophets and advisors. No longer would Israel have the UT's word-for-word accuracy in their revelation. Fittingly, David's first consultation with a prophet in this capacity was subject to erroneous human judgment. This trend continued until the cessation of prophecy at the beginning of the Second Temple period.

This is where R. Zadok's analysis begins. According to this progression, the spiritual leadership of the nation went from absolute divine revelation (Moses), to a word-for-word revelation requiring priestly inspiration (UT), to prophecy (which had a human dimension), to the Oral Law.

With every decrease in overt revelation, there was an increase in human participation in the acquisition of God's word, culminating in Torah study as the highest means of reaching that Truth. As Ben Sira would observe in an age lacking prophecy, "A man of understanding will trust in the law; for him the law is as dependable as an inquiry by means of Urim."[65]

---

65   Ben Sira 33:3

By definition, each stage is a step forward and backward. While the decline of overt revelation distances us from God's Will, it simultaneously enables full and active human participation in the mutual covenant between God and humanity.

This religious struggle is captured poignantly by the classic talmudic passage:[66]

> And they stood under the mount: R. Abdimi b. Hama b. Hasa said: This teaches that the Holy One, blessed be He, overturned the mountain upon them like an [inverted] cask, and said to them, 'If you accept the Torah, it is well; if not, there shall be your burial.' R. Aha b. Jacob observed: This furnishes a strong protest against the Torah. Said Raba, Yet even so, they re-accepted it in the days of Ahasuerus, for it is written, [the Jews] confirmed, and took upon them [etc.]: [i.e.,] they confirmed what they had accepted long before.

Rather than attempting to explain R. Aha's question away, Raba understood that revelation in fact did cripple an aspect of free will. Therefore, he proposed Purim as the antidote, since that represents the age when revelation ceased.

These are necessary conflicts in true religious experience. The study of the use and the discontinuation of the UT represent a vital stage in this development from childlike dependency to the more mature model of wisdom, learning, and growth.[67]

---

66   *Shabbat* 88a

67   For recent scholarly literature on UT, see Victor Avigdor Hurowitz, "True Light on the Urim and Thummim" (review essay on Van Dam's book), *JQR* 88 (1998), pp. 263-274. A.M. Kitz, "The Plural Form of Urim and Thummim," *JBL* 116 (1997), pp. 401-410. Wayne Horowitz & Victor Avigdor Hurowitz, "Urim and Thummim in Light of a Psephomancy Ritual from Assur (LKA 137)," *JANES* 21 (1992), pp. 95-115. C. Houtman, "The Urim and Thummim: A New Suggestion," *VT* 40 (1990), pp. 229-232. Herbert B. Huffmon, "Priestly Divination in Israel," in *The Word of the Lord Shall Go Forth: Essays in Honor of David Noel Freedman in Celebration of his Sixtieth Birthday*, ed. Carol L. Myers & M. O'Connor (Winona Lake IN: Eisenbrauns, 1983), pp. 355-359. Edward Robertson, "The Urim and Thummim: What Were They?" *VT* 14 (1964), pp. 67-74.

YCT Tanakh Companion

Why David did not kill Saul: Insights from Psalms

Rabbi Hayyim Angel

The relationship between Saul and David is among the most conflicted and the most dramatic in all of Tanakh.

As a youth, David serves as Saul's arms-bearer and musician. Saul, however, afflicted with "an evil spirit," hurls spears at David, attempts to set his children Jonathan and Michal against him, and personally leads the royal army in pursuit of David.

David's restraint with Saul

Despite Saul's violent behavior, David maintains his love and compassion for Saul. The first time David has the chance to kill Saul, David's men view the opportunity as a divine blessing. David, however, emphatically rejects his men's request:

I Samuel 24

4 David's men said to him, 'This is the day of which the LORD said to you: I will deliver your enemy into your hands; you can do with him as you please.'

5 But afterward David reproached himself for having cut off the corner of Saul's cloak.

ד וַיֹּאמְרוּ אַנְשֵׁי דָוִד אֵלָיו הִנֵּה הַיּוֹם
אֲשֶׁר-אָמַר יְיָ אֵלֶיךָ הִנֵּה אָנֹכִי
נֹתֵן אֶת-איביך (אֹיִבְךָ) בְּיָדֶךָ
וְעָשִׂיתָ לּוֹ כַּאֲשֶׁר יִטַב בְּעֵינֶיךָ:
וַיָּקָם דָּוִד וַיִּכְרֹת אֶת-כְּנַף-
הַמְּעִיל אֲשֶׁר-לְשָׁאוּל בַּלָּט.

ה וַיְהִי אַחֲרֵי-כֵן וַיַּךְ לֵב-דָּוִד אֹתוֹ: עַל
אֲשֶׁר כָּרַת אֶת-כָּנָף אֲשֶׁר לְשָׁאוּל.

6 He said to his men 'The LORD forbid that I should do such a thing to my lord-the LORD's anointed-that I should raise my hand against him; for he is the LORD's anointed.'

וַיֹּאמֶר לַאֲנָשָׁיו חָלִילָה לִּי מֵיְיָ אִם-אֶעֱשֶׂה אֶת-הַדָּבָר הַזֶּה לַאדֹנִי לִמְשִׁיחַ יְיָ לִשְׁלֹחַ יָדִי בּוֹ: כִּי-מְשִׁיחַ יְיָ הוּא.

7 David rebuked his men and did not permit them to attack Saul. And Saul rose up out of the cave, and went on his way.

וַיְשַׁסַּע דָּוִד אֶת-אֲנָשָׁיו בַּדְּבָרִים וְלֹא נְתָנָם לָקוּם אֶל-שָׁאוּל: וְשָׁאוּל קָם מֵהַמְּעָרָה וַיֵּלֶךְ בַּדָּרֶךְ.

8 David also arose afterward, and went out of the cave, and cried after Saul, saying: 'My lord the king.' And when Saul looked behind him, David bowed with his face to the earth, and prostrated himself.

וַיָּקָם דָּוִד אַחֲרֵי-כֵן וַיֵּצֵא מִן המערה (מֵהַמְּעָרָה) וַיִּקְרָא אַחֲרֵי-שָׁאוּל לֵאמֹר אֲדֹנִי הַמֶּלֶךְ: וַיַּבֵּט שָׁאוּל אַחֲרָיו וַיִּקֹּד דָּוִד אַפַּיִם אַרְצָה וַיִּשְׁתָּחוּ.

David settles for cutting off the corner of Saul's coat, and later regrets even having perpetrated this act against God's anointed.

Two chapters later, David again is presented with an opportunity to eliminate Saul. One of David's supporters wants to deliver the fatal blow to Saul; but again David strongly opposes such an action:

I Samuel 26

8 And Avishai said to David, 'God has delivered your enemy into your hands today. Let me pin him to the ground with a single thrust of the spear. I will not have to strike him twice.'

וַיֹּאמֶר אֲבִישַׁי אֶל-דָּוִד סִגַּר אֱלֹהִים הַיּוֹם אֶת-אוֹיִבְךָ בְּיָדֶךָ: וְעַתָּה אַכֶּנּוּ נָא בַּחֲנִית וּבָאָרֶץ פַּעַם אַחַת וְלֹא אֶשְׁנֶה לוֹ.

9 But David said to Avishai, 'Don't do him violence! No one can lay hands on the LORD's anointed with impunity.'

וַיֹּאמֶר דָּוִד אֶל-אֲבִישַׁי אַל-תַּשְׁחִיתֵהוּ: כִּי מִי שָׁלַח יָדוֹ בִּמְשִׁיחַ יְיָ וְנִקָּה.

David expresses his allegiance to Saul most poignantly after Saul perishes in battle.

The eulogy reveals David's love for Saul.

II Samuel 1
19 Your glory, O Israel, lies
slain on your heights; How
the mighty have fallen!

יט הַצְּבִי יִשְׂרָאֵל עַל-בָּמוֹתֶיךָ
חָלָל: אֵיךְ נָפְלוּ גִבּוֹרִים.

David directly avenges Saul's death, promptly ordering the execution of the youth who claims to have killed Saul.[1] Similarly, David acts swiftly against the assassins of Saul's son, Ish-boshet.[2]

It is difficult to imagine that David could have harbored no resentment towards Saul. Accordingly, some rabbinic authorities[3] suggest David also has a utilitarian motive for sparing the king: David knows that he is to succeed Saul as King of Israel. David reasons that if he assassinates the first king, perhaps someone else might decide to assassinate the *second* king: David himself. They[4] assert that this is the reason that David orders the execution of Saul's murderer—David wants to make it clear that regicide is an unforgivable crime.[5] While affirming that David is largely motivated by piety, Ralbag and Abarbanel maintain that this more practical impetus also factors into his exceptional restraint.

While there are questions as to whether David was motivated purely by respect for God's (first) anointed king, or whether he also had utilitarian motivations, there is another source we can turn to for insight into King David: the Psalms.

Psalms with historical superscriptions

It is unusual for Tanakh to supply the feelings or motivations for biblical characters. Instead, the Bible generally focuses on actions, leaving the reader to speculate about the deeper aspects of a character's soul. David, however, is an exception. We have a primary record of what David feels while being pursued by Saul, and how he reacts when the king is killed in battle. The Book of Psalms provides another perspective of the relationship between David and Saul. In this essay, we will consider the psalms that David composed while fleeing Saul, and see how these psalms refine our understanding of the Saul/David relationship.

---

1 II Samuel 1:13-16
2 II Samuel 4:9-12
3 R. Yeshayah D'Trani, Ralbag, and Abarbanel on I Samuel 24:5.
4 Ralbag and Abarbanel on II Samuel 1:14.
5 See also II Samuel 4:9-12, where David had Ish-boshet's assassins executed as well. See Abarbanel *ad loc.*

There are at least seven psalms whose superscription indicates a specific event during Saul's pursuit of David.[6]

Psalm 18[7]

1 For the leader. Of David, the servant of the LORD, who addressed the words of this song to the LORD after the LORD had saved him from the hands of all his enemies, and from the clutches of Saul.

א לַמְנַצֵּחַ לְעֶבֶד יְיָ–לְדָוִד:
אֲשֶׁר דִּבֶּר לַיָי אֶת-דִּבְרֵי הַשִּׁירָה
הַזֹּאת:
בְּיוֹם הִצִּיל-יְיָ אוֹתוֹ מִכַּף
כָּל-אֹיְבָיו וּמִיַּד שָׁאוּל.

Psalm 52[8]

1 For the leader. A *maskil* of David,
2 when Doeg the Edomite came and informed Saul, telling him, 'David came to Achimelekh's house.'

א לַמְנַצֵּחַ מַשְׂכִּיל לְדָוִד.
ב בְּבוֹא דּוֹאֵג הָאֲדֹמִי וַיַּגֵּד לְשָׁאוּל:
וַיֹּאמֶר לוֹ: בָּא דָוִד
אֶל-בֵּית אֲחִימֶלֶךְ

Psalm 54[9]

1 For the leader; with instrumental music. A *maskil* of David,
2 when the Ziphites came and told Saul, 'Know, David is hiding among us.'

א לַמְנַצֵּחַ בִּנְגִינֹת מַשְׂכִּיל לְדָוִד.
ב בְּבֹא הַזִּיפִים וַיֹּאמְרוּ לְשָׁאוּל:
הֲלֹא דָוִד מִסְתַּתֵּר עִמָּנוּ.

---

6   It is difficult to ascertain the exact chronological order of the composition of these psalms, especially since some of the events referred to occur more than once. For example, David hid in caves (Psalms 57, 142) both in I Samuel 22:1 and 24:3; he hid in the Wilderness of Judah (Psalm 63) in I Samuel 23:14; 23:24; 24:1; and 25:1. The Ziphites informed Saul of David's whereabouts (Psalm 54) in I Samuel 23:19 and 26:1. On several occasions, commentators attempt to pinpoint the specific events mentioned, but these efforts generally are uncompelling.

7   See I Samuel 31:6.
8   See I Samuel 22:9-10.
9   See I Samuel 23:14; 26:1.

Psalm 57[10]

1 For the leader; *al tashchet*. Of David. A *michtam*; when he fled from Saul into a cave.

א לַמְנַצֵּחַ אַל-תַּשְׁחֵת לְדָוִד מִכְתָּם: בְּבָרְחוֹ מִפְּנֵי-שָׁאוּל בַּמְּעָרָה.

Psalm 59[11]

1 For the leader; *al tashchet*. Of David. A *michtam*; when Saul sent men to watch his house in order to put him to death.

א לַמְנַצֵּחַ אַל-תַּשְׁחֵת לְדָוִד מִכְתָּם בִּשְׁלֹחַ שָׁאוּל: וַיִּשְׁמְרוּ אֶת-הַבַּיִת לַהֲמִיתוֹ.

Psalm 63[12]

1 A psalm of David, when he was in the Wilderness of Judah.

א מִזְמוֹר לְדָוִד: בִּהְיוֹתוֹ בְּמִדְבַּר יְהוּדָה.

Psalm 142[13, 14]

1 A *maskil* of David, while he was in the cave. A prayer.

א מַשְׂכִּיל לְדָוִד: בִּהְיוֹתוֹ בַמְּעָרָה תְפִלָּה.

Although one might assume that the prayers expressed in these seven psalms reflect David's feelings towards Saul and his men (with the exception of Psalm 52 which discusses Doeg, and 54 which criticizes the Ziphites), the matter is not so simple. There are two methodological questions we must address:

First, are these psalms personal prayers which later became canonized for others to use, or does David consider his prayers as a formula for prayer as he writes them?

Secondly, what is the relationship of the main body of a psalm to its superscription? Do we assume that the entire psalm reflects the event

---

10   See I Samuel 22:1; 24:3.

11   See I Samuel 19:11-17.

12   See I Samuel 23:14; 23:24; 24:1; 25:1.

13   See I Samuel 22:1; 24:3.

14   One might also include Psalms 34 and 60, which David composed in Philistia, while in flight from Saul.

specified in the superscription, or may a psalm move beyond the original event which inspired its composition?

Purpose of the Psalms

The Talmud leaves our first question unresolved:

> Our rabbis have taught: all the songs and hymns which David said in the Book of Psalms, R. Eliezer says, he wrote them for himself. R. Yehoshua says, he wrote them for the community. The Sages say, some are for the community, and others are for himself: those in the singular voice are for himself, while those in the plural voice are for the community (*Pesahim* 117a).

The five psalms we will consider (18, 57, 59, 63 and 142) are all written in the first person singular. According to both R. Eliezer and the Sages, these psalms are private prayers, in which David pleads to God to be saved from Saul and his men. However, according to R. Yehoshua, even these five psalms are communal prayers, addressing crises beyond David's personal life.

The contrast between the two positions is striking: if these psalms are private prayers, then one may assume that references to "enemies" allude specifically to Saul and his men. If, however, the psalms are prayers for the entire community, then David may be including more generic elements, including details not directly relevant to Saul's pursuit of David.

Relationship of superscriptions to the psalm body

Closely related to the issue of the original intent of a psalm is whether the entire body of a psalm corresponds to the introductory verse, or superscription. For example, the superscription to Psalm 59, "When Saul sent men to watch his house in order to put him to death," alludes to the narrative where Michal helps her husband David escape Saul's men.[15]

The beginning of this psalm reads:

Psalm 59

2 Save me from my enemies,
   O my God; secure me
   against my assailants.

ב הַצִּילֵנִי מֵאֹיְבַי אֱלֹהָי
מִמִּתְקוֹמְמַי תְּשַׂגְּבֵנִי.

---

15   I Samuel 19:11-17

3 Save me from evildoers,
deliver me from murderers.

ג הַצִּילֵנִי מִפֹּעֲלֵי אָוֶן וּמֵאַנְשֵׁי דָמִים הוֹשִׁיעֵנִי.

4 For see, they lie in wait for
me; fierce men plot against me
for no offense of mine, for no
transgression, O LORD;

ד כִּי הִנֵּה אָרְבוּ לְנַפְשִׁי יָגוּרוּ עָלַי עַזִּים: לֹא-פִשְׁעִי וְלֹא-חַטָּאתִי יי.

5 for no guilt of mine do they
rush to array themselves
against me. Look,

ה בְּלִי-עָוֺן יְרֻצוּן וְיִכּוֹנָנוּ: עוּרָה לִקְרָאתִי וּרְאֵה.

6 rouse Yourself on my behalf! You,
O LORD God of hosts, God of
Israel, bestir Yourself to bring all
nations to account; have no mercy
on any treacherous villain. Selah!

ו וְאַתָּה יי-אֱלֹהִים צְבָאוֹת אֱלֹהֵי יִשְׂרָאֵל הָקִיצָה לִפְקֹד כָּל-הַגּוֹיִם: אַל-תָּחֹן כָּל-בֹּגְדֵי אָוֶן סֶלָה.

In general, with the exception of the superscription, the psalms do not make reference to specific events in David's life.[16] It is possible that these psalms were initially composed with these formulations; it also is possible that they may have been subsequently reworked, deliberately omitting David's specific references so that the prayers may be applied universally. In either case, the assumption of a direct relationship between a psalm's superscription and its main body leads one to believe that references to "enemies" here would refer specifically to Saul and his men. If, on the other hand, the subject of the main body of the psalm spins beyond the superscription, then we may not necessarily associate every reference to David's feelings towards Saul and his men. Instead, this psalm would be seen as a general prayer asking God to save oppressed people from their enemies.

This issue comes to the fore in verse six, where David is apparently referring to other nations. This is also true for a later verse:

Psalm 59

9 But You, O LORD, shall
laugh at them; You shall have
all the nations in derision.

ט וְאַתָּה יי תִּשְׂחַק-לָמוֹ: תִּלְעַג לְכָל-גּוֹיִם.

These references seem to support those who contend that the body of a psalm may refer to a wider scope of events than those mentioned in the

16   See Amos Hakham (*Da'at Mikra, Psalms* [Hebrew] [Jerusalem: Mossad HaRav Kook, 1979], vol. l), pp. 15-18, for a fuller discussion of this topic.

superscription.

Yet, several exegetes maintain that even these ostensibly explicit references to other nations still refer to Saul and his men: Rashi on verse 6 of this psalm, states: "Bestir Yourself to bring all nations to account"—may You judge the wicked people *as You would the nations.* On them You should have no mercy.

Ibn Ezra on verse 6 of this psalm, states: "Do not have mercy on traitors"—from whichever nation they derive (i.e., even if they *are* from Israel). Radak on verse 9 of this psalm, states: As You mock all the nations who deny You—annulling their [evil] thoughts and plots, so too may You mock these [i.e., Saul and his men].[17] It would appear that in this case, Rashi, Ibn Ezra, and Radak espouse the view that David originally composed this psalm as a personal prayer for salvation from Saul and his men; and *all* references to enemies in this psalm allude to Saul and his men (even where the plain sense of the text may seem to indicate otherwise).

Evidently, the methodological issues involved in an analysis of Psalms, even those with specific historical superscriptions, are difficult to resolve. As we consider the five psalms that David addresses towards Saul and his men, we will begin with the assumption that David has composed these psalms as private prayers, and that the main bodies of the psalms generally follow their superscriptions. Even were one to follow the opinion of R. Yehoshua, that all psalms were composed originally for the community, one still may argue that David drew his inspiration from the personal events that were occurring as he composed those psalms.

The Psalms

Psalm 142

1 A *maskil* of David, while he was in the cave. A prayer.

א מַשְׂכִּיל לְדָוִד:
בִּהְיוֹתוֹ בַמְּעָרָה תְפִלָּה.

2 With my voice I cry to the LORD; with my voice I make supplication to the LORD.

ב קוֹלִי אֶל-יי אֶזְעָק: קוֹלִי
אֶל-יי אֶתְחַנָּן.

3 I pour out my complaint before Him, I declare before Him my trouble;

ג אֶשְׁפֹּךְ לְפָנָיו שִׂיחִי:
צָרָתִי לְפָנָיו אַגִּיד.

---

17   On verse 6, Radak suggests that David is praying for the Day of Judgment in Messianic times. He avers that the entire verse does not fit into the general framework of the psalm.

4 When my spirit faints within
me–You know my path–in
the way wherein I walk have
they hidden a snare for me.

ד בְּהִתְעַטֵּף עָלַי רוּחִי וְאַתָּה
יָדַעְתָּ נְתִיבָתִי בְּאֹרַח-זוּ
אֲהַלֵּךְ: טָמְנוּ פַח לִי.

5 Look at my right and see–I have
no friend, there is nowhere I can
flee, no one cares about me.

ה הַבֵּיט יָמִין וּרְאֵה וְאֵין-לִי מַכִּיר:
אָבַד מָנוֹס מִמֶּנִּי: אֵין
דּוֹרֵשׁ לְנַפְשִׁי.

6 I have cried unto You, O
LORD; I have said: 'You
are my refuge, my portion
in the land of the living.'

ו זָעַקְתִּי אֵלֶיךָ יְיָ
אָמַרְתִּי אַתָּה מַחְסִי:
חֶלְקִי בְּאֶרֶץ הַחַיִּים.

7 Listen to my cry, for I have
been brought very low; save
me from my pursuers, for
they are too strong for me.

ז הַקְשִׁיבָה אֶל-רִנָּתִי כִּי-דַלּוֹתִי-מְאֹד:
הַצִּילֵנִי מֵרֹדְפַי: כִּי אָמְצוּ מִמֶּנִּי.

8 Free me from my prison, that
I may praise Your Name. The
righteous shall glory in me for
Your gracious dealings with me.

ח הוֹצִיאָה מִמַּסְגֵּר נַפְשִׁי
לְהוֹדוֹת אֶת-שְׁמֶךָ בִּי יַכְתִּרוּ
צַדִּיקִים: כִּי תִגְמֹל עָלָי.

Psalm 142 reveals a pious image of David. While hiding in a cave from Saul and his men,[18] David feels isolated and frightened. Despite the great threat to his life, he does not ask that God obliterate his enemies, nor does he ridicule them; instead, he asks only that God deliver him from danger.

Reading this, we hear the terrible anguish that plagues David as he flees from his father-in-law, King Saul. Yet, we also hear David's resolve, and sense of purpose, as he asks to be spared so that God's Name will be sanctified among righteous people.

Psalm 142 stands alone in conveying this theme of pure graciousness. In Psalm 57, David laments in a different, more hostile, tone:

Psalm 57

1 For the leader; *al tashchet*. Of
David. A *michtam*; when he
fled from Saul into a cave.

א לַמְנַצֵּחַ אַל-תַּשְׁחֵת לְדָוִד מִכְתָּם:
בְּבָרְחוֹ מִפְּנֵי-שָׁאוּל בַּמְּעָרָה.

18   Either in I Samuel 22:1 or 24:3.

2 Have mercy on me, O God,
have mercy on me, for I
seek refuge in You.

ב חָנֵּנִי אֱלֹהִים חָנֵּנִי כִּי בְךָ
חָסָיָה נַפְשִׁי וּבְצֵל־כְּנָפֶיךָ
אֶחְסֶה: עַד יַעֲבֹר הַוּוֹת.

3 I will cry to God most exalted; to
God that accomplishes for me.

ג אֶקְרָא לֵאלֹהִים עֶלְיוֹן:
לָאֵל גֹּמֵר עָלָי.

4 He will reach down from
heaven and deliver me: God
will send down His steadfast
love; my persecutor reviles.

ד יִשְׁלַח מִשָּׁמַיִם וְיוֹשִׁיעֵנִי חֵרֵף שֹׁאֲפִי
סֶלָה: יִשְׁלַח אֱלֹהִים חַסְדּוֹ וַאֲמִתּוֹ.

5 As for me, I lie down among
man-eating lions whose teeth
are spears and arrows, whose
tongue is a sharp sword.

ה נַפְשִׁי בְּתוֹךְ לְבָאִם אֶשְׁכְּבָה לֹהֲטִים
בְּנֵי־אָדָם שִׁנֵּיהֶם חֲנִית וְחִצִּים:
וּלְשׁוֹנָם חֶרֶב חַדָּה.

6 Be exalted, O God, above
the heavens; Your glory
is above all the earth.

ו רוּמָה עַל־הַשָּׁמַיִם אֱלֹהִים:
עַל כָּל־הָאָרֶץ כְּבוֹדֶךָ.

7 They prepared a net for my feet
to ensnare me; they dug a pit
for me, but they fell into it.

ז רֶשֶׁת הֵכִינוּ לִפְעָמַי כָּפַף נַפְשִׁי:
כָּרוּ לְפָנַי שִׁיחָה: נָפְלוּ בְתוֹכָהּ סֶלָה.

8 My heart is firm, O God;
my heart is firm; I will sing,
I will chant a hymn.

ח נָכוֹן לִבִּי אֱלֹהִים נָכוֹן לִבִּי:
אָשִׁירָה וַאֲזַמֵּרָה.

9 Awake, my glory; awake, psaltery
and harp; I will awake the dawn.

ט עוּרָה כְבוֹדִי עוּרָה הַנֵּבֶל
וְכִנּוֹר אָעִירָה שָּׁחַר.

10 I will give thanks to You, O
LORD, among the peoples;
I will sing praises to You
among the nations.

י אוֹדְךָ בָעַמִּים יי: אֲזַמֶּרְךָ בַּלְאֻמִּים.

11 For Your mercy is extends
to the heavens, and Your
truth to the skies.

יא כִּי־גָדֹל עַד־שָׁמַיִם חַסְדֶּךָ
וְעַד־שְׁחָקִים אֲמִתֶּךָ.

12 Be exalted, O God, above
the heavens; Your glory
is above all the earth.

יב רוּמָה עַל־שָׁמַיִם אֱלֹהִים
עַל כָּל־הָאָרֶץ כְּבוֹדֶךָ.

Here, David continues the themes from Psalm 142, praying for salvation, and remaining steadfastly focused on God and His reputation. But
now, David describes his pursuers in negative terms with verses 4 and 5,
particularly depicting their brutality and viciousness. Additionally, David

is gratified in verse 7 that his antagonists fall into the snare which they have set for him.

David appears even more resentful in Psalm 59, when Saul sends men to surround David's house:[19]

Psalm 59

7 They come each evening growling
like dogs, roaming the city.

ז יָשׁוּבוּ לָעֶרֶב יֶהֱמוּ כַכָּלֶב
וִיסוֹבְבוּ עִיר.

8 Behold, they rave with their
mouths; swords are in their
lips: 'For who hears?'

ח הִנֵּה יַבִּיעוּן בְּפִיהֶם–חֲרָבוֹת
בְּשִׂפְתוֹתֵיהֶם: כִּי-מִי שֹׁמֵעַ.

9 But You, O LORD, laugh
at them You shall hold all
the nations in derision.

ט וְאַתָּה יי תִּשְׂחַק-לָמוֹ:
תִּלְעַג לְכָל-גּוֹיִם.

10 Because of his strength,
I will wait for You; for
God is my high tower.

י עֻזּוֹ אֵלֶיךָ אֶשְׁמֹרָה:
כִּי-אֱלֹהִים מִשְׂגַּבִּי.

11 The God of my mercy will come
to meet me; God will let me
gaze upon mine adversaries.

יא אֱלֹהֵי חסדו (חַסְדִּי) יְקַדְּמֵנִי:
אֱלֹהִים יַרְאֵנִי בְשֹׁרְרָי.

12 Do not kill them lest my
people be unmindful; with
Your power make wanderers
of them; bring them low, O
our Shield, the LORD.

יב אַל-תַּהַרְגֵם פֶּן יִשְׁכְּחוּ עַמִּי–
הֲנִיעֵמוֹ בְחֵילְךָ וְהוֹרִידֵמוֹ: מָגִנֵּנוּ יי.

13 Let them be trapped by their
pride, and by the imprecations
and lies they utter.

יג חַטַּאת-פִּימוֹ דְּבַר-שְׂפָתֵימוֹ
וְיִלָּכְדוּ בִגְאוֹנָם: וּמֵאָלָה
וּמִכַּחַשׁ יְסַפֵּרוּ.

14 Your fury put an end to them;
put an end to them that they be
no more; that it may be known
to the ends of the earth that God
does rule over Jacob. Selah.

יד כַּלֵּה בְחֵמָה כַּלֵּה וְאֵינֵמוֹ
וְיֵדְעוּ כִּי-אֱלֹהִים מֹשֵׁל בְּיַעֲקֹב:
לְאַפְסֵי הָאָרֶץ סֶלָה.

15 And they return at evening,
they howl like a dog, and
go round about the city;

טו וְיָשֻׁבוּ לָעֶרֶב יֶהֱמוּ
כַכָּלֶב וִיסוֹבְבוּ עִיר.

16 They wander up and down
to devour, and tarry all night
if they have not their fill.

טז הֵמָּה ינועון (יְנִיעוּן) לֶאֱכֹל:
אִם-לֹא יִשְׂבְּעוּ וַיָּלִינוּ.

---

19   See I Samuel 19.

17 But as for me, I will sing of
Your strength; yea, I will sing
aloud of Your mercy in the
morning; for You have been
my high tower, and a refuge
in the day of my distress.

יז וַאֲנִי אָשִׁיר עֻזֶּךָ וַאֲרַנֵּן לַבֹּקֶר
חַסְדֶּךָ כִּי-הָיִיתָ מִשְׂגָּב לִי:
וּמָנוֹס בְּיוֹם צַר-לִי.

18 O my strength, to You will I
sing praises; for God is my high
tower, the God of my mercy.

יח עֻזִּי אֵלֶיךָ אֲזַמֵּרָה: כִּי-אֱלֹהִים
מִשְׂגַּבִּי אֱלֹהֵי חַסְדִּי.

This psalm contains the elements we have seen in the others: prayer for salvation from enemies, verses 2-3, and 10-11, and a request for the sanctification of God's name in verse 4. However, David displays even more hostility, calling Saul and his men dogs, in biblical parlance the lowliest of all animals.[20] Even more astonishingly, David calls on God to destroy his enemies slowly, so that everyone can witness that God is against them. One begins to sense that David indeed harbors much resentment towards Saul.

Psalm 63, written when David was in the Wilderness of Judah, minces no words in asking for the death of Saul and his men:

Psalm 63

10 May those who seek to
destroy my life enter the
depths of the earth.

י וְהֵמָּה לְשׁוֹאָה יְבַקְשׁוּ נַפְשִׁי:
יָבֹאוּ בְּתַחְתִּיּוֹת הָאָרֶץ.

11 May he be gutted by the sword;
may they be prey for jackals.

יא יַגִּירֻהוּ עַל-יְדֵי-חָרֶב:
מְנָת שֻׁעָלִים יִהְיוּ.

12 But the king [i.e., David[21]] shall
rejoice in God; all who swear
by Him shall exult, when the
mouth of liars is stopped.

יב וְהַמֶּלֶךְ יִשְׂמַח בֵּאלֹהִים:
יִתְהַלֵּל כָּל-הַנִּשְׁבָּע בּוֹ: כִּי
יִסָּכֵר פִּי דוֹבְרֵי-שָׁקֶר.

Radak (on verse 11) explains that David asks for Saul (his singular foe) to be killed by the sword, and then for Saul's men to be prey for jackals.

Psalm 18 (found in variant form in II Samuel 22) is a song of triumph,

---

20   See, e.g., I Samuel 17:43; 24:14; II Samuel 3:8; 9:8; 16:9; Ecclesiastes 9:4.

21   Rashi and Radak on 63:12 explain that this refers to David himself, who already was anointed (and therefore viewed himself as a king already). Cf. *Megillah* 14a-b.

apparently reflecting David's excitement at Saul's death:[22]

Psalm 18

1 For the leader. Of David, the servant of the LORD, who addressed the words of this song to the LORD: in the day that the LORD had saved him from the hands of all his enemies, and from the clutches of Saul.

א לַמְנַצֵּחַ לְעֶבֶד יְיָ לְדָוִד אֲשֶׁר דִּבֶּר
לַיי אֶת-דִּבְרֵי הַשִּׁירָה הַזֹּאת:
בְּיוֹם הִצִּיל-יְיָ אוֹתוֹ מִכַּף
כָּל-אֹיְבָיו וּמִיַּד שָׁאוּל.

This psalm is a fitting epilogue to the other Saul-related psalms of David.[23]

If we take these psalms as expressing David's personal feelings, then we see that throughout the period that David was chased by Saul and his men, David expresses deep bitterness towards his enemies and wishes them dead. He maintains allegiance to God and prays for his own personal salvation as well as the sanctification of God's name. Finally, he rejoices at Saul's demise.

New light on the Samuel text

After reading and analyzing these psalms, we may reconsider some of the passages in the Book of Samuel pertaining to the relationship between David and Saul. When Saul's son, Ish-boshet, is murdered,[24] David has the assassins put to death.[25] Consistent with his position discussed earlier, Abarbanel maintains that David wishes to protect the institution of monarchy.

More significant, however, is David's avowed reason for killing Ish-boshet's assassins:

---

22   Rashi (on Psalm 18:1) writes that David composed this psalm towards the end of his life. He singled out Saul because the king pursued David more than any other individual enemy. Ibn Ezra asserts that David wrote this psalm after his men told him to remain home during battles, lest he be killed (see II Samuel 22:17). With this view, Ibn Ezra can explain the position of the psalm as it appears in II Samuel 22, immediately following the request of David's men in the text.

23   It is noteworthy that in *Mo'ed Katan* 16b, God castigates David for singing a hymn of glory at the downfall of the righteous Saul.

24   II Samuel 4

25   As with the Amalekite youth in II Samuel 1.

II Samuel 4

10 The man who told me in Ziklag that Saul was dead thought he was bringing good news. But instead of rewarding him for the news, I seized him and killed him.

11 How much more, then, when wicked people have killed a blameless man in bed in his own house! I will certainly avenge his blood on you, and I will rid the earth of you.

י כִּי הַמַּגִּיד לִי לֵאמֹר הִנֵּה-מֵת
שָׁאוּל וְהוּא-הָיָה כִמְבַשֵּׂר בְּעֵינָיו
וָאֹחֲזָה בוֹ וָאֶהְרְגֵהוּ בְּצִקְלָג:
אֲשֶׁר לְתִתִּי-לוֹ בְּשֹׂרָה.

יא אַף כִּי-אֲנָשִׁים רְשָׁעִים הָרְגוּ
אֶת-אִישׁ-צַדִּיק בְּבֵיתוֹ עַל-מִשְׁכָּבוֹ:
וְעַתָּה הֲלוֹא אֲבַקֵּשׁ אֶת-דָּמוֹ
מִיֶּדְכֶם וּבִעַרְתִּי אֶתְכֶם מִן-הָאָרֶץ.

From this statement, we may infer that David believes that Saul was *not* righteous (he deserves his fate), whereas Ish-bosheth—a "blameless man"—is killed unjustly. Although David's reasoning may be understood in other ways, this explanation is consistent with the language of the psalms. Perhaps David still harbors anger towards Saul.

We find further evidence of David's continued resentment towards Saul when Michal (Saul's daughter and David's wife) becomes enraged at seeing David dancing immodestly around the Ark.[26] After Michal censures David for his undignified mode of dress and behavior, David snaps at her:

II Samuel 6

21 And David said to Michal: It was before the LORD who chose me instead of your father and all his family and appointed me ruler over the LORD's people Israel!

כא וַיֹּאמֶר דָּוִד אֶל-מִיכַל לִפְנֵי יְיָ
אֲשֶׁר בָּחַר-בִּי מֵאָבִיךְ וּמִכָּל-
בֵּיתוֹ לְצַוֹּת אֹתִי נָגִיד עַל-עַם יְיָ
עַל-יִשְׂרָאֵל: וְשִׂחַקְתִּי לִפְנֵי יְיָ.

Let us now return to David's stunning restraint from killing Saul:

---

26   *Midrash Shemuel* 25:6: "Said Michal, 'My father's kingdom was more becoming than yours, for far be it from any of [his family] to be viewed with even a forearm or calf exposed...' Answered David, '... [The members of] your father's household sought but their own honor, forsaking the honor of Heaven. And I do not do so....' "

Both text and midrash capture David's rancor which he apparently nurtures against Saul long after Saul's death.

I Samuel 26

10 And David said: 'As the LORD
lives, the LORD Himself will
strike him down, or his time will
come and he will die; or he will
go down to battle and perish.

11 But the LORD forbid that I
should lay a hand on the LORD's
anointed but now take, please,
the spear that is at his head, and
the cruse of water and let us go.'

י וַיֹּאמֶר דָּוִד חַי-יְיָ כִּי אִם-יְיָ
יִגְּפֶנּוּ: אוֹ-יוֹמוֹ יָבוֹא וָמֵת אוֹ
בַּמִּלְחָמָה יֵרֵד וְנִסְפָּה.

יא חָלִילָה לִּי מֵיְיָ מִשְּׁלֹחַ יָדִי
בִּמְשִׁיחַ יְיָ: וְעַתָּה קַח-נָא
אֶת-הַחֲנִית אֲשֶׁר מְרַאֲשֹׁתָו
וְאֶת-צַפַּחַת הַמַּיִם וְנֵלְכָה-לָּנוּ.

Although David stops Avishai from assassinating Saul, he simultaneously prays for the death of the monarch through natural causes! These
verses, read in light of Psalms, capture the powerful emotional conflict
David feels at those moments.

The text captures David's mixed feelings towards Saul when David has
an opportunity to hurt the vulnerable monarch:

I Samuel 24

11 Please, father, take a close look at
the corner of your cloak my hand;
for when I cut off the corner of
your cloak, I did not kill you. You
must see plainly that I have done
nothing evil or rebellious, and
I have never wronged you. Yet
you are bent on taking my life.

12 **May the LORD judge between
you and me! And may He take
vengeance upon you for me, but
my hand will never touch you...**

13 **As the proverb of the ancients
says: Out of the wicked cometh
forth wickedness; but my
hand shall not be upon you.**

14 Against whom has the king
of Israel come out? Whom
are you pursuing? A dead
dog? A single flea?

יא וְאָבִי רְאֵה גַּם רְאֵה אֶת-כְּנַף
מְעִילְךָ בְּיָדִי: כִּי בְּכָרְתִי אֶת-כְּנַף
מְעִילְךָ וְלֹא הֲרַגְתִּיךָ דַּע וּרְאֵה כִּי
אֵין בְּיָדִי רָעָה וָפֶשַׁע וְלֹא-חָטָאתִי
לָךְ-וְאַתָּה צֹדֶה אֶת-נַפְשִׁי לְקַחְתָּהּ.

יב יִשְׁפֹּט יְיָ בֵּינִי וּבֵינֶךָ וּנְקָמַנִי יְיָ
מִמֶּךָּ: וְיָדִי לֹא תִהְיֶה-בָּךְ.

יג כַּאֲשֶׁר יֹאמַר מְשַׁל הַקַּדְמֹנִי
מֵרְשָׁעִים יֵצֵא רֶשַׁע:
וְיָדִי לֹא תִהְיֶה-בָּךְ.

יד אַחֲרֵי מִי יָצָא מֶלֶךְ יִשְׂרָאֵל
אַחֲרֵי מִי אַתָּה רֹדֵף: אַחֲרֵי
כֶּלֶב מֵת אַחֲרֵי פַּרְעֹשׁ אֶחָד.

15 May the LORD be arbiter
and may He judge between
you and me! May He take note
and uphold my cause, and
vindicate me against you.

טו וְהָיָה יְיָ לְדַיָּן וְשָׁפַט בֵּינִי וּבֵינֶךָ
וְיֵרֶא וְיָרֵב אֶת-רִיבִי וְיִשְׁפְּטֵנִי מִיָּדֶךָ.

David, in his extended plea to Saul, oscillates between a position of love
and humility ("please, father," "against whom has the king of Israel come
out?"), and one of hostility and vengeance ("May the Lord judge...")!
From our above analysis, it seems that David is caught between his profound love for his father-in-law (and God's anointed), and his equally
potent hostility towards his ruthless pursuer.

Mixed Feelings

From the psalms David composes while being pursued by Saul, we
find that David's feelings towards Saul are far more complex than a casual
reading of the Book of Samuel would suggest. Additionally, we have seen
that David does not quickly forget Saul's conduct toward him: David's
outburst at Michal and the more subtle reference in the story of Ish-boshet indicate some lasting bitterness even beyond Saul's lifetime.

We may now return to our original inquiry—why does David spare
Saul? Once we have established that David does not have a purely forgiv-
ing attitude towards Saul, it appears that David is partially motivated by
utilitarian interests.

Be that as it may, David's love and loyalty to King Saul influence events
as well. David is tormented constantly by the king. Psalms and the Book
of Samuel render a portrait of David as a desperate fugitive who reacts
as one pursued—with animosity, exasperation, and feelings of destruc-
tiveness. However, perhaps due to David's remembered feelings for Saul,
David is capable of responding with even greater restraint than one might
expect from another man in similar circumstances.[27]

David confronts Saul possibly only hours after composing the most
militant of all his psalms. Yet, he is able to transcend his potent emotions
and control himself. It is difficult to imagine that the desire to protect
the monarchy fully explains David's ability to stifle his burning desire
to eliminate Saul. It is far more plausible that it is David's piety inter-

---

27   *Vayikra Rabbah* 23:11 and *Ruth Rabbah* 6:4 both compare David's restraint in his not killing Saul to that of Joseph's restraint in his avoiding an affair
with Potiphar's wife.

vening at those critical moments: David could not imagine killing God's anointed.[28]

In fact, some commentators explain the superscription, *al tashchet*[29] in reference to the dual nature of David's prayer. Looking purely at the literal meaning: "Do not destroy," some assert that David is praying for Saul not to destroy David, but others aver that David is praying that *he* not destroy Saul.[30] Rashi appears to combine these two approaches in his commentary on the double language used in the second verse:

Psalm 57

2 **Have mercy on me, O God, have mercy on me,** for in You has my soul taken refuge, yea, in the shadow of Your wings will I take refuge, until calamities be past.

ב חָנֵּנִי אֱלֹהִים חָנֵּנִי כִּי בְךָ חָסָיָה נַפְשִׁי
וּבְצֵל-כְּנָפֶיךָ אֶחְסֶה:
עַד יַעֲבֹר הַוּוֹת.

According to Rashi the repetition in the phrase, "Have mercy on me, have mercy"—signifies "have mercy on me that **I will not kill**; *and* have mercy on me that **I not be killed**."

This reflects the comment of the midrash that says, just as David prayed that he should not fall into the hands of Saul, so too he prayed that Saul should not fall into his hands.[31]

While these psalms demonstrate David's hostility towards Saul, this conclusion only serves to highlight David's restraint. David has passionate human drives, and instinctively wishes to lash out at his enemies. Our reading of the synthesized portrait of David from the Book of Samuel and the Book of Psalms shows a tormented, conflicted individual, one who simultaneously loves and resents his pursuer.

David's self-control, in the heat of such potent emotions, truly places him as one of the righteous people in our tradition.[32]

---

28 The explanation of R. Yeshayah D'Trani, Ralbag, and Abarbanel does seem apt, however, concerning David's executions of the Amalekite youth and Ish-bosheth's assassins.

29 Psalms 57:1; 58:1; 59:1

30 Malbim agrees with Alsheikh's interpretation of "*al tashchet*," deriving its meaning from David's command to Avishai (I Samuel 26:9), *al tashhitehu* ("Don't do him violence").

31 *Midrash Shoher Tov* 7:13

32 An earlier version of this article appeared in *From Strength to Strength: Lectures from Shearith Israel*, ed. Rabbi Marc D. Angel (Brooklyn, NY: Sefer Hermon Press, 1998), pp. 163-183. This modified version is reprinted with permission from the editor.

Avigayil: Savior of David
I Samuel 25

Rabbi Avraham Weiss

It is my contention that Avigayil was one of the most pivotal influences in David's life. In fact, were it not for Avigayil, David may very well never have become king.

Our study focuses on I Samuel 25. Let us first lay out the text of the chapter and its narrative thread, starting with the death of Samuel.

I Samuel 25

1 And Samuel died; and all Israel gathered themselves together, and lamented him, and buried him in his house at Ramah. And David arose, and went down to the wilderness of Paran.

א וַיָּמָת שְׁמוּאֵל וַיִּקָּבְצוּ כָל־יִשְׂרָאֵל וַיִּסְפְּדוּ־לוֹ וַיִּקְבְּרֻהוּ בְּבֵיתוֹ בָּרָמָה: וַיָּקָם דָּוִד וַיֵּרֶד אֶל־מִדְבַּר פָּארָן.

2 And there was a man in Ma'on, whose possessions were in Carmel; and the man was very great, and he had three thousand sheep, and a thousand goats; and he was shearing his sheep in Carmel.

ב וְאִישׁ בְּמָעוֹן וּמַעֲשֵׂהוּ בַכַּרְמֶל וְהָאִישׁ גָּדוֹל מְאֹד וְלוֹ צֹאן שְׁלֹשֶׁת־אֲלָפִים וְאֶלֶף עִזִּים וַיְהִי בִּגְזֹז אֶת־צֹאנוֹ בַּכַּרְמֶל.

3 Now the name of the man was Naval; and the name of his wife Avigayil; and the woman was of good understanding, and of a beautiful form; but the man was churlish and evil in his doings; and he was of the house of Caleb.

ג וְשֵׁם הָאִישׁ נָבָל וְשֵׁם אִשְׁתּוֹ אֲבִגָיִל: וְהָאִשָּׁה טוֹבַת־שֶׂכֶל וִיפַת תֹּאַר וְהָאִישׁ קָשֶׁה וְרַע מַעֲלָלִים וְהוּא כלבו (כָלִבִּי).

After the death of Samuel, we meet Naval and his wife, Avigayil. We learn some details: she is beautiful and wise; he is difficult and evil.

I Samuel 25

4 And David heard in the wilderness that Naval was shearing his sheep.

ד וַיִּשְׁמַע דָּוִד בַּמִּדְבָּר: כִּי־
גָזַז נָבָל אֶת־צֹאנוֹ.

5 And David sent ten young men, and David said to the young men: 'Get you up to Carmel, and go to Naval, and greet him in my name;

ה וַיִּשְׁלַח דָּוִד עֲשָׂרָה נְעָרִים
וַיֹּאמֶר דָּוִד לַנְּעָרִים: עֲלוּ
כַרְמֶלָה וּבָאתֶם אֶל־נָבָל
וּשְׁאֶלְתֶּם־לוֹ בִשְׁמִי לְשָׁלוֹם.

6 and so shall you say: All hail! and peace be to you, and peace be to your house, and peace be to all that is yours.

ו וַאֲמַרְתֶּם כֹּה לֶחָי: וְאַתָּה שָׁלוֹם
וּבֵיתְךָ שָׁלוֹם וְכֹל אֲשֶׁר־לְךָ שָׁלוֹם.

7 And now I have heard that you have shearers; your shepherds have now been with us, and we did them no hurt, neither was there anything missing unto them, all the while they were in Carmel.

ז וְעַתָּה שָׁמַעְתִּי כִּי גֹזְזִים לָךְ: עַתָּה
הָרֹעִים אֲשֶׁר־לְךָ הָיוּ עִמָּנוּ
לֹא הֶכְלַמְנוּם וְלֹא־נִפְקַד לָהֶם
מְאוּמָה כָּל־יְמֵי הֱיוֹתָם בַּכַּרְמֶל.

8 Ask your young men, and they will tell you; and let the young men find favor in your eyes; for we come on a good day; give, I pray you, whatsoever comes to your hand, to your servants, and to your son David.'

ח שְׁאַל אֶת־נְעָרֶיךָ וְיַגִּידוּ לָךְ וְיִמְצְאוּ
הַנְּעָרִים חֵן בְּעֵינֶיךָ כִּי־עַל־יוֹם
טוֹב בָּנוּ: תְּנָה־נָּא אֵת אֲשֶׁר
תִּמְצָא יָדְךָ לַעֲבָדֶיךָ וּלְבִנְךָ לְדָוִד.

9 And when David's young men came, they spoke to Naval according to all those words in the name of David, and ceased.

ט וַיָּבֹאוּ נַעֲרֵי דָוִד וַיְדַבְּרוּ
אֶל־נָבָל כְּכָל־הַדְּבָרִים
הָאֵלֶּה בְּשֵׁם דָּוִד: וַיָּנוּחוּ.

David sends ten lads to Naval to ask for provisions, making use of particularly beautiful language.

I Samuel 25

10 And Naval answered David's servants, and said: 'Who is David? and who is the son of

י וַיַּעַן נָבָל אֶת־עַבְדֵי דָוִד וַיֹּאמֶר מִי
דָוִד וּמִי בֶן־יִשָׁי: הַיּוֹם רַבּוּ עֲבָדִים

Jesse? there are many servants
now-a-days that break away
every man from his master;

הַמִּתְפָּרְצִים אִישׁ מִפְּנֵי אֲדֹנָיו.

11 shall I then take my bread, and
my water, and my flesh that
I have killed for my shearers,
and give it to men of whom I
know not whence they are?'

יא וְלָקַחְתִּי אֶת־לַחְמִי וְאֶת־מֵימַי
וְאֵת טִבְחָתִי אֲשֶׁר טָבַחְתִּי
לְגֹזְזָי: וְנָתַתִּי לַאֲנָשִׁים אֲשֶׁר
לֹא יָדַעְתִּי אֵי מִזֶּה הֵמָּה.

12 So David's young men turned
on their way, and went back,
and came and told him
according to all these words.

יב וַיַּהַפְכוּ נַעֲרֵי־דָוִד לְדַרְכָּם: וַיָּשֻׁבוּ
וַיָּבֹאוּ וַיַּגִּדוּ לוֹ כְּכֹל הַדְּבָרִים הָאֵלֶּה.

Naval turns down David's emissaries, sharply rejecting their request
and recalling David's rebelliousness against Saul.

I Samuel 25

13 And David said unto his men:
'Gird every man his sword.'
And they girded every man
his sword; and David also
girded on his sword; and there
went up after David about
four hundred men; and two
hundred abode by the baggage.

יג וַיֹּאמֶר דָּוִד לַאֲנָשָׁיו חִגְרוּ אִישׁ
אֶת־חַרְבּוֹ וַיַּחְגְּרוּ אִישׁ אֶת־חַרְבּוֹ
וַיַּחְגֹּר גַּם־דָּוִד אֶת־חַרְבּוֹ: וַיַּעֲלוּ
אַחֲרֵי דָוִד כְּאַרְבַּע מֵאוֹת אִישׁ
וּמָאתַיִם יָשְׁבוּ עַל־הַכֵּלִים.

Upon hearing of Naval's refusal, David becomes irate and prepares to
battle Naval with four hundred men.

I Samuel 25

14 But one of the young men told
Avigayil, Naval's wife, saying:
'Behold, David sent messengers
out of the wilderness to salute our
master; and he flew upon them.

יד וְלַאֲבִיגַיִל אֵשֶׁת נָבָל הִגִּיד
נַעַר־אֶחָד מֵהַנְּעָרִים לֵאמֹר: הִנֵּה
שָׁלַח דָּוִד מַלְאָכִים מֵהַמִּדְבָּר
לְבָרֵךְ אֶת־אֲדֹנֵינוּ וַיָּעַט בָּהֶם.

15 But the men were very good
to us, and we were not hurt,
neither missed we any thing,
as long as we went with them,
when we were in the fields;

טו וְהָאֲנָשִׁים טֹבִים לָנוּ מְאֹד:
וְלֹא הָכְלַמְנוּ וְלֹא־פָקַדְנוּ
מְאוּמָה כָּל־יְמֵי הִתְהַלַּכְנוּ
אִתָּם בִּהְיוֹתֵנוּ בַּשָּׂדֶה.

16 they were a wall to us both
by night and by day, all the
while we were with them
keeping the sheep.

17 Now know and consider
what you will do; for evil is
determined against our master,
and against all his house; for
he is such a base fellow, that
one cannot speak to him.'

18 Then Avigayil made haste, and
took two hundred loaves, and
two bottles of wine, and five
sheep ready dressed, and five
measures of parched corn, and
a hundred clusters of raisins,
and two hundred cakes of figs,
and laid them on donkeys.

19 And she said to her young men:
'Go on before me; behold, I
come after you.' But she told
not her husband Naval.

20 And it was so, as she rode on
her donkey, and came down
by the covert of the mountain,
that, behold, David and his
men came down towards
her; and she met them.

טז חוֹמָה הָיוּ עָלֵינוּ גַּם-לַיְלָה
גַּם-יוֹמָם: כָּל-יְמֵי הֱיוֹתֵנוּ
עִמָּם רֹעִים הַצֹּאן.

יז וְעַתָּה דְּעִי וּרְאִי מַה-תַּעֲשִׂי כִּי-
כָלְתָה הָרָעָה אֶל-אֲדֹנֵינוּ וְעַל כָּל-
בֵּיתוֹ: וְהוּא בֶּן-בְּלִיַּעַל מִדַּבֵּר אֵלָיו.

יח וַתְּמַהֵר אבוגיל (אֲבִיגַיִל) וַתִּקַּח
מָאתַיִם לֶחֶם וּשְׁנַיִם נִבְלֵי-יַיִן וְחָמֵשׁ
צֹאן עשוות (עֲשׂוּיוֹת) וְחָמֵשׁ
סְאִים קָלִי וּמֵאָה צִמֻּקִים וּמָאתַיִם
דְּבֵלִים: וַתָּשֶׂם עַל-הַחֲמֹרִים.

יט וַתֹּאמֶר לִנְעָרֶיהָ עִבְרוּ
לְפָנַי הִנְנִי אַחֲרֵיכֶם בָּאָה:
וּלְאִישָׁהּ נָבָל לֹא הִגִּידָה.

כ וְהָיָה הִיא רֹכֶבֶת עַל-הַחֲמוֹר וְיֹרֶדֶת
בְּסֵתֶר הָהָר וְהִנֵּה דָוִד וַאֲנָשָׁיו
יֹרְדִים לִקְרָאתָהּ: וַתִּפְגֹּשׁ אֹתָם.

Avigayil is informed about David's plans. She understands that she must intercede, or else Naval and the entire family will be wiped out.

I Samuel 25

21 Now David had said: 'Surely
in vain have I kept all that this
fellow has in the wilderness, so
that nothing was missed of all
that pertained unto him; and he
has returned me evil for good.

כא וְדָוִד אָמַר אַךְ לַשֶּׁקֶר שָׁמַרְתִּי
אֶת-כָּל-אֲשֶׁר לָזֶה בַּמִּדְבָּר
וְלֹא-נִפְקַד מִכָּל-אֲשֶׁר-לוֹ מְאוּמָה:
וַיָּשֶׁב-לִי רָעָה תַּחַת טוֹבָה

22 God do so to the enemies
of David, and more also, if
I leave of all that pertain to
him by the morning light
so much as one male.'

כב כֹּה-יַעֲשֶׂה אֱלֹהִים לְאֹיְבֵי דָוִד וְכֹה
יֹסִיף: אִם-אַשְׁאִיר מִכָּל-אֲשֶׁר-לוֹ
עַד-הַבֹּקֶר מַשְׁתִּין בְּקִיר.

David explains why he is outraged with Naval.

I Samuel 25

23 And when Avigayil saw David,
she made haste, and alighted
from her donkey, and fell
before David on her face, and
bowed down to the ground.

כג וַתֵּרֶא אֲבִיגַיִל אֶת-דָּוִד וַתְּמַהֵר
וַתֵּרֶד מֵעַל הַחֲמוֹר: וַתִּפֹּל לְאַפֵּי
דָוִד עַל-פָּנֶיהָ וַתִּשְׁתַּחוּ אָרֶץ.

Avigayil intercedes. She falls on her face before David and gives one of
the great orations in Tanakh.

I Samuel 25

24 And she fell at his feet, and
said: 'Upon me, my lord, upon
me be the iniquity; and let
your handmaid, I pray you,
speak in your ears, and hear
the words of your handmaid.

כד וַתִּפֹּל עַל-רַגְלָיו וַתֹּאמֶר בִּי-אֲנִי
אֲדֹנִי הֶעָוֹן: וּתְדַבֶּר-נָא אֲמָתְךָ
בְּאָזְנֶיךָ וּשְׁמַע אֵת דִּבְרֵי אֲמָתֶךָ.

25 Let not my lord, I pray you,
regard this base fellow, even
Naval; for as his name is, so
is he: Naval is his name, and
churlishness is with him; but I
your handmaid saw not the young
men of my lord, whom you sent.

כה אַל-נָא יָשִׂים אֲדֹנִי אֶת-לִבּוֹ
אֶל-אִישׁ הַבְּלִיַּעַל הַזֶּה עַל-נָבָל כִּי
כִשְׁמוֹ כֶּן-הוּא–נָבָל שְׁמוֹ וּנְבָלָה
עִמּוֹ: וַאֲנִי אֲמָתְךָ לֹא רָאִיתִי
אֶת-נַעֲרֵי אֲדֹנִי אֲשֶׁר שָׁלָחְתָּ.

26 Now therefore, my lord, as
the LORD lives, and as your
soul lives, seeing the LORD
has withheld you from
bloodguiltiness, and from
finding redress for yourself with
your own hand, now let your
enemies, and them that seek
evil to my lord, be as Naval.

כו וְעַתָּה אֲדֹנִי חַי-יְיָ וְחֵי-נַפְשְׁךָ אֲשֶׁר
מְנָעֲךָ יְיָ מִבּוֹא בְדָמִים וְהוֹשֵׁעַ
יָדְךָ לָךְ: וְעַתָּה יִהְיוּ כְנָבָל אֹיְבֶיךָ
וְהַמְבַקְשִׁים אֶל-אֲדֹנִי רָעָה.

27 And now this present which
your maidservant has brought to
my lord, let it be given unto the
young men that follow my lord.

28 Forgive, I pray you, the trespass
of your handmaid; for the LORD
will certainly make my lord a sure
house, because my lord fights the
battles of the LORD; and evil is
not found in you all your days.

29 And though man be risen up
to pursue you, and to seek your
soul, yet the soul of my lord
shall be bound in the bundle of
life with the LORD your God;
and the souls of your enemies,
them shall He sling out, as
from the hollow of a sling.

30 And it shall come to pass,
when the LORD shall have
done to my lord according to all
the good that He has spoken
concerning you, and shall have
appointed you prince over Israel;

31 that this shall be no stumbling-
block to you, nor offence of
heart to my lord, either that
you have shed blood without
cause, or that my lord has
found redress for himself. And
when the LORD shall have
dealt well with my lord, then
remember your handmaid.

כז וְעַתָּה הַבְּרָכָה הַזֹּאת אֲשֶׁר-הֵבִיא
שִׁפְחָתְךָ לַאדֹנִי: וְנִתְּנָה לַנְּעָרִים
הַמִּתְהַלְּכִים בְּרַגְלֵי אֲדֹנִי.

כח שָׂא נָא לְפֶשַׁע אֲמָתֶךָ: כִּי
עָשֹׂה-יַעֲשֶׂה יְיָ לַאדֹנִי בַּיִת נֶאֱמָן
כִּי-מִלְחֲמוֹת יְיָ אֲדֹנִי נִלְחָם
וְרָעָה לֹא-תִמָּצֵא בְךָ מִיָּמֶיךָ.

כט וַיָּקָם אָדָם לִרְדָפְךָ וּלְבַקֵּשׁ
אֶת-נַפְשֶׁךָ: וְהָיְתָה נֶפֶשׁ אֲדֹנִי
צְרוּרָה בִּצְרוֹר הַחַיִּים אֶת
יְיָ אֱלֹהֶיךָ וְאֵת נֶפֶשׁ אֹיְבֶיךָ
יְקַלְּעֶנָּה בְּתוֹךְ כַּף הַקָּלַע.

ל וְהָיָה כִּי-יַעֲשֶׂה יְיָ לַאדֹנִי כְּכֹל
אֲשֶׁר-דִּבֶּר אֶת-הַטּוֹבָה עָלֶיךָ:
וְצִוְּךָ לְנָגִיד עַל-יִשְׂרָאֵל.

לא וְלֹא תִהְיֶה זֹאת לְךָ לְפוּקָה
וּלְמִכְשׁוֹל לֵב לַאדֹנִי וְלִשְׁפָּךְ-דָּם
חִנָּם וּלְהוֹשִׁיעַ אֲדֹנִי לוֹ: וְהֵיטִב
יְיָ לַאדֹנִי וְזָכַרְתָּ אֶת-אֲמָתֶךָ.

Avigayil offers all kinds of arguments begging David for mercy and to
forgive Naval. It is here that she says the famous line, *Naval, ki khe-shmo
ken hu* – his name reflects him.[1] Then Avigayil tries a different argument.
She implies that perhaps she herself is at fault, having been unaware of
David's request.

---

1   I Samuel 25:25, Naval literally means "filth": in Tanakh, names are not
just names, they are descriptions of the Biblical character.

She then blesses David with long life, including another famous line, "May the soul of my lord be bound in the bonds of everlasting life, *tzrurah be-tzror ha-hayyim*."[2] Today, it is normally recited at funerals, and appears often on headstones; but it originates in Avigayil's speech to David. Here the line has a conclusion that we don't hear much at funerals: "the souls of your enemies, may He fling them out as from the hollow of a sling."

With her parting words, "Remember your maidservant,"[3] she figuratively winks at David. One wonders about her motives.

David accepts Avigayil's words and gifts, adding that her intervention saved Naval and his men from death. When David says he would have killed every male, he uses the harsh, vulgar phrase *mashtin be-kir*, literally, "one who urinates against a wall."[4]

I Samuel 25

32 And David said to Avigayil: 'Blessed be the LORD, the God of Israel, who sent you this day to meet me;

לב וַיֹּאמֶר דָּוִד לַאֲבִיגַל: בָּרוּךְ יְיָ אֱלֹהֵי יִשְׂרָאֵל אֲשֶׁר שְׁלָחֵךְ הַיּוֹם הַזֶּה לִקְרָאתִי.

33 and blessed be your discretion, and blessed be you, that has kept me this day from bloodguiltiness, and from finding redress for myself with my own hand.

לג וּבָרוּךְ טַעְמֵךְ וּבְרוּכָה אָתְּ: אֲשֶׁר כְּלִתִנִי הַיּוֹם הַזֶּה מִבּוֹא בְדָמִים וְהֹשֵׁעַ יָדִי לִי.

34 For in very deed, as the LORD, the God of Israel, lives, who has withheld me from hurting you, except you made haste to come meet me, surely there had not been left to Naval by the morning light so much as one male.'

לד וְאוּלָם חַי-יְיָ אֱלֹהֵי יִשְׂרָאֵל אֲשֶׁר מְנָעַנִי מֵהָרַע אֹתָךְ: כִּי לוּלֵי מִהַרְתְּ וַתָּבֹאת (וַתָּבֹאת) לִקְרָאתִי כִּי אִם-נוֹתַר לְנָבָל עַד-אוֹר הַבֹּקֶר מַשְׁתִּין בְּקִיר.

35 So David received of her hand that which she had brought him; and he said to her: 'Go up in peace to your house; see, I have hearkened to your voice, and have accepted your person.'

לה וַיִּקַּח דָּוִד מִיָּדָהּ אֵת אֲשֶׁר-הֵבִיאָה לוֹ וְלָהּ אָמַר עֲלִי לְשָׁלוֹם לְבֵיתֵךְ רְאִי שָׁמַעְתִּי בְקוֹלֵךְ וָאֶשָּׂא פָּנָיִךְ.

The story comes to its completion with Avigayil telling her husband Naval what has occurred, at which point he turns into a stone and dies.

---

2   I Samuel 25:29
3   I Samuel 25:31
4   I Samuel 25:34

David thanks God: justice is meted to Naval, but David is not guilty of any wrongdoing.

I Samuel 25

36 And Avigayil came to Naval; and, behold, he held a feast in his house, like the feast of a king; and Naval's heart was merry within him, for he was very drunken; wherefore she told him nothing, less or more, until the morning light.

לו וַתָּבֹא אֲבִיגַיִל אֶל-נָבָל וְהִנֵּה-לוֹ מִשְׁתֶּה בְּבֵיתוֹ כְּמִשְׁתֵּה הַמֶּלֶךְ וְלֵב נָבָל טוֹב עָלָיו וְהוּא שִׁכֹּר עַד-מְאֹד: וְלֹא-הִגִּידָה לּוֹ דָּבָר קָטֹן וְגָדוֹל–עַד-אוֹר הַבֹּקֶר.

37 And it came to pass in the morning, when the wine was gone out of Naval, that his wife told him these things, and his heart died within him, and he became as a stone.

לז וַיְהִי בַבֹּקֶר בְּצֵאת הַיַּיִן מִנָּבָל וַתַּגֶּד-לוֹ אִשְׁתּוֹ אֶת-הַדְּבָרִים הָאֵלֶּה: וַיָּמָת לִבּוֹ בְּקִרְבּוֹ וְהוּא הָיָה לְאָבֶן.

38 And it came to pass about ten days after, that the LORD smote Naval, so that he died.

לח וַיְהִי כַּעֲשֶׂרֶת הַיָּמִים: וַיִּגֹּף יְי אֶת-נָבָל וַיָּמֹת.

39 And when David heard that Naval was dead, he said: 'Blessed be the LORD, that has pleaded the cause of my reproach from the hand of Naval, and has kept back His servant from evil; and the evil-doing of Naval has the LORD returned upon his own head.' And David sent and spoke concerning Avigayil, to take her to him for wife.

לט וַיִּשְׁמַע דָּוִד כִּי מֵת נָבָל וַיֹּאמֶר בָּרוּךְ יְי אֲשֶׁר רָב אֶת-רִיב חֶרְפָּתִי מִיַּד נָבָל וְאֶת-עַבְדּוֹ חָשַׂךְ מֵרָעָה וְאֵת רָעַת נָבָל הֵשִׁיב יְי בְּרֹאשׁוֹ: וַיִּשְׁלַח דָּוִד וַיְדַבֵּר בַּאֲבִיגַיִל לְקַחְתָּהּ לוֹ לְאִשָּׁה.

When David finds out what happened, he sends messengers to propose on his behalf to Avigayil. David and Avigayil marry.

I Samuel 25

40 And when the servants of David were come to Avigayil to Carmel, they spoke to her, saying: 'David has sent us to you, to take you to him to wife.'

מ וַיָּבֹאוּ עַבְדֵי דָוִד אֶל-אֲבִיגַיִל הַכַּרְמֶלָה: וַיְדַבְּרוּ אֵלֶיהָ לֵאמֹר דָּוִד שְׁלָחָנוּ אֵלַיִךְ לְקַחְתֵּךְ לוֹ לְאִשָּׁה.

41 And she arose, and bowed down
with her face to the earth, and
said: 'Behold, your handmaid
is a servant to wash the feet
of the servants of my lord.'

42 And Avigayil hastened, and
arose, and rode upon an
donkey, with five maidens of
hers that followed her; and she
went after the messengers of
David, and became his wife.

43 David also took Achino'am
of Jezreel; and they became
both of them his wives.

44 Now Saul had given Michal
his daughter, David's wife,
to Palti the son of Laish,
who was of Gallim.

מא וַתָּקׇם וַתִּשְׁתַּחוּ אַפַּיִם אָרְצָה:
וַתֹּאמֶר הִנֵּה אֲמָתְךָ לְשִׁפְחָה
לִרְחֹץ רַגְלֵי עַבְדֵי אֲדֹנִי.

מב וַתְּמַהֵר וַתָּקׇם אֲבִיגַיִל וַתִּרְכַּב
עַל-הַחֲמוֹר וְחָמֵשׁ נַעֲרֹתֶיהָ
הַהֹלְכוֹת לְרַגְלָהּ: וַתֵּלֶךְ אַחֲרֵי
מַלְאֲכֵי דָוִד וַתְּהִי-לוֹ לְאִשָּׁה.

מג וְאֶת-אֲחִינֹעַם לָקַח דָּוִד מִיִּזְרְעֶאל:
וַתִּהְיֶיןָ גַּם-שְׁתֵּיהֶן לוֹ לְנָשִׁים.

מד וְשָׁאוּל נָתַן אֶת-מִיכַל בִּתּוֹ אֵשֶׁת
דָּוִד: לְפַלְטִי בֶן-לַיִשׁ אֲשֶׁר מִגַּלִּים.

Five Questions

Let us return to the story and try to understand it on a deeper level
with these five questions:

- Was David correct in demanding provisions?
- Was Naval correct in refusing?
- How are we to understand David's willingness
  to wipe out Naval?
- What is Avigayil's role in this story?
- How are we to assess Avigayil's actions?

In the process of answering these specific questions, we will examine
the broader narrative, which begins with I Samuel 21 and reaches its conclusion in chapter 26.

Was David correct in demanding provisions?

In chapter 21, we are told the story of David arriving in the city of Nob.
He meets Achimelekh the Priest and makes his first request for food.

I Samuel 21

4 Now what do you have under your hand? five loaves of bread? give them in my hand, or whatsoever there is present.'

ד וְעַתָּה מַה-יֵּשׁ תַּחַת-יָדְךָ חֲמִשָּׁה-לֶחֶם תְּנָה בְיָדִי: אוֹ הַנִּמְצָא.

On the run from Saul, David desperately needs food in order to survive.

I Samuel 21

9 And David said unto Achimelekh: 'And is there peradventure here under your hand spear or sword? for I have neither brought my sword nor my weapons with me, because the king's business required haste.'

ט וַיֹּאמֶר דָּוִד לַאֲחִימֶלֶךְ וְאִין יֶשׁ-פֹּה תַּחַת-יָדְךָ חֲנִית אוֹ-חָרֶב: כִּי גַם-חַרְבִּי וְגַם-כֵּלַי לֹא-לָקַחְתִּי בְיָדִי כִּי-הָיָה דְבַר-הַמֶּלֶךְ נָחוּץ.

10 And the priest said: 'The sword of Goliath the Philistine, whom you slew in the vale of Elah, behold, it is here wrapped in a cloth behind the *ephod*; if you will take that, take it; for there is no other save that here.' And David said: 'There is none other like it; give it to me.'

י וַיֹּאמֶר הַכֹּהֵן חֶרֶב גָּלְיָת הַפְּלִשְׁתִּי אֲשֶׁר-הִכִּיתָ בְּעֵמֶק הָאֵלָה הִנֵּה-הִיא לוּטָה בַשִּׂמְלָה אַחֲרֵי הָאֵפוֹד אִם-אֹתָהּ תִּקַּח-לְךָ קָח כִּי אֵין אַחֶרֶת זוּלָתָהּ בָּזֶה: וַיֹּאמֶר דָּוִד אֵין כָּמוֹהָ תְּנֶנָּה לִּי.

David also asks Achimelekh for something with which to defend himself. Achimelekh gives him the sword of Goliath which lies behind the *ephod*, the breastplate from where God speaks.

Supplying David with food and a sword, Achimelekh certainly acts like a supporter of David. Moreover, Achimelekh leaves the impression that he sees David as having the support of God. That may not have been his intention, but the sword is brought forth from behind the *ephod* – God territory.[5]

The act of requesting food of Achimelekh, the priest of Nob, meets two goals. First of all, David requires food to survive. Secondly, he is looking for supporters. To whom can he turn? He needs to know. Certainly, receiving Goliath's sword from behind the *ephod* is a signal to the people that David has support.

---

5   See I Samuel 22:15 where Achimelekh declares: "Did I begin today to inquire for him of God?"

Here in the narrative of Avigayil, the same dynamic unfolds. David turns to Naval for food. That's the bottom line. But he also seeks political support. In this particular case, the political component of his request is even more pronounced than it was in chapter 21.

By the time David reaches out to Naval in chapter 25, David's position has been dramatically changed by the events of chapter 24, in which David finds Saul in a vulnerable position in Ein Gedi, and, in a dramatic moment, cuts Saul's coat.

Reading through that passage, one concludes that the image of David holding a corner cut from Saul's coat should prove to Saul the purity of David's intentions. David is in a position to kill Saul, and he does not. David then pleads his innocence to Saul, whom he calls "Father."

I Samuel 24

11 Moreover, my father, see, see the skirt of your robe in my hand; for I cut off the skirt of your robe, and killed you not, know you and see that there is neither evil nor transgression in my hand, and I have not sinned against you, though you lay in wait for my soul to take it.

יא וְאָבִי רְאֵה גַּם רְאֵה אֶת־כְּנַף
מְעִילְךָ בְּיָדִי: כִּי בְּכָרְתִי אֶת־כְּנַף
מְעִילְךָ וְלֹא הֲרַגְתִּיךָ דַּע וּרְאֵה כִּי
אֵין בְּיָדִי רָעָה וָפֶשַׁע וְלֹא־חָטָאתִי
לָךְ־וְאַתָּה צֹדֶה אֶת־נַפְשִׁי לְקַחְתָּהּ.

That is the way the text looks on the simplest level.

Rabbi David Silber sees it very differently. He says that David's cutting of Saul's coat is the key, notwithstanding that in the next verse David regrets his actions.

I Samuel 24

4 And the men of David said to him: 'Behold the day in which the LORD said to you: Behold, I will deliver your enemy into your hand, and you shall do to him as it shall seem good to you.' Then David arose, and cut off the skirt of Saul's robe privily.

5 And it came to pass afterward, that David's heart smote him, because he had cut off Saul's skirt.

ד וַיֹּאמְרוּ אַנְשֵׁי דָוִד אֵלָיו הִנֵּה הַיּוֹם
אֲשֶׁר־אָמַר יְיָ אֵלֶיךָ הִנֵּה אָנֹכִי
נֹתֵן אֶת־איביך (אֹיִבְךָ) בְּיָדֶךָ
וְעָשִׂיתָ לּוֹ כַּאֲשֶׁר יִטַב בְּעֵינֶיךָ:
וַיָּקָם דָּוִד וַיִּכְרֹת אֶת־כְּנַף־
הַמְּעִיל אֲשֶׁר־לְשָׁאוּל בַּלָּט.

ה וַיְהִי אַחֲרֵי־כֵן וַיַּךְ לֵב־דָּוִד אֹתוֹ: עַל
אֲשֶׁר כָּרַת אֶת־כָּנָף אֲשֶׁר לְשָׁאוּל.

<table>
<tr>
<td>

6 And he said to his men: 'The
LORD forbid me, that I should
do this thing to my lord, the
LORD'S anointed, to put forth
my hand against him, seeing
he is the LORD'S anointed.'

</td>
<td dir="rtl">

ו וַיֹּאמֶר לַאֲנָשָׁיו חָלִילָה לִּי מֵיְיָ
אִם־אֶעֱשֶׂה אֶת־הַדָּבָר הַזֶּה
לַאדֹנִי לִמְשִׁיחַ יְיָ לִשְׁלֹחַ יָדִי
בּוֹ: כִּי־מְשִׁיחַ יְיָ הוּא.

</td>
</tr>
</table>

David cuts Saul's coat when he catches Saul in a vulnerable position. He then feels pangs of remorse and blocks his men from doing harm to Saul. But the deed is still done. The coat has been rent.

It has been noted that coats in Tanakh symbolize leadership. The one wearing the coat is the leader. Removing or cutting the coat indicates that the leadership has been terminated. Thus when Jacob wants to elevate Joseph, he gives him a special coat, the *ketonet pasim*.[6] And when the brothers wish to sell Joseph, they must first remove the coat.[7] Only then can Joseph be sold. Having one's coat removed signifies the loss of one's claim to leadership.

Once Saul's coat is cut, notwithstanding David's remorse, Saul's leadership has come to its end. Although David is not yet officially king, it is as if he has assumed the kingship. Note that when David displays the cut corner of Saul's coat, King Saul admits as much to David:

I Samuel 24

<table>
<tr>
<td>

20 And now, behold, I know that
you shall surely be king, and
that the kingdom of Israel shall
be established in your hand.

</td>
<td dir="rtl">

כ וְעַתָּה הִנֵּה יָדַעְתִּי כִּי מָלֹךְ תִּמְלוֹךְ:
וְקָמָה בְּיָדְךָ מַמְלֶכֶת יִשְׂרָאֵל.

</td>
</tr>
</table>

So while Saul retained formal control when David sought aid from Achimelekh, Saul has virtually lost the kingship by the time we come to the story of Naval. David is now Saul's clear successor. This may also explain why the Avigayil chapter begins with the death of Samuel. Samuel is linked to Saul. Samuel anoints Saul, he teaches him, he encourages him, he rebukes him. Once Saul's kingship is *de facto* over, Samuel dies.[8]

Make no mistake about it: Saul is still king. But on an emotional and spiritual level, at this point Saul is out and David is in. As a consequence, when arguing for provisions from Naval, David does so as the virtual

---

6   Genesis 37:3
7   Genesis 37:23
8   Note that Samuel's death is also recorded in I Samuel 28:3.

king. With Saul marginalized and Samuel gone, David's demand for provisions is effectively a form of taxation and statement of loyalty.

ᴈ❧ Was Naval correct to refuse David?

Let us analyze Naval's refusal.

Methodologically, whenever one looks at an event in a narrative, it is always good to see parallels to similar events; how they intersect and how they diverge. This leads us to compare the stories of Naval and Achimelekh of Nob.

There are two ways of looking at Naval's refusal. On the one hand, we can view his rebuff as an act of *nibul*, ugliness. As Avigayil says, "He is as his name is."[9] And that is Naval. His act is despicable. After all, David and his men had protected him. He should have expressed support for David.

On the other hand, it could be argued that Naval's actions are very understandable. He knows well the fate of Achimelekh and the Priests of Nob. Let's look at the episode in chapter 22.

After giving David succor, Achimelekh and the Priests of Nob are confronted by none other than Saul, who is furious that Achimelekh helped David. As a result, Saul orchestrates the slaughter of the whole priestly city at the hands of Doeg the Edomite.

I Samuel 22

18 And the king said to Doyeg (Doeg): 'Turn, and fall upon the priests.' And Doyeg (Doeg) the Edomite turned, and he fell upon the priests, and he slew on that day fourscore and five persons that did wear a linen *ephod*.

19 And Nob, the city of the priests, smote he with the edge of the sword, both men and women, children and sucklings, and oxen and asses and sheep, with the edge of the sword.

יח וַיֹּאמֶר הַמֶּלֶךְ לדויג (לְדוֹאֵג)
סֹב אַתָּה וּפְגַע בַּכֹּהֲנִים:
וַיִּסֹּב דויג (דּוֹאֵג) הָאֲדֹמִי
וַיִּפְגַּע־הוּא בַּכֹּהֲנִים וַיָּמֶת
בַּיּוֹם הַהוּא שְׁמֹנִים וַחֲמִשָּׁה
אִישׁ נֹשֵׂא אֵפוֹד בָּד.

יט וְאֵת נֹב עִיר־הַכֹּהֲנִים הִכָּה לְפִי־
חֶרֶב מֵאִישׁ וְעַד־אִשָּׁה מֵעוֹלֵל וְעַד־
יוֹנֵק וְשׁוֹר וַחֲמוֹר וָשֶׂה לְפִי־חָרֶב.

---

9   I Samuel 25:25

In chapter 25, although Saul's coat is cut, he is still king and quite capable of exacting punishment on anyone who helps David. After all, David is a threat to Saul.

This may motivate Naval's refusal. Note the language where Naval rejects David's request saying: "There are many slaves who break from their masters," which in Hebrew is *"rabu avadim ha-mitpartzim ish mipnei adonav."*[10] It has been noted that the term *mitpartzim*, which means to break away, is from the word *peretz*, a term which reminds the reader of Peretz the son of Judah, the ancestor of David.[11]

Naval is arguing that many vie for power but he dares not support any of these individuals, including David, as they are challenging the leadership of Saul. And if he supports them, he stands to be punished by Saul in the same way that Saul punished Achimelekh and the city of Nob. So Naval may be simply, and perhaps sagaciously, protecting himself from Saul's wrath.

❧ What of David's readiness to destroy Naval?

This question is the heart of the matter: David's intention to go to war against Naval. David's reaction seems to be disproportionate to Naval's cold response. Had David not been stopped by Avigayil, he would have annihilated Naval.

David's actions are particularly problematic when one takes into account chapter 23, the story of David in the city of Ke'ilah. After demolishing the Philistines who had attacked Ke'ilah, God tells David that the people of Ke'ilah will hand him over to Saul.

And what does David do? Instead of destroying Ke'ilah, David leaves the city:

I Samuel 23

13 Then David and his men, who were about six hundred, arose and departed out of Ke'ilah, and went wherever they could

יג וַיָּקָם דָּוִד וַאֲנָשָׁיו כְּשֵׁשׁ-מֵאוֹת אִישׁ וַיֵּצְאוּ מִקְּעִלָה וַיִּתְהַלְּכוּ בַּאֲשֶׁר

---

10   I Samuel 25:10

11   See Ruth 4:18-22 for David's ancestry. I first heard the connection between *mitpartzim* and Peretz from Rabbi David Silber. Professor Robert Alter argues that here Naval was rebuking David for rebelling against Saul. In his words, "David himself is a slave or subject (the same word in Hebrew) who has rebelled against his master Saul." Alter, Robert, *The Book of David: A Commentary on Samuel I-II*, (William and Norton, 1999) p.154.

go. And it was told Saul that David was escaped from Ke'ilah; and he forbore to go forth.	יִתְהַלָּכוּ וּלְשָׁאוּל הֻגַּד כִּי-נִמְלַט דָּוִד מִקְּעִילָה וַיֶּחְדַּל לָצֵאת.

In Ke'ilah, David recognizes that he cannot randomly annihilate a city, but here in the Naval story he seems prepared to do just that.

Note the words of the lad to Avigayil warning of the impending doom: "for evil is determined against our master" – "*ki kholtah hara'ah el adoneinu.*"[12] This recalls the statement in the Book of Esther, when the text says concerning Haman:[13]

Esther 7

7 And the king arose in his wrath from the banquet of wine and went into the palace garden; but Haman remained to make request for his life to Esther the queen; for he saw that **there was evil determined against him** by the king.	ז וְהַמֶּלֶךְ קָם בַּחֲמָתוֹ מִמִּשְׁתֵּה הַיַּיִן אֶל-גִּנַּת הַבִּיתָן וְהָמָן עָמַד לְבַקֵּשׁ עַל-נַפְשׁוֹ מֵאֶסְתֵּר הַמַּלְכָּה כִּי רָאָה כִּי-כָלְתָה אֵלָיו הָרָעָה מֵאֵת הַמֶּלֶךְ.

"*Ki kholtah*" is a foreboding term.

What has changed in David's character? Why would David destroy Naval, after acting with appropriate restraint in sparing Ke'ilah? A close analysis of David indicates that he is in constant struggle with himself. He is a personality struggling between peaceful and warlike tendencies, passive and aggressive, and, yes, moral and immoral.

In Tanakh, this is expressed through personality qualities which correspond to those of either Jacob or Esau. (Elsewhere we can discuss Esau in a more positive light. There is much good that can be said about him.) One broad way to view Esau is as an aggressive personality. Jacob's is the more passive personality.

Who was David? Does he most resemble Jacob or Esau? Our approach will be to analyze the first time David is described, when we meet him as a young shepherd.[14] This may reveal much about his personality, as the locus of meaning for any word, or term, or Biblical character, resides in the place of first encounter. Additionally, we will analyze the first time we

---

12   I Samuel 25:17
13   See *Mesorat Ha-Tanakh* by Rabbi Chaim Heller, *zt"l*, who points out this parallel.
14   I Samuel 16:12

encounter David as a warrior,[15] as well as the first description of the forces David gathers around him.[16] This may reveal much about his character, as one of the major tasks of the king is to go to battle to defend his people.[17]

David as Jacob

There are many different Davids. Amongst his many personas is the David who is the sweet singer of Israel. He is God's poet, the composer of Psalms. As such, he must have been pure and holy, much like Jacob who is described as an *ish tam*, a "wholesome man."[18]

This portrayal is evident when we first meet David. There he is described as "goodly to look upon," "*tov ro'i.*" The word *ro'eh*, "sight," in the book of Genesis is a covenantal term. In the life of Abraham, the word "*ro'eh*" brackets his covenantal experience: his first stop in Canaan is at Alon **Moreh**,[19] and his story reaches its crescendo with the binding of Isaac on Mount **Moriah**.[20] By referring to David as "*tov ro'i*" when we first meet him, the text is attesting to his role as the one who is to lead the covenantal mission of the Jewish people.

David's first battle, his battle against Goliath, reveals a Jacob-like warrior. He fights with stealth rather than brute strength. He fights much like Jacob who finesses the blessings from Esau with guile. He is subtle. He is quick. As Esau says upon hearing that Jacob had taken the blessings:

Genesis 27

36 And he said: 'Is not he rightly
named **Jacob** (*ya'akov*)? for he
has **supplanted** me (*ya'kveini*)
these two times: he took away
my birthright; and, behold, now
he has taken away my blessing.'
And he said: 'Have you not
reserved a blessing for me?'

לו וַיֹּאמֶר הֲכִי קָרָא שְׁמוֹ יַעֲקֹב
וַיַּעְקְבֵנִי זֶה פַעֲמַיִם אֶת-בְּכֹרָתִי
לָקָח וְהִנֵּה עַתָּה לָקַח בִּרְכָתִי:
וַיֹּאמַר הֲלֹא-אָצַלְתָּ לִּי בְּרָכָה?

Similarly, the description of the way David battles Goliath is laced with Jacob terminology:

15   I Samuel 17
16   I Samuel 22:2
17   See Deuteronomy 17:14-20.
18   Genesis 25:27
19   Genesis 12:6
20   Genesis 22:2

I Samuel 17

49 And David reached his hand into the bag, and took from there a **stone**, and **slung** it, and smote the Philistine in his forehead; and the **stone** sank into his forehead, and **he fell upon his face to the ground**.

מט וַיִּשְׁלַח דָּוִד אֶת-יָדוֹ אֶל-הַכֶּלִי וַיִּקַּח מִשָּׁם אֶבֶן וַיְקַלַּע וַיַּךְ אֶת-הַפְּלִשְׁתִּי אֶל-מִצְחוֹ: וַתִּטְבַּע הָאֶבֶן בְּמִצְחוֹ וַיִּפֹּל עַל-פָּנָיו אָרְצָה.

Note that David takes a stone – which brings to mind an important stone from the Jacob story. Jacob takes stones for his pillow[21] when fleeing from Esau. And after dreaming his dream that night, several stones become, according to the Midrash, one stone which remains as a monument to God.[22] Then Jacob rises and declares, "If I return in peace, this stone monument will become a house of God."[23]

Even the term *va-yekal'a*–ויקלע–looks like and sounds like and has letters similar to the "*Ya'akov*"–יעקב, Jacob's name in Hebrew.

A the end of this verse, it says "he fell upon his face (*panav*) to the ground." This reminds the reader of Jacob, who, in the midst of his challenge with Esau, wrestles an angel in the place he names "Peni'el," "for I have seen God face to face, (*panim el panim*), and my life is preserved."[24]

So there is a side of David's personality which is Jacobean.

David as Esau

But David also has aspects of the Esau personality. In general terms, David, like Esau, is very powerful and strong and adept at overcoming his enemies. More specifically, the first description of David contains hints of

21   Genesis 28:11

22   Genesis 28:18. See Rashi Genesis 28:11 *va-yasem meirashotav*; Genesis Rabbah 68:11; Midrash Tanchuma *Va-Yetze* 1. The Hebrew word for stone, *even*, may be a compound of *av*, "father," and *ben*, "son." When Jacob leaves his home, he is feuding with his brother Esau about who will inherit the blessing of the birthright from their father. Hence, according to the Midrash, many stones are vying with each other. In the end, the stones merge – a sign of the hope that Esau and Jacob will one day reconcile. Only then can a true monument be built to the Lord.

23   Genesis 28:22

24   Genesis 32:31. Note also the term *keli* (כלי) which in Hebrew script looks like *kaf* (כף), reminding the reader of how Jacob was struck in the hollow, "*kaf*," of the thigh by the mysterious man. See Genesis 32:26.

Esau. David, like Esau, is described as a redhead, *admoni*.[25] In fact, the word appears in Tanakh only in the verses which introduce these two characters.[26]

Consider also the first description of the forces that David gathers around him:

I Samuel 22

2 And every one that was **in distress**, and every one that was in **debt**, and every one that was **embittered**, gathered themselves to him; and he became captain over them; and there were with him about **four hundred men**.

ב וַיִּתְקַבְּצוּ אֵלָיו כָּל־אִישׁ מָצוֹק וְכָל־אִישׁ אֲשֶׁר־לוֹ נֹשֶׁא וְכָל־אִישׁ מַר־נֶפֶשׁ וַיְהִי עֲלֵיהֶם לְשָׂר: וַיִּהְיוּ עִמּוֹ כְּאַרְבַּע מֵאוֹת אִישׁ.

This is a ragtag army. David is the leader, and with him are four hundred men. Similarly, when Esau is marching to Jacob, he marches with four hundred men.[27]

Consider also how David's men are described: every one that was "in distress," *matzok* – "in debt," *noshe* – and "embittered," *mar nefesh*. These terms appear when the Torah describes Esau's reaction when informed that Jacob had taken his blessing.

Genesis 27

34 When Esau **heard** the words of his father, he **cried** with an exceeding great and **bitter** cry,

לד כִּשְׁמֹעַ עֵשָׂו אֶת־דִּבְרֵי אָבִיו וַיִּצְעַק צְעָקָה גְּדֹלָה וּמָרָה עַד־מְאֹד

---

25   I Samuel 16:12; and Genesis 25:25. It has been argued that *admoni* may mean ruddy of skin, rather than hair.

26   The entire first description of David reads: *Ve-hu admoni, im yefeh ein-ayim, ve-tov ro'i* – "and he was ruddy, with beautiful eyes, and of good appearance." I Samuel 16:12. Thus, our introduction to David reveals his inner struggle. *Admoni* describes David's "Esau" side; *tov ro'i* his "Jacob" side.

There is one other descriptive term here: *yefeh einayim*. Note that the letters *peh heh* (פה) in *yefeh* remind the reader of Esau, who fooled his father with his "mouth," *peh* (פה) (see Genesis 25:28 and Rashi, ad loc.) *Einayim*, "eyes," may remind the reader of Jacob because the function of an eye is to see, and "see," *ro'eh*, is a covenantal term. Alternatively, *einayim* sounds like *ma'ayan*, "fountain" or "well," recalling the episode when Jacob meets Rachel at the well. See Genesis 29:1-11.

27   Genesis 32:7, 33:1

and said to his father: 'Bless me,
even me also, O my father.'

וַיֹּאמֶר לְאָבִיו בָּרֲכֵנִי גַם-אָנִי אָבִי.

Consider the Hebrew for Esau's scream: *va-yitz'ak tze'akah*. It is the same as the Hebrew for "distressed," in describing David's followers – *matzok*. The meaning and sound of both words are similar. And, of course, there is a direct parallel between *marah*, the bitter cry in the Esau narrative, and *mar nefesh*, the embittered men in the David story. Even the term *noshe* describing David's men as debt-ridden, sounds like *kishmo'ah* in the Esau verse. It is not a coincidence that the terms *matzok, noshe, mar nefesh* parallel *va-yitz'ak, ki-shmo'ah, u-marah*. David's men may be purposefully described in terms that remind the reader of Esau, hinting that David has aspects of Esau.

David at war with himself

Unmistakably, David is struggling. There is conflict between the covenantal/Jacob side of his personality, and the warrior/Esau side. That struggle reaches its crescendo right here in our text, chapter 25. Is David capable, in the spirit of Esau, of killing the ungrateful Naval and his followers? It would certainly seem so.

Were David to destroy the city along with Naval and everyone around Naval, it would not be the first time that such a massacre has occurred in the Book of Samuel.

We witness a terrible massacre when Saul instructs Doeg the Edomite to destroy Achimelekh and the rest of the priests for aiding David.[28] In that verse, Doeg becomes "Doyeg," the spelling changes and the *aleph* (א) becomes a *yud* (י). The Midrash says that he lost the *aleph* because it was an "oy!" There was a moan; for goodness sake, how could you *do* this terrible thing? That Nob, city of Priests, should be put to the sword![29]

One wonders: who was Doeg the Edomite? Edomite means a descendant of Edom – that is, Esau. In Hebrew, "Edomite" is *"adomi"* – almost *"admoni,"* redhead. And *"Doeg"* means a worrier. *"Doeg ha-'Adomi"* might make a nickname for David: the worrying redhead.[30] In other words, *Doeg*

---

28   I Samuel 22:18

29   Yalkut Shimoni, 1 Samuel, Section 231

30   Note the incident when Meirav, Saul's eldest daughter, was given to Adriel ha-Mecholati after she had been promised to David (I Samuel 18:19). Adriel ha-Mecholati may be a nickname for David as well. Adriel is a compound of *eder El*, flocks of the Lord, and David was a shepherd who followed God's way. *Ha-Mecholati* reminds the reader of the dancing women (*me-cholot*) who

ha-ʾAdomi could be a description of David, the redhead who is worrying about his welfare as he battles Saul.

Don't get me wrong. Of course Doeg is a distinct character in the story. David had nothing to do with the slaughter in chapter 22. Nothing. But I am suggesting that the text is hinting that David has the capacity to *become* a Doeg. He has the same capacity for murder as Doeg the Edomite. After Naval defies him, David without hesitation sets out to kill Naval.

It takes a lot of somersaults to prove that Naval deserves death for the act of withholding support from David. If David follows through, he will be repeating Saul's mistake in ordering death for the Priests of Nob.[31] David will become a Doeg. If David is such an indiscriminate killer, perhaps he is not truly worthy of the kingship.

And that is the significance of this moment.

᠔ What is Avigayil's role?

It is here that Avigayil steps in. Through her brilliant oratory skills, she becomes the teacher par excellence, advising against this dangerous course of action. Robert Alter[32] points out that the encounter between Avigayil and David echoes the encounter of Jacob and Esau, with David playing the role of Esau. This places Avigayil in the role of Jacob.

David is marching toward Naval with four hundred men. Esau is also accompanied by four hundred men.

Avigayil intercepts David, and she does exactly what Jacob does when he prepares to meet Esau. She prepares gifts for David,[33] much like Jacob

---

sing: "Saul has slain his thousands, and David his tens of thousands" (I Samuel 18:6-7). Here, too, Adriel ha-Mecholati is not David. Still, the text may be hinting that David, like Adriel, could become involved in taking unfair advantage of women. And in the end, David has improper relations with Batsheva (1I Samuel 11:2-4).

Thus, Doeg ha-ʾAdomi and Adriel ha-Mecholati represent the two great challenges facing David: the temptations to commit murder and to act in a sexually immoral way.

I first heard the name similarities of Doeg ha-ʾAdomi and Adriel ha-Mecholati to David from Rabbi David Silber. The implications of these similarities, as well as the formula and development of the theory presented here, are my own.

31   Note the similarity between the name, "Naval" and the place, "Nob," which is *"Nov"* in the Hebrew. Naval presents, for David, a challenge similar to the challenge faced by Saul in Nob.

32   Alter, Robert, *The Book of David: A Commentary on Samuel 1-2*, (William and Norton, 1999), p. 157.

33   I Samuel 25:18

prepares gifts for Esau.[34] As a matter of fact, there's a very unusual phrase which shows up in both stories: "pass before me," (*ivru le-fanay)*.[35] Thus Jacob instructs those who are carrying his gifts to Esau, and Avigayil uses the same language.

When Avigayil offers gifts to David, what is the language used for the word "gifts?" It is not "*matanah*," it is not "*minchah*." The language used is "*berakhah*," generally translated "blessing." Here is the blessing,[36] or here is the present, your maidservant is giving to you. Jacob does the same and uses the same language of *berakhah*[37] when he offers a present to Esau.

Additionally, when speaking to David, Avigayil in effect implores him not to repeat Saul's mistake with Doeg in Nob. In effect, she says to David: Be a Jacob, don't be an Esau. It is here that Avigayil originates the famous line used to bless the souls of the departed, *ve-haytah nefesh adoni tzrura be-tzror ha-chayyim et Hashem Elohekha*, may my lord's soul be bound up in the bonds of life with the Lord your God.[38] Avigayil tells David, if you act like Jacob, you will be one with the Lord.

She then proclaims: "*ve'et nefesh oyvekha **yekal'enah** be-tokh **kaf hakala‘***, And He will **fling away** (יְקַלְּעֶנָּה) the lives of your enemies as from the **hollow of a sling** (כַּף הַקֶּלַע)."[39] Here, Avigayil's language is laced with Jacob imagery. As previously noted, hollow, *kaf*, כַּף reminds us of Jacob being struck by the mysterious man in the hollow *kaf*, כַּף of his thigh.[40] Even the term for "fling away," "*yekal'enah*" (יְקַלְּעֶנָּה), may remind the reader of the name Jacob, *Ya'akov* יַעֲקֹב , as they look and sound the same. As David leans towards the Esau influence, Avigayil steps in and reminds him of the way to achieve his destiny within Israel. The way to be God-like, she tells him, is to follow the way of Jacob.

David heeds Avigayil's advice

What is extraordinary here is that David accepts Avigayil's lesson. In the end, Avigayil convinces David.

---

34   Genesis 32:14-16

35   Compare Genesis 32:17 and I Samuel 25:19.

36   I Samuel 25:27. "And now, this **blessing** that your maidservant has brought to my lord," *ve-'atah ha-brakha ha-zot asher hevi shifchatkha la'adoni*.

37   Genesis 33:11. 'Take, I pray you, **my gift** (*birkhati* בִּרְכָתִי) that is brought to you; because God hath dealt graciously with me, and because I have enough.' And he urged him, and he took it. קַח-נָא אֶת-בִּרְכָתִי אֲשֶׁר הֻבָאת לָךְ, כִּי-חַנַּנִי אֱלֹהִים וְכִי יֶשׁ-לִי-כֹל; וַיִּפְצַר-בּוֹ, וַיִּקָּח.

38   I Samuel 25:29

39   Ibid.

40   Genesis 32:26 *Va-yiga‘ be-khaf yereicho.*

Consider the sentence describing David's acquiescence to Avigayil's words. David takes the blessing, the present from her hands which she has brought to him. And he says to her, "Go up in peace to your house. See, I have heard your voice, *re'ei shama'ti ve-kolekh*."[41]

The words "hear," *shema,* and "voice," *kol,* together have powerful resonance. The first time they are found together is in the Eden story. There, the Torah states: "And [Adam and Eve] **heard** the **voice** of the Lord, God, moving about in the garden – *Va-yishme'u et kol Hashem Elokim mithalekh ba-gan.*"[42] Thus, *kol* is not just the voice from the larynx, it is the deeper voice that comes from God Himself.

That is why, when on Rosh Hashanah we blow shofar, the ram's horn, the wording of the blessing is: "to **hear** the **voice** of the shofar, *li-shmo'a kol shofar.*" No wonder: The shofar sound is produced by the inner breath, the inner Godliness, the inner soul. To blow shofar, we breathe out the breath that God breathed into Adam when the human being was first created.[43] Thus, *lishmo'a kol shofar,* takes us back to Eden. Similarly, David's words here – "I have **heard** your **voice,** *shamati ve-kolekh*" – indicate that he recognizes that Avigayil's teaching is suffused with Godliness.

When we come across Biblical heroes we have a sense that they are absolutely good. What could we possibly have in common with such paragon personalities? After all, the rest of us struggle. We're all pulled in very different directions. The truth is that great people of Tanakh are often pulled in opposing directions as well.[44]

This is precisely what is occurring here. David is conflicted. He is both Jacob *and* Esau, and the Esau part of him is about to prevail. Avigayil steps in and says, stop, remember the greater mission, remember the message of Jacob.

---

41   I Samuel 25:35

42   Genesis 3:8

43   Genesis 2:7

44   It often occurs that biblical personalities experience inner turmoil. A good example is Moses. Nursed by his Jewish mother, and raised by Pharaoh's daughter, he must have been in tension: was he Jewish or Egyptian? The Bible then records (Exodus 2:12) that when Moses saw an Egyptian smiting a Jew, he turned "this way and that, and seeing no one, he struck down the Egyptian." This could refer to Moses' looking within himself, at his own Jewish and Egyptian sides. Seeing that he was not a whole person true to one particular mission, Moses then smote his Egyptian side and emerged as the leader of the Jewish people. So, too, David is pulled by inner Jacob and Esau forces. In the end, thanks to Avigayil, Jacob prevails.

🙿 Assessing Avigayil

It could be argued that Avigayil's motives were not so pure. Her last words to David, "Remember your handmaid,"[45] sound like a wink. Although married, she seems very interested in David.

It has been pointed out that when Avigayil comes down the mountain, she comes down the "hidden" part of the mountain.[46] The word "hidden" evokes the text concerning a woman accused of infidelity (*sotah*): "and the matter is **hidden**, and she is impure," "*ve-nisterah ve-hi nitma'ah.*"[47] The term "hidden side of the mountain," in the Naval story, may allude to Avigayil's wish to betray her husband and take up with David.

This is apparent in the text. Consider the listing of David's wives.[48] His second wife is Avigayil, the wife of Naval the Carmeli. Extraordinary: although she is married to King David, she is still identified as the wife of Naval the Carmeli. In fact, they have a son together, Khilav.

For this reason, Khilav, David's second child, was not a candidate to be the next king, as opposed to Amnon and Absalom, David's first and third sons. Perhaps this has something to do with the feud that erupted between the first and third child.[49] Some explain that Amnon's rape of Tamar, the full-blood sister of Absalom, was Amnon's way of establishing his right to rulership. Sexual acts in Tanakh are often political in nature.[50] But Khilav, the second son, never gets involved in any of these struggles; he is simply not in the running. Rabbi David Silber has pointed out that simply identifying Khilav's mother as the wife of someone other than the king meant that Khilav would never even be considered for the throne. End of story.

Despite Avigayil's seemingly ulterior motives when she first encounters David, she can still be seen as having performed a glorious and holy act.

Note that the language used to describe Avigayil's initial approach to David is reminiscent of the phrasing used in the story of Rebeccah's courtship with Isaac.[51] Avigayil hurries (*va-temaher*) and alights (*va-tered*) from her donkey;[52] Rebeccah hurries (*va-temaher*) and lowered (*va-tored*)

---

45   I Samuel 25:31
46   I Samuel 25:20
47   Numbers 5:13
48   1I Samuel 3:2-5
49   1I Samuel 13
50   See Genesis 35:22, 1I Samuel 16:20-22.
51   Genesis 24:10-27. Many thanks to my dear friend Hillel Jaffe for planting the seed of this idea.
52   I Samuel 25:23

her jug.[53] Avigayil fell before David (*va-tipol*);[54] Rebeccah fell from the camel (*va-tipol*) upon meeting Isaac.[55]

Avigayil must work around her husband Naval; Rebeccah must deal with her brother Lavan. Naval and Lavan are both questionable characters, indeed, Naval's name is Lavan spelled backward.

In the end, Avigayil saves David from becoming a murderer, which might have resulted in David's losing the kingship. If she had been present, perhaps she could have saved the city of Nob, and even Saul. Who knows? Maybe the real nail in the coffin of Saul's kingship was the massacre at Nob. [56]

The meaning of Avigayil's name

Literally, what does the word "Avigayil" mean? Avigayil means, *av*, "father," or more loosely, the "parent," of *gal*, which is a "wave." A *galgal* is a wheel which constantly revolves. Avigayil is like a wave that turns things upside down. She turns David upside down, setting him right.

Avigayil is similar to another biblical character, Tamar. In the Genesis narrative, Tamar becomes the great teacher who inspires Judah to say those great words, "She is more righteous than I."[57] Avigayil is the one who teaches David that he ought to be the spiritual heir to Jacob, not Esau. And her efforts seem to succeed. David backs off from Naval.

In the very next chapter, David is once again in a position to take advantage of Saul. Avishai says to David, "Let me kill him [Saul]."[58] Without hesitation, David responds with the words, "Do not destroy him."[59]

Now, this differs dramatically from David's instincts in chapter 24, when he impulsively cuts Saul's coat. Many people see David's actions in chapter 26, when he takes Saul's spear and a cruse of water from Saul as he sleeps,[60] as worse behavior than he exhibits in chapter 24.

---

53   Genesis 24:18
54   I Samuel 25:23
55   Genesis 24:64
56   While the text indicates that Saul's kingship is terminiated for having spared Amalek (I Samuel 15:10-29), the midrash attributes Saul's death to his order to kill the priests of Nob. As the midrash notes, one of the reasons why Saul was slain was "because he slew the inhabitants of Nob, the city of priests," (Leviticus Rabbah 26:7).
57   Genesis 38:26 *tzadkah mimeni*
58   I Samuel 26:8
59   I Samuel 26:9 *al tashchiteihu*
60   I Samuel 26:12

The opposite may in fact be true. In chapter 24 David effectively does away with Saul's kingship. While some say chapter 26 echoes chapter 24, the two narratives are quite different. David displays a different attitude in chapter 26. His instinct in the later story leads him to tell Avishai not to harm Saul. True, in chapter 26 he expresses the hope that one day Saul will die through other means – maybe war, maybe old age.[61] He does say that. But there is no mention of David himself killing Saul; here, David leaves Saul's fate to God.

Thus, there is a major difference between chapters 24 and 26. In the former, David takes the kingdom, in the latter, he backs off. This may be due to the influence of Avigayil.

In fact, from the Avigayil story until the end of the first book of Samuel, which describes the death of Saul, David will not confront Saul again. He escapes to Philistia to plunder the enemies of Israel: The Geshuri, The Grizi, and Amalek[62] – but steers clear of Saul. Avigayil has softened David. Whether or not Avigayil's teaching remains with David after Saul's death is, in fact, the question of the second book of Samuel.[63]

---

61   I Samuel 26:10 *o yomo yavo va-met, o va-milchamah yered ve-nispah.*

62   I Samuel 27:8

63   This essay was originally delivered at the Yeshivat Chovevei Torah Rabbinical School Yemei Iyun on Bible and Jewish Thought in June, 2005. I am grateful to Rabbi David Silber, whose classes in Tanakh have given me much joy, and whose teachings have influenced my overall approach to understanding the Book of Samuel. Many thanks also to my Tanakh students at The Bayit, the Hebrew Institute of Riverdale, who in our weekly classes have challenged me and offered insights that helped shape this study.

Uzzah and the Ark
II Samuel 6

based on a lecture by **Rabbi Jack Bieler**

The Tanakh is generally concerned only with external manifestations of emotional reactions. People are depicted as disappointed, frustrated, angry, and happy. Emotional reactions are described but very seldom do characters have their motivations spelled out.

To fill in these gaps, to try to understand what motivates biblical characters, the Sages use midrash and legend.

The standard commentaries and the classic Rabbinic interpreters were very sophisticated in terms of approaches to text and use of psychology. Many commentaries reflect a highly developed sensitivity and sensibility to character motivation. Rabbi Aharon Lichtenstein once said that vast parts of Tanakh are closed to rabbis who haven't studied psychology. Such modes of thinking equip us to appreciate stories in far greater complexity.

We will attempt to bring this sensitivity to our study of what happened in Beit Shemesh after the Ark was returned by the Philistines.

The story begins with David's decision to move the Ark to Jerusalem.

II Samuel 6

1 And David again gathered together all the chosen men of Israel, thirty thousand.

א וַיֹּסֶף עוֹד דָּוִד אֶת-כָּל-בָּחוּר בְּיִשְׂרָאֵל שְׁלֹשִׁים אָלֶף.

2 And David arose, and went with all the people that were with him, from Ba'alei-Yehudah, to bring up from there the Ark of God, whereupon is called the Name, even the name of the LORD of hosts that sits upon the cherubim.

ב וַיָּקָם וַיֵּלֶךְ דָּוִד וְכָל-הָעָם אֲשֶׁר אִתּוֹ מִבַּעֲלֵי יְהוּדָה: לְהַעֲלוֹת מִשָּׁם אֵת אֲרוֹן הָאֱלֹהִים אֲשֶׁר-נִקְרָא שֵׁם שֵׁם יי צְבָאוֹת יֹשֵׁב הַכְּרֻבִים עָלָיו.

3 And they set the Ark of God
upon a new cart, and brought
it out of the house of Avinadav
that was in the hill; and
Uzzah and Achyo, the sons of
Avinadav, drove the new cart.

ג וַיַּרְכִּבוּ אֶת-אֲרוֹן הָאֱלֹהִים
אֶל-עֲגָלָה חֲדָשָׁה וַיִּשָּׂאֻהוּ
מִבֵּית אֲבִינָדָב אֲשֶׁר בַּגִּבְעָה:
וְעֻזָּא וְאַחְיוֹ בְּנֵי אֲבִינָדָב
נֹהֲגִים אֶת-הָעֲגָלָה חֲדָשָׁה.

They use a new wagon to move the Ark, not one that is grimy and dis-
gusting. You could say they are being respectful because it is brand new
– or disrespectful because it is, after all, only an ordinary wagon.

4 And they carried it out of the
house of Avinadav, which was in
the hill, with the Ark of God,
and Achyo went before the Ark.

ד וַיִּשָּׂאֻהוּ מִבֵּית אֲבִינָדָב אֲשֶׁר
בַּגִּבְעָה עִם אֲרוֹן הָאֱלֹהִים:
וְאַחְיוֹ הֹלֵךְ לִפְנֵי הָאָרוֹן.

"Carried" – What does this mean, if the Ark has already been placed
on the wagon? It is unclear what exactly is going on, and who is doing
what. We are told that Achyo is in front of the wagon, but where is Uzzah?

5 And David and all the house of
Israel played before the LORD
with all manner of instruments
made of cypress-wood, and
with harps, and with psalteries,
and with timbrels, and with
sistra, and with cymbals.

ה וְדָוִד וְכָל-בֵּית יִשְׂרָאֵל מְשַׂחֲקִים
לִפְנֵי יי בְּכֹל עֲצֵי בְרוֹשִׁים:
וּבְכִנֹּרוֹת וּבִנְבָלִים וּבְתֻפִּים
וּבִמְנַעַנְעִים וּבְצֶלְצֶלִים.

David and the people celebrate. The band plays and they dance before
the Ark.

6 And when they came to the
threshing-floor of Nakhon,
Uzzah put forth his hand to
the Ark of God, and took hold
of it; for the oxen stumbled.

ו וַיָּבֹאוּ עַד-גֹּרֶן נָכוֹן: וַיִּשְׁלַח
עֻזָּה אֶל-אֲרוֹן הָאֱלֹהִים וַיֹּאחֶז
בּוֹ-כִּי שָׁמְטוּ הַבָּקָר.

Why does Uzzah grab the Ark? The animals pulling the wagon have
caused the Ark to be unstable. Uzzah is worried that the Ark will fall off
of the wagon, so he tries to take hold of it. Perhaps he is in that very position to prevent such a circumstance. He wants to protect the Ark from

falling, so, instead of leading the wagon with Achyo, he travels alongside the wagon to make sure the Ark is properly supported.

7 And the anger of the LORD was kindled against Uzzah; and God smote him there for his error; and there he died by the Ark of God.

ז וַיִּחַר-אַף יי בְּעֻזָּה וַיַּכֵּהוּ שָׁם הָאֱלֹהִים עַל-הַשַּׁל: וַיָּמָת שָׁם עִם אֲרוֹן הָאֱלֹהִים.

God does not like Uzzah's actions. Uzzah is struck down in the the presence of the Ark when he tries to protect it. Somehow, this angers God. Would it have been preferable for the Ark to fall off the wagon? What did Uzzah do that was so bad?

8 And David was displeased, because the LORD had broken forth upon Uzzah; and that place was called Peretz-Uzzah, unto this day.

ח וַיִּחַר לְדָוִד עַל אֲשֶׁר פָּרַץ יי פֶּרֶץ בְּעֻזָּה: וַיִּקְרָא לַמָּקוֹם הַהוּא פֶּרֶץ עֻזָּה עַד הַיּוֹם הַזֶּה.

The word translated here as "displeased," "*va-yichar*," is an interesting word. What, exactly, is David feeling? *Charon af* is anger.[1] *Va-yichar* is something different. It is a certain type of disturbance, a disorientation. David's equanimity has been disturbed. He is upset. He is depressed. He feels that something is very wrong. Although we see David's emotional response, we are not told the cause. We are not told why David feels Uzzah's death so strongly, or why David memorializes the place forever as "*Peretz Uzzah*," literally, "Uzzah's Breach."

9 And David was afraid of the LORD that day; and he said: 'How shall the Ark of the LORD come to me?'

ט וַיִּרָא דָוִד אֶת-יי בַּיּוֹם הַהוּא: וַיֹּאמֶר אֵיךְ יָבוֹא אֵלַי אֲרוֹן יי.

David now fears God. This implies that earlier, he wasn't fearing God. Was that somehow wrong of David?

At this point, David fears that moving the Ark again may cause another disaster.

---

1   *Charon* is "heat" in Hebrew, and *af* is "nose." *Charon af* denotes the heavy, hot breathing (through the nose) during anger.

10 So David would not remove the
Ark of the LORD to him into
the city of David; but David
carried it aside into the house
of Oved-Edom the Gittite.

י וְלֹא-אָבָה דָוִד לְהָסִיר אֵלָיו
אֶת-אֲרוֹן יי עַל-עִיר דָּוִד: וַיַּטֵּהוּ
דָוִד בֵּית עֹבֵד-אֱדֹם הַגִּתִּי.

So David wonders: Maybe God does not want the Ark taken to Jerusalem.

Note that there is no prophet instructing David in how to proceed.
David, left to his own devices, is at a loss. He had assumed it was a good
thing to bring the Ark to Jerusalem, and now it is not so clear.

David interprets Uzzah's death as a message from God that something
is wrong. But what?

One possibility is that David should not have moved the Ark at all, or
at least not tried to bring it to Jerusalem. So David decides to take a time-
out and store the Ark in the closest place alongside the road.

Of course, that is also risky. Remember, 57,000 people died for gazing
at the Ark in Beit Shemesh.[2] In Ashdod, the Philistines were smitten
when they had the Ark in their possession.[3] So. it takes a good deal of
courage to house the Ark – although it does not sound as if David consults at all with the Ark's new host, Oved-Edom.

11 And the Ark of the LORD
remained in the house of
Oved-Edom the Gittite three
months; and the LORD blessed
Oved-Edom, and all his house.

יא וַיֵּשֶׁב אֲרוֹן יי בֵּית עֹבֵד אֱדֹם
הַגִּתִּי–שְׁלֹשָׁה חֳדָשִׁים: וַיְבָרֶךְ יי
אֶת-עֹבֵד אֱדֹם וְאֶת-כָּל-בֵּיתוֹ.

The result of the experiment is that Oved-Edom prospers. In Genesis,
we learned that success is a sign of God's blessing. Avimelekh perceived
that God was with Avraham because he was very successful.[4] So David
makes the following calculation: If Oved-Edom's crops die and everyone
perishes of plagues, this is not a good place for the Ark.

But if everything goes well, and Oved-Edom is blessed by the Ark's
presence – maybe that means the Ark should be left there. Maybe this is
truly the Ark's proper place, and not Jerusalem.

---

2   I Samuel 6:19
3   I Samuel 5:6
4   Genesis 21:22

12 And it was told to King David: 'The LORD has blessed the house of Oved-Edom, and all that is his, because of the Ark of God.' And David went and brought up the Ark of God from the house of Oved-Edom into the city of David with joy.

יב וַיֻּגַּד לַמֶּלֶךְ דָּוִד לֵאמֹר בֵּרַךְ יי אֶת-בֵּית עֹבֵד אֱדֹם וְאֶת-כָּל-אֲשֶׁר-לוֹ בַּעֲבוּר אֲרוֹן הָאֱלֹהִים: וַיֵּלֶךְ דָּוִד וַיַּעַל אֶת-אֲרוֹן הָאֱלֹהִים: מִבֵּית עֹבֵד אֱדֹם עִיר דָּוִד בְּשִׂמְחָה.

David comes to an interesting conclusion: Because Oved-Edom prospered when the Ark was in his possession, the Ark may now be brought to Jerusalem. That is clearly David's line of reasoning – although no argument is given as to why Oved-Edom's prosperity might not mean the precise opposite; namely, that God wants the Ark to remain with Oved-Edom.

13 And so it was , that when those who carried the Ark of the LORD had gone six paces, he sacrificed an ox and a fatling.

יג וַיְהִי כִּי צָעֲדוּ נֹשְׂאֵי אֲרוֹן-יי שִׁשָּׁה צְעָדִים: וַיִּזְבַּח שׁוֹר וּמְרִיא.

In moving the Ark this time, much care is employed. After completing six steps, sacrifices are offered to God. With every six steps, another sacrifice is offered. It is a tentative journey, each step is a question: Can we go this far? Nothing is taken for granted.

14 And David danced before the LORD with all his might; and David was girded with a linen *ephod*.

יד וְדָוִד מְכַרְכֵּר בְּכָל-עֹז לִפְנֵי יי: וְדָוִד חָגוּר אֵפוֹד בָּד.

David dances with all of his strength before God. He is attired in a special costume; the apron with shoulder straps reminiscent of the garment worn by the High Priest. This all implies that David did not conduct himself in this fashion the first time around. These changes in procedure seem to be working.

15 So David and all the house of Israel brought up the Ark of the LORD with shouting, and with the sound of the horn.

טו וְדָוִד וְכָל-בֵּית יִשְׂרָאֵל מַעֲלִים אֶת-אֲרוֹן יי: בִּתְרוּעָה וּבְקוֹל שׁוֹפָר.

The use of the shofar is also interesting. We don't normally associate the sound of a shofar with rejoicing. On Rosh Hashanah the voice of the shofar is not a voice of happiness. The Talmud says that Sisera's keening mother produced the shofar sound when, while waiting in vain for Sisera, she realized that he would never return.[5]

Apparently, the procedural changes employed in this second move are significant enough to transfer the Ark successfully. There is no plague; no one dies. The dangerous situation seems to have passed.

So that is the story as it appears in Samuel.

Protocol Overhaul

How are we to understand this story?

It seems that no rules were set forth for moving the sacred Ark, and David had to muddle through as best he could. If Uzzah's punishment was an indication to David of problematic behavior, then David's challenge was to interpret the significance of events in order to determine God's response.

As Nachmanides explains,[6] most activities with which people occupy themselves are not written down in any book. It is simply impossible for the Torah to describe every action ever performed since the creation of the world. A certain amount of extrapolation is required for those times when events are not clearly delineated, as with our present story.

In the Book of Chronicles,[7] David explicitly draws the conclusion that to move the Ark successfully, the transportation protocol must be changed.

In Chronicles,[8] by the way, the Ark's three month stint on Oved-Edom's farm is not directly connected to David's decision to complete the Ark's passage to Jerusalem. Chronicles instead speaks in terms of David's military success against the Philistines. In this scenario, in order to take the measure of his status with God, David uses his success in warfare as the yardstick. That, rather than the welfare of Oved Edom's farm, may indeed be a more accurate gauge of God's disposition towards David with regard to the Ark. Oved-Edom is, after all, a third party, tangential to the story taking place between David and God.

---

5   Rosh Hashanah 33b, referencing Judges 5:28
6   Commentary to Deuteronomy 6:18
7   I Chronicles 15:11-13
8   I Chronicles 13-15

Causality and Misfortune

Why does David take Uzzah's death personally? Is this egocentricity or solipsism? If something bad happens to somebody else, is it generally David's fault?

Well, when David took a census without God's approval, the whole Israelite nation suffered.[9] There *is* a sense that the buck stops with the CEO, with David, the king.

There is no evidence from the text that there might be another reason for Uzzah's death. Without any intimation of illness or accident regarding Uzzah, David concludes that his death is a sign of Divine displeasure. In the wake of Uzzah's tragic death, David feels that the only proper course of action is to change the manner in which the Ark is accompanied. It is a huge leap on David's part to interpret incidents as a critique from God, and such interpretations can be very dangerous.

When the Talmud[10] says that a person should examine his deeds when bad things happen in his life, this is a challenge. It is not always easy to pinpoint the exact behavior that may have offended God. Some people say it is good enough to check whether the *mezuzot* on our doorposts[11] are in good shape, to see whether their scrolls are still kosher. I think that to check something external downplays personal responsibility for one's own actions. It is certainly easier to project internal realities onto the outside world – like searching for one's keys under a streetlamp, simply because the light is better, than to search in the dark alley where they actually fell.

In fact, I want to note that the notion of causality, that misfortune should be seen as a punishment for wrongdoing, is very problematic, particularly when discussing a text in an educational setting. Within the context of David and the Ark, when God is acting directly, it makes plenty of sense. However, we find this view of causality throughout the Torah, the Tanakh, and the works of the Sages and it can be dangerous. Extrapolating from the premise that there are rewards for doing good, and punishments for doing bad, one might think that if something bad is happening it must be due to one's sins. But that kind of thinking becomes very psychologically punishing. You have to be very careful, particularly if you're teaching children, to temper that idea of causality with plenty of other possible interpretations to explain difficult events.

---

9 II Samuel 24:17
10 Eruvin 13b
11 cf. Deuteronomy 6:9

Dangers of the Holy

If we want to consider this more closely, we need to review the Ark's immediate past prior to the move.

At this point in time, the Ark has already caused major problems in certain circles, beginning from the time Eli's sons take it out to war.[12]

God is already angry with Eli's sons when they set out to battle. God swears that they will not be forgiven even if they repent.[13] I think God manipulates them, much as He manipulated Pharaoh. Israel's spirit is at a very low ebb and God wants to teach them a lesson. Eli's sons die in battle and the Ark is appropriated by the Philistines.

For seven months the Philistines try to hold onto the Ark. They suffer plagues and catastrophes and their idols are inexplicably smashed. Finally, they say, "Enough!"

The Ark is placed upon a new wagon, and, lo and behold, it finds its way back to the Israelites. People in Beit Shemesh say: "Oh, look at that," and go right back to work.

Apparently this is an inappropriate response. A plague follows and everybody dies. People in Beit Shemesh say: "Get this Ark out of here! We don't know how to handle it." They send for help. You can imagine that people are very afraid of the Ark at this point.

So when Uzzah dies, this is not the first indication that the Ark is very potent and everyone must be very careful in their behavior when approaching the Holy.

There are several other examples throughout Tanakh of the importance of keeping a respectful distance from the sacred.

Obviously the story of Nadav and Avihu[14] is a cautionary tale[15] that there is no room for error when confronting the sacred, especially on the part of the priests.

---

12   I Samuel 4:4

13   I Samuel 3:14

14   Leviticus 6

15   The idea that arrogance motivated Nadav and Avihu, is an interpretation. Looking at the text, it just says that they "offered strange fire." It's not clear what that is and why they did it. So, that fits my original thesis about the unexplained motivations of biblical characters. Why did Nadav and Avihu do what they did? The Sages have different views about this and they try to base their opinions on various hints in the text. But there is no way to answer questions like these. It can be frustrating, yet compelling as well. Large powerful things happen and they are puzzles to us. There are all sort of hypotheses generated and we are not sure whether any or all of them are really correct. It is very engaging

There is the prohibition against getting too close to Mount Sinai.[16] The rules received right before the Revelation had the effect of creating a buffer between the people and holy space. No one could touch the mountain. Anyone who passed a certain line would die. The lesson is that one must be very careful in coming close to God's location.

According to Maimonides, the *mishkan*, the Tabernacle which held the Ark, was considered a portable Mount Sinai. In fact, according to him, during the course of the desert years, additional commandments were revealed. There is a debate as to whether these were actually new commandments that had not been revealed on Mt. Sinai, or whether the Ark was delivering a review of already received teachings. The fact is, if the *mishkan* was a continuation of Mt. Sinai, that would mean that the same rules that applied to Mt. Sinai, including the limitations of who could approach, would continue to apply.

In the Book of Daniel, it states explicitly in the text that Belshazzar, the king of Babylon, used the utensils from the Beit Hamikdash for a party[17] – and that night the Persians and the Medes came and killed him.[18]

Also, the Talmud states that were one to put the wrong ingredient into the incense, one would be liable for the death penalty.[19]

So there is an aura of danger that is associated with the *mishkan* and its utensils. There is little margin for error when one approaches them.

Similarly, the Talmud tells how when the priesthood had become a political appointment, every year the High Priest would be dragged from the Holy of Holies, because he would make some sort of mistake and die inside. So, on a certain level, one might ask, who would want that job? Who would want to take such chances? Priests were supposed to be very, very careful, but there is no denying that there was considerable danger attached to these prestigious duties.

The story of Uzzah fits into this framework. The Ark is always potentially destructive, and getting close to it is a dangerous undertaking.

---

and, with the proper basis, one has the right to suggest opinions about Nadav and Avihu, and Uzzah for that matter, but there has to be textual proof.

16   Exodus 19:10-13
17   Daniel 5:2
18   Daniel 5:30
19   Keritut 6a. Some people say that when one recites the listing of the ingredients of the incense, one must make no mistakes. They say that since we can no longer perform the ritual incense burning and in it's place we can only recite the ingredients, then saying the wrong word is comparable to inserting the wrong ingredient – which would render one liable for the death penalty. Some people would just as soon not recite the incense ingredients for this reason.

One detail that the text mentions is that the Ark is placed on a new wagon.[20] This mirrors the Philistine's behavior with the Ark.[21] Could it be that David thought – and some commentaries say this – that if this worked for the Philistines, maybe this was God's preference? Are standards to be framed according to immediate anecdotal evidence[22] – or is there an overriding standard to follow because the Torah discusses how to transport the Ark?

The Torah, remember, specifically states that the priests must bear the Ark on their shoulders.[23] Accordingly, poles are required to remain fixed on the Ark[24] and the Ark should not be touched, even by the Levites who are charged to carry it. They had to carry it on their shoulders, touching only the poles, and never the Ark itself.

When assigning the Levitical clan of Kehat as bearers of the holy things, the Torah is explicit: "and they should not touch the Holy and die."[25] Even amongst the people who are empowered and charged to perform this service, no accident will be tolerated. "Oops, sorry, I just bumped into it," is unacceptable.

Nepotism and Regret

All we know about Uzzah is his family genealogy and the fact that when he accompanies the Ark, at some point it begins to slip and Uzzah puts out his hand to steady it.

It sounds as if Uzzah acts completely within the bounds of proper behavior, yet a very powerful negative response is generated. Had Uzzah merely collapsed we might have speculated that he had some kind of health problem, but the text insists that God smote him. God was clearly angry. Some implication begs to be drawn from this story.

One explanatory approach is that David initially created the wrong kind of atmosphere for moving the Ark, and tragically, Uzzah suffered the consequences. In other words, David is disturbed because he realizes that Uzzah is a casualty of the mistaken way David originally undertook the maneuver. David, in this scenario, misjudged the logistics of trans-

---

20   II Samuel 6:3

21   I Samuel 6:7

22   Perhaps we have no business emulating the Philistines at all, even when they get things right.

23   Numbers 7:9

24   Exodus 25:14

25   Numbers 4:15

porting the Ark. In the wake of Uzzah's death, David carefully tries to correct his error.

Later, in Chronicles, we discover exactly who Uzzah is. He is not a Levite; he hails from Judah.[26] That's a problem – transporting the Ark is a job for Levites.

It happened that the Ark was in Uzzah's father's territory.[27] Although it was convenient for someone from that family to see to the transport, it was a tragic miscalculation.

Further, we note that Uzzah is kin to David. Perusing the genealogy,[28] one discovers that Uzzah's father, Avinadav, is David's older brother. Avinadav is the second son and David is the youngest. And of course, these are Avinadav's sons who are designated to take care of the Ark. So it is the loss of his own nephew that David takes so personally.

Uzzah's kinship to David adds extra drama. Perhaps David chose this family for the job because of his connection. Once it turns out badly, it might be appropriate for David to say: "This is something for which I must take responsibility, and must repair."

I've tried to demonstrate that it is extremely difficult to discern from the text itself precisely what sort of error took place. And so, therefore, something has to be derived, something has to be teased out of the text.

We will now turn our attention to different theories offered about the error involved in the initial attempt to move the Ark. These theories can be divided into different general approaches.

An intellectual mistake

The first approach is to explain that David's procedural mistakes were intellectual in origin.

Radak, for instance, presents this point of view. He explains that David's mistakes boil down to misinterpreting the arrival of the Ark. When the Philistines sent the Ark, it arrived without any problems. The Philistines did the best they could without the benefit of the Torah teachings on how to treat the Ark of God. Out of respect for the God of the Ark, the Philistines sent along offerings of gold. Therefore, God did not object.

Israel, however, had a responsibility to look for the precedence within their own tradition. Instead, they only looked at the immediate history with the Philistines. God's answer to this was: "This is wrong. The Ark

---

26   I Chronicles 2:13 (Avinadav is Uzzah's father)
27   II Samuel 6:3
28   I Chronicles 2:3-15

is unstable because the whole situation is precarious." Uzzah tried to support the Ark, but the enterprise was misguided from the start.

Was David unaware of the Torah's rules of how to transport the Ark?

Radak explains David's mistake as one of reasoning – although David knew what the Torah said, he thought it would be okay to move the Ark differently this time.

David had figured that the Ark had to be carried upon the shoulders of the Levites in the desert in order to distinguish it from the Tabernacle, an item less holy than the Ark which was regularly transported on wagons.

David inferred: When I have both the Tabernacle and the Ark, the Ark has to be treated in a qualitatively finer manner than the Tabernacle. Here, I am only transporting the Ark (the Tabernacle had already been moved to Jerusalem). Since it is not necessary to make a distinction between the two items, the Ark may now rest on a wagon.

Or maybe he thought: It got this far on a wagon; let it continue on a wagon.

Another suggestion is that David made this erroneous decision because he was comparing his generation's spiritual level to that of the Israelites in the desert. He assumed that it was appropriate for the generation of the desert – which had experienced Revelation – to carry the Ark on their shoulders. But, reasoned David, the present generation cannot claim the right to get that close to the Ark. Therefore, it is better to keep the Ark at a respectful remove. This is the same principle we use today when we kiss a Torah scroll with an intermediate object (like a prayer book), or when we use a prayer shawl to handle a parchment that has accidentally separated from its Torah scroll. Indirect handling is considered the most respectful method.

The commentary *Eitz Yosef* says the Ark was empty. David made sure to take out the Tablets of the Law before he moved it. Given that the Ark was empty, David thought: "The Ark is only a receptacle. Once emptied, I can put it in the moving van. Levites need not carry it on their shoulders; that only applies when the Ark is laden with the holy things."

And there are surely other possibilities. One can probably imagine plenty more lines of reasoning that might lead to the same mistaken conclusion.[29]

---

29   These explanations of David's error, which involve arriving at a plausible but wrong explanation of the law, remind us of the Talmudic explanation of the dramatic error of Solomon, his son. The Torah says the king should not have too many wives or too many horses. And Solomon says: "I'm too smart to make mistakes – breaking these rules won't affect me." And of course, Solomon loses his direction and becomes corrupted. The Talmud uses this to indict the

So one approach to the question of Uzzah's death is that a mistaken conclusion was drawn. There are different conjectures presented here about how this can have happened, and one can make up another five or ten more. The point is that a miscalculation took place.

Seen this way, the whole Uzzah story is a cautionary tale about drawing erroneous conclusions from assumptions and then manipulating those conclusions to take shortcuts. Uzzah's death resulted from David's intellectual mistake.

An emotional mistake

A second approach, offered by the commentary *Akeidat Yitzchak* contrasts the two verses in the story that describe celebrations before the Ark. First:

II Samuel 6

5 And David and all the house of Israel **played before the LORD** with all manner of instruments made of cypress-wood, and with harps, and with psalteries, and with timbrels, and with sistra, and with cymbals.

ה וְדָוִד וְכָל-בֵּית יִשְׂרָאֵל מְשַׂחֲקִים לִפְנֵי יי בְּכֹל עֲצֵי בְרוֹשִׁים: וּבְכִנֹּרוֹת וּבִנְבָלִים וּבְתֻפִּים וּבִמְנַעַנְעִים וּבְצֶלְצֶלִים.

But later:

II Samuel 6

12 And it was told to King David: 'The LORD has blessed the house of Oved-Edom, and all that is his, because of the Ark

יב וַיֻּגַּד לַמֶּלֶךְ דָּוִד לֵאמֹר בֵּרַךְ יי אֶת-בֵּית עֹבֵד אֱדֹם וְאֶת-כָּל- אֲשֶׁר-לוֹ בַּעֲבוּר אֲרוֹן הָאֱלֹהִים:

---

whole notion of supplying *ta'amei ha-mitzvot*, the underlying reasons for the commandments.

Saul also manipulates legal reasoning to his own advantage. Kings may be particularly susceptible to this type of thinking. They're extremely self-centered and are used to having their commands obeyed and may think that they understand everything.

Certainly Rabbinic tradition prefers an explicit Divine decree over any sort of logical derivation. If there is a choice between proving something written in the text or by interpretive methodologies, the written command is considered more reliable and solid. It may be less interesting, but it is also less subject to error.

of God.' And David went and
brought up the Ark of God from
the house of Oved-Edom into
the city of David **with joy**.

וַיֵּלֶךְ דָּוִד וַיַּעַל אֶת-אֲרוֹן הָאֱלֹהִים
מִבֵּית עֹבֵד אֱדֹם עִיר דָּוִד בְּשִׂמְחָה.

Is there a difference between these two celebrations?

The *Akeidat Yitzchak* reminds us of another verse, this one from Exodus, from the story of the golden calf:

Exodus 32

6 And they rose up early on
the morrow, and offered
burnt-offerings, and brought
peace-offerings; and the
people sat down to eat and to
drink, **and rose up to play**.

ו וַיַּשְׁכִּימוּ מִמָּחֳרָת וַיַּעֲלוּ עֹלֹת
וַיַּגִּשׁוּ שְׁלָמִים: וַיֵּשֶׁב הָעָם
לֶאֱכֹל וְשָׁתוֹ וַיָּקֻמוּ לְצַחֵק.

The word translated "play" in Exodus is not exactly the same word used to describe David and his musicians – but it's very close. They only differ in one very similarly-sounding letter – a (שׁ) *sin* and a (צ) *tzaddi*.

There is a negative connotation attached to the Exodus phrasing, *le-tzachek*, and the *Akeidat Yitzhak* applies that connotation to David's first celebration, deducing that it was unbridled and lacking in holiness. The celebration may have been very enthusiastic and emotional, but it was not sufficiently elevated.

Note that the word "play" is not used in the description for the second attempt to move the Ark. Instead it says,[30] "And David brought the Ark into the city with **joy**," "*be-simchah*." It doesn't say "*me-sachakim*" any more. It is a different kind of celebration.

Another difference between the two celebrations is leadership.

Describing the first attempt to move the Ark, it says:[31] "David and all the House of Israel." The people share equal billing with David. It is possible that the celebration of the throng may not have been appropriate.

The second time, David leads and sets the proper tone. The proof is that the people are blasting on rams' horns.[32] Rather than playing on "all manner of instruments made of cypress-wood," harps, psalteries, timbrels, sistra, and cymbals like before,[33] the instruments now being played

30 II Samuel 6:12
31 II Samuel 6:5
32 II Samuel 6:15
33 II Samuel 6:5

are those used in religious ritual and martial situations: rams' horns. This celebration is informed by a greater sense of divinity. This is no longer a self-serving emotional experience in which people lose all sense of discipline and propriety.

So originally, there was an emotional problem. David hadn't set the proper tone – and the moving of the Ark was reduced to an excuse for a party.

David learned that, as leader, it was up to him to maintain a certain tone, and he worked to meet that expectation the next time around.

Combination intellectual/emotional error

There is another position which combines the previous two.

In the Talmud[34] Rava asks: "Why was David punished?" (Note the phrasing of the question: Nothing happened to David personally. If Uzzah was his nephew, at most, this was an indirect blow. But from Rava's perspective, this blow was directed at David.)

Talmud Bavli, Sotah 35a

Rava expounded: Why was David punished? Because he called words of Torah 'songs', as it is said (Psalms 119:54): 'Your statutes have been my songs in the house of my pilgrimage.' The Holy One, blessed be He, said to him, 'Words of Torah, of which it is written (Proverbs 23:5): "Will you set your eyes upon it? It is gone," you recite as songs! I will cause you to stumble in a matter which even school-children know.' For it is written (Numbers 7:9): "But to the sons of Kehat he gave none, because the service of the sanctuary etc." and yet [David] brought it in a wagon.

דרש רבא מפני מה נענש דוד מפני שקרא לדברי תורה זמירות שנאמר (תהילים קיט) זמירות היו לי חוקיך בבית מגורי אמר לו הקב"ה ד"ת שכתוב בהן (משלי כג) התעיף עיניך בו ואיננו אתה קורא אותן זמירות הריני מכשילך בדבר שאפילו תינוקות של בית רבן יודעין אותו דכתיב (במדבר ז) ולבני קהת לא נתן כי עבודת הקודש וגו' ואיהו אתייה בעגלתא

---

34   Sotah 35a

What is Rava saying? Here is the verse from Psalms which equates Torah to songs:

Psalms 119

54 Your statutes have been my songs in the house of my pilgrimage

נד זְמִרוֹת הָיוּ-לִי חֻקֶּיךָ בְּבֵית מְגוּרָי.

Why was this wrong? If people see the commandments as something musical, isn't that attractive?

Rava says that David was making a real mistake. Calling laws "songs" indicates a lack of seriousness for something understood by Rava (citing Proverbs) to be difficult to grasp. If you divert your attention from words of Torah, they can just vanish. Rava is alerting the student of Torah to the fact that one's sober attention must remain fixed upon Torah, and that romanticising Torah will result in the teachings slipping away from the unwary student.[35]

So God decrees that David will stumble on something "familiar to every schoolchild," a law that everyone who has memorized the Torah[36] will know: That the Ark was to be carried on the shoulders of the sons of Kehat. But David, unaware, brings the Ark on a wagon. David's untoward light-heartedness concerning words of Torah leads to ignorance, an ignorance that proves fatal.

According to this view, the problem is not orgiastic dancing or celebrations out of control. It is simply that David did not approach the matter with the proper gravity, a reflection of David's own inclinations toward the aesthetic. It was not appropriate for David to project his personal values onto God's legal system. Doing so was a fundamental mistake. It showed a lack of respect. If David had had more respect, he would have checked for precedent.

Instead, David made a spontaneous decision on how to move the Ark. It seemed beautiful and wonderful and right to have the people at hand move the Ark and to take out the instruments and dance. David didn't understand the frame of mind with which commandments must be approached, and this led him to a tragic miscalculation. These actions reflect David's global conception of Torah.

---

35   Compare the teaching in Chapter 24 of Avot D'Rabbi Natan, the famous book of midrash on The Ethics of the Fathers: "Words of Torah are as hard to acquire as fine gold, and as easy to lose as delicate crystal." This saying is appropriately attributed to Elisha Ben Avuyah, who is well known for having lost faith with the words of the Torah.

36   Whether our schoolchildren should know the Book of Numbers by heart is an interesting pedagogical discussion for another occasion.

David was a poet and a musician. He was the one who played when Saul was depressed; David charmed Saul out of his moods of melancholy. Being musical imparts a certain perspective on life. However, no matter how talented David was and no matter how profound was the music that informed him, he had a duty to contain himself. It was not David's place to impose his language upon God's language. The music was apparently more important to David than the Ark of the Lord. It was not appropriate: The mitzvah comes before the music, and not the other way around.

When David was in exile, the Torah was still beautiful to him and it sang to him. This is a very beautiful idea, illustrating his righteousness. But Rava sees something else, too. He sees that David loses balance. Balance is a particular requirement for the leader of the people.

Summary

We've seen different explanations for Uzzah's death. The story of Uzzah is very mysterious. It is still not clear what really happened. Uzzah makes a mistake. David also errs. David recognizes something is wrong and he changes the way the Ark is brought into Jerusalem. But it is important to try to establish the precise dynamics here and attempt to pinpoint the nature of the mistake.

This brings us to an important pedagogical question.

When one simply teaches the facts of the story: Uzzah does wrong, David feels bad, and he fixes it... what do we learn from that? Seen this way, the story is reduced to bits of information which I irreverently refer to as "holy trivia."

Who touched the Ark and died? Uzzah. Whose fault was it? David's. What happened? David went back and escorted the Ark more respectfully. These are all inert pieces of information that certainly do not speak to me, or to many other people.

The important questions – the "why" questions – don't have just one answer. There are many answers. One of my favorite examples of this is in the Talmud's discussion of why Haman was invited to Esther's wine parties.[37] Would it not have been better for Esther to snub Haman and speak to Ahasuerus alone? Thirteen different positions are presented! And the last position states that all of the preceding explanations are true.

In other words, a person's motivations can be extremely complex, with multiple ideas and strategies occurring on either a conscious or a subconscious level.

---

37   Megillah 15b

If instead of focusing on the details, we focus on the motivations, on the "why," we can have a living discussion, because there is no fixed answer to that question. There are many answers.

When a student says to me, "The answer is..." I say, "No. *An* answer is..." Whenever I present a topic, I never present only one correct way of viewing it. But if someone comes up with an opinion and there's nothing to disprove it, then it is valid.

The study of Tanakh is a conversation. Those who base ideas on the text may participate, and the understanding added to the conversation by these new ideas is legitmate.

David's Request to Build the Temple
II Samuel 7

Rabbi Joshua Berman

It is nearly impossible to fully grasp the very confusing chapter of the Book of Samuel dealing with David's request to build a Temple unless we first turn our attention to some of the underlying concepts of the Temple. These concepts are not addressed in the standard commentaries. We will begin by reading the chapter and raising a number of difficulties. Then we will examine the purpose of the Temple and see whether we can shed some new light on the subject.

After David establishes his kingdom, wins some wars and builds his palace, we read the following:

II Samuel 7

1 And it came to pass, when the king dwelt in his house, and the LORD had given him rest from all his enemies round about,

א וַיְהִי כִּי-יָשַׁב הַמֶּלֶךְ בְּבֵיתוֹ: וַיי הֵנִיחַ-לוֹ מִסָּבִיב מִכָּל-אֹיְבָיו.

2 that the king said to Nathan the prophet: 'See now, I dwell in a house of cedar, but the ark of God dwells within curtains.'

ב וַיֹּאמֶר הַמֶּלֶךְ אֶל-נָתָן הַנָּבִיא רְאֵה נָא אָנֹכִי יוֹשֵׁב בְּבֵית אֲרָזִים: וַאֲרוֹן הָאֱלֹהִים יֹשֵׁב בְּתוֹךְ הַיְרִיעָה.

The Ark is still in the Tabernacle (*mishkan*), constructed by Moses generations earlier.

II Samuel 7

3 And Nathan said to the king: 'Go, do all that is in your heart; for the LORD is with you.'

ג וַיֹּאמֶר נָתָן אֶל-הַמֶּלֶךְ כֹּל אֲשֶׁר בִּלְבָבְךָ לֵךְ עֲשֵׂה: כִּי יי עִמָּךְ.

4 And it came to pass the same night, that the word of the LORD came to Nathan, saying:

ד וַיְהִי בַּלַּיְלָה הַהוּא: וַיְהִי דְּבַר-יי אֶל-נָתָן לֵאמֹר.

5 'Go and tell My servant
David: Thus says the LORD:
Shall you build Me a house
for Me to dwell in?

ה לֵךְ וְאָמַרְתָּ אֶל-עַבְדִּי אֶל-
דָּוִד כֹּה אָמַר יְיָ: הַאַתָּה
תִּבְנֶה-לִּי בַיִת לְשִׁבְתִּי?

Nathan tells David he will be able to build the Temple. And then, that night, God tells Nathan to give David a very different message. This implies that prophets are sometimes wrong. Prophetic fallibility appears several places in Tanakh, and is an interesting topic, but our purpose to-day is to understand why God does not want David to build the Temple. God does not give Nathan a simple veto to pass on to David, but rather a detailed response:

II Samuel 7

6 for I have not dwelt in a
house since the day that I
brought up the children of
Israel out of Egypt, even to
this day, but have walked in
a tent and in a tabernacle.

ו כִּי לֹא יָשַׁבְתִּי בְּבַיִת לְמִיּוֹם
הַעֲלֹתִי אֶת-בְּנֵי יִשְׂרָאֵל
מִמִּצְרַיִם וְעַד הַיּוֹם הַזֶּה: וָאֶהְיֶה
מִתְהַלֵּךְ בְּאֹהֶל וּבְמִשְׁכָּן.

7 In all places wherein I have
walked among all the children of
Israel, spoke I a word with any
of the tribes of Israel, whom I
commanded to feed My people
Israel, saying: Why have you
not built Me a house of cedar?

ז בְּכֹל אֲשֶׁר-הִתְהַלַּכְתִּי בְּכָל-בְּנֵי
יִשְׂרָאֵל הֲדָבָר דִּבַּרְתִּי אֶת-אַחַד
שִׁבְטֵי יִשְׂרָאֵל אֲשֶׁר צִוִּיתִי לִרְעוֹת
אֶת-עַמִּי אֶת-יִשְׂרָאֵל לֵאמֹר:
לָמָּה לֹא-בְנִיתֶם לִי בֵּית אֲרָזִים?

In other words, "I had a dwelling." There was a tabernacle, *mishkan*, but not a proper house, *bayit*. And further: God had never complained about the status quo. Still, it is not clear why God says no.

II Samuel 7

8 Now therefore thus shall you
say to My servant David:
Thus says the LORD of
hosts: I took you from
the sheepcote, from following the
sheep, that you should be prince
over My people, over Israel.

ח וְעַתָּה כֹּה-תֹאמַר לְעַבְדִּי לְדָוִד
כֹּה אָמַר יְיָ צְבָאוֹת אֲנִי לְקַחְתִּיךָ
מִן-הַנָּוֶה מֵאַחַר הַצֹּאן: לִהְיוֹת
נָגִיד עַל-עַמִּי עַל-יִשְׂרָאֵל.

9 And I have been with you
wherever you went, and have cut
off all your enemies from before
you; and I will make you a great
name, like the name of the great
ones that are in the earth.

ט וָאֶהְיֶה עִמְּךָ בְּכֹל אֲשֶׁר הָלַכְתָּ
וָאַכְרִתָה אֶת-כָּל-אֹיְבֶיךָ
מִפָּנֶיךָ: וְעָשִׂתִי לְךָ שֵׁם גָּדוֹל
כְּשֵׁם הַגְּדֹלִים אֲשֶׁר בָּאָרֶץ.

10 And I will appoint a place for
My people Israel, and will plant
them, that they may dwell
in their own place, and be
disquieted no more; neither shall
the children of wickedness afflict
them any more, as at the first,

י וְשַׂמְתִּי מָקוֹם לְעַמִּי לְיִשְׂרָאֵל
וּנְטַעְתִּיו וְשָׁכַן תַּחְתָּיו וְלֹא יִרְגַּז
עוֹד: וְלֹא-יֹסִיפוּ בְנֵי-עַוְלָה
לְעַנּוֹתוֹ כַּאֲשֶׁר בָּרִאשׁוֹנָה.

11 even from the day that I
commanded judges to be over My
people Israel; and I will cause you
to rest from all your enemies...

יא וּלְמִן-הַיּוֹם אֲשֶׁר צִוִּיתִי
שֹׁפְטִים עַל-עַמִּי יִשְׂרָאֵל
וַהֲנִיחֹתִי לְךָ מִכָּל-אֹיְבֶיךָ...

God promises good things for David and Israel. There will be peace.

It is not clear what this review of David's career trajectory has to do with his request, other than restating facts that for David are obvious.

So far, we've had some expression of surprise from God that David wants to build a temple, a review of David's personal history, but no explanation as to why David's request is rejected.

II Samuel 7

11 ... Moreover the LORD
tells you that the LORD
will make you a house.

יא ... וְהִגִּיד לְךָ יי כִּי-בַיִת
יַעֲשֶׂה-לְּךָ יי.

Changing the subject entirely, God says, "Oh, and by the way, you are asking Me if you can build a house for Me – which I am not so interested in – well, I want to tell you at precisely this juncture, that, guess what, I want to build a house for *you*." House, *bayit*, of course means dynasty. The dynasty will continue through the House of David. What is the relationship between these things? We still don't know why God doesn't want a temple.

II Samuel 7

12 When your days are fulfilled, and
you sleep with your fathers, I will
set up your seed after you, that
will proceed out of your innards,
and I will establish his kingdom.

13 He shall build a house for My
name, and I will establish the
throne of his kingdom for ever.

יב כִּי יִמְלְאוּ יָמֶיךָ וְשָׁכַבְתָּ אֶת-
אֲבֹתֶיךָ וַהֲקִימֹתִי אֶת-זַרְעֲךָ
אַחֲרֶיךָ אֲשֶׁר יֵצֵא מִמֵּעֶיךָ:
וַהֲכִינֹתִי אֶת-מַמְלַכְתּוֹ.

יג הוּא יִבְנֶה-בַּיִת לִשְׁמִי: וְכֹנַנְתִּי
אֶת-כִּסֵּא מַמְלַכְתּוֹ עַד-עוֹלָם.

God declares that David will have a son who will be king and build
the Temple. It seems that God does want a house after all, but not yet.
Not from David.

Why should that be?

II Samuel 7

14 I will be to him for a father,
and he shall be to Me for a
son; if he commit iniquity, I
will chasten him with the rod
of men, and with the stripes
of the children of men;

15 but My mercy shall not depart
from him, as I took it from Saul,
whom I put away before you.

16 And your house and your
kingdom shall be made sure
for ever before you; your throne
shall be established for ever.'

17 According to all these words,
and according to all this vision,
so did Nathan speak to David.

יד אֲנִי אֶהְיֶה-לּוֹ לְאָב וְהוּא יִהְיֶה-לִּי
לְבֵן: אֲשֶׁר בְּהַעֲוֹתוֹ וְהֹכַחְתִּיו
בְּשֵׁבֶט אֲנָשִׁים וּבְנִגְעֵי בְּנֵי אָדָם.

טו וְחַסְדִּי לֹא-יָסוּר מִמֶּנּוּ:
כַּאֲשֶׁר הֲסִרֹתִי מֵעִם שָׁאוּל
אֲשֶׁר הֲסִרֹתִי מִלְּפָנֶיךָ.

טז וְנֶאְמַן בֵּיתְךָ וּמַמְלַכְתְּךָ עַד-עוֹלָם
לְפָנֶיךָ: כִּסְאֲךָ יִהְיֶה נָכוֹן עַד-עוֹלָם.

יז כְּכֹל הַדְּבָרִים הָאֵלֶּה וּכְכֹל הַחִזָּיוֹן
הַזֶּה: כֵּן דִּבֶּר נָתָן אֶל-דָּוִד.

So David has been rejected, but he's getting a consolation prize. He
won't get a temple-building permit, but he will have a dynasty. And what
is David's response?

II Samuel 7

18 Then David the king went in,
and sat before the LORD; and
he said: 'Who am I, O Lord

יח וַיָּבֹא הַמֶּלֶךְ דָּוִד וַיֵּשֶׁב לִפְנֵי יְיָ:
וַיֹּאמֶר מִי אָנֹכִי אֲדֹנָי יְיָ וּמִי

GOD, and what is my house, that
You have brought me thus far?

בֵיתִי כִּי הֲבֵאֹתַנִי עַד-הֲלֹם?

He's just blown away. "Wow, I'm going to have a dynasty!" He seems to forget all about his original request and goes on to give praise because he's going to have a dynasty.

We're left with this really big puzzle. Why does God reject David's request to build a temple? Why must the task be relegated to David's son?

The obvious answer to reach for is that David was a "man of blood," *ish damim*. That answer, however, is problematic.

As you see (or rather *don't* see), there's no such explanation here in II Samuel 7 for David's rejection. The notion that David has blood on his hands is from Chronicles.[1] Many Torah Sages will claim that words of Torah that are sparse in one place, may be rich in another[2] – if it is not written here, it is written there. While that position has great merit, generally speaking, it cannot help us understand the chapter at hand. Let me explain why.

The Perspective of the Book of Samuel

Our Sages of Blessed Memory tell us that the Book of Samuel was written by the prophets Samuel, Gad, and Nathan, and that Chronicles was written by Ezra the Scribe.[3] Samuel, Gad, and Nathan are basically contemporaries, but there were about 500 years between the three of them and Ezra.

My aim is to try to understand the Book of Samuel on its own terms, without Chronicles, which would not exist for another 500 years. The Book of Samuel must yield its own answer to this question. And within the Book of Samuel there is no mention that David cannot build the Temple because of bloody hands. So throughout the first Temple period, before Chronicles was written, how was David's rejection understood? How did people make sense of this part of the story?

Very often we look to integrate the "royal" books: Samuel, Chronicles, and Kings. If something isn't in Samuel, we often look in Chronicles or Kings. In the Book of Kings, there is no explanation for why Uziyahu got skin disease, but if you read Chronicles on the subject, you will find

---

1   I Chronicles 22:8; I Chronicles 28:3

2   *divrei Torah aniyim bimkoman, ve-ashirim bemakom acher,* Yerushalmi Rosh Hashanah 3:5

3   Talmud Baba Batra, 15a

out what Uziyahu did inside the Temple.[4] And so forth. I think it is very helpful to recognize that there are places where the Book of Samuel and Chronicles are irreconcilable. It is not just that there's a gap. There are portions where they actually contradict one another. One need only compare the genealogies at the beginning of Chronicles with their counterparts elsewhere to see the truth of this.

And I want to throw out an idea. It is probably a bold one but I think that it is an honest one and I think that it is accurate. Because Chronicles is written so many years later, it could well be that we need to relate to it in the same way that we relate to other midrashic literature. Midrashim often add details to a story. Upon reading midrashim, we sometimes ask: If that is *really* what happened, how come it is not written in the Bible itself? With maturity, we understand that the Sages are underscoring ideas that they want to highlight. They take opportunities to create new stories, as it were, by adding pertinent details. (The issue of whether the stories are historically accurate is not really so important.)

I wonder whether, in fact, Chronicles already begins that Midrashic process. In other words, might the editor of Chronicles have had a certain agenda? Many themes in Chronicles are absent from the earlier books of Samuel and Kings. It could be that concepts that we first find in Chronicles are, perhaps, an early form of Midrash. The idea that spilling blood prevents David from building the Temple may be a concept that did not even exist during the time of the Book of Samuel.

So, if we cross "bloody hands" off our list of reasons to exclude David from building God's house in the Book of Samuel, then how do we account for the rejection?

Perhaps we may find an answer in the reason God gives David as the purpose for which He will allow David's son to build the Temple – His name.[5]

A single entity may have several names. For example, my university students call me Dr. Berman, my seminary students call me Rabbi Berman and my three-year-old calls me *Abbaleh*. My wife, also has a name for me. All these names reflect different aspects of who I am. The same is true for the Temple, which goes by many names. It is "Holy House," *Beit Hamikdash*, and "God's House," *Beit Hashem*. The Sages refer to it as "Chosen House," *Beit Habechirah*.

In Deuteronomy, the Temple has only one name, which appears many times with slightly different variations: "the Place where God will choose

---

4   II Chronicles 26
5   II Samuel 7:13

for the resting place of His name."[6]

Now, what exactly does that mean?

"The Place where God will choose" – that's easy enough.

"As a resting place for his name" – does that mean that you have to take a big chisel to engrave God's name in letters and find a place to put it?[7]

Looking at the key word "name" throughout the Torah, we see that it has a very interesting career, indeed.

Tower of Babel – The Anti-Temple

I want to start by looking in Genesis, at what might be described as the anti-Temple, the Tower of Babel, and see the use of the word "name" in that story.

Genesis 11

1 And the whole earth was of one language and of one speech.

א וַיְהִי כָל-הָאָרֶץ שָׂפָה אֶחָת: וּדְבָרִים אֲחָדִים.

2 And it came to pass, as they journeyed east, that they found a plain in the land of Shinar; and they dwelt there.

ב וַיְהִי בְּנָסְעָם מִקֶּדֶם: וַיִּמְצְאוּ בִקְעָה בְּאֶרֶץ שִׁנְעָר וַיֵּשְׁבוּ שָׁם.

3 And they said one to another: 'Come, let us make brick, and burn them thoroughly.' And they had brick for stone, and slime had they for mortar.

ג וַיֹּאמְרוּ אִישׁ אֶל-רֵעֵהוּ הָבָה נִלְבְּנָה לְבֵנִים וְנִשְׂרְפָה לִשְׂרֵפָה: וַתְּהִי לָהֶם הַלְּבֵנָה לְאָבֶן וְהַחֵמָר הָיָה לָהֶם לַחֹמֶר.

4 And they said: 'Come, let us build us a city, and a tower, with its top in heaven, and let us **make us a name**; lest we be scattered abroad upon the face of the whole earth.'

ד וַיֹּאמְרוּ הָבָה נִבְנֶה-לָּנוּ עִיר וּמִגְדָּל וְרֹאשׁוֹ בַשָּׁמַיִם וְנַעֲשֶׂה-לָּנוּ שֵׁם: פֶּן-נָפוּץ עַל-פְּנֵי כָל-הָאָרֶץ.

Abraham ibn Ezra and many others commentators ask, what does it mean "to make us a name?"

He answers: They want to build an edifice that will be impressive. They were thinking like Donald Trump. Everyone who looks at Trump Tower says, "That Trump must be something!" They want to make a name for themselves, a reputation. As in: "A good name is better than good oil."[7]

---

6   "*Hamakom asher yivchar Hashem lishakane shimo sham.*" Deuteronomy12:5; 12:11; 12:21; 14:23; 14:24; 16:2; 16:6; 16:11 26:2

7   Ecclesiates 7:1 טוֹב שֵׁם, מִשֶּׁמֶן טוֹב

In fact, you can see this even from the scant details the text provides.

For example, the people choose to build the tower from bricks. What is the difference between using bricks as a building material, or stone and wood? The answer is that bricks are manufactured; every brick can be labeled "made in Babel." If they use stone, every stone basically says on it: "Hand crafted by God." They want to build a structure that will be completely man made. They use those materials deliberately.

There's even something in the rhythm, the meter, of the end of verse three. What does this sound like? "Let's do something," and then, "and it was." It sounds like Creation. At the beginning of Genesis, God says, "Let Us do this," and then it happens. Why does the Bible cast the desire of the tower builders in such a fashion, as Creation-like? It is because they imagine themselves as creators. They see themselves in the place of God. He created His world; they are creating their building. And so the edifice that they build is for their own grandeur.

So, the anti-Temple is something that is devoted to creating a great name for a group of people, not for God.

Calling in God's Name

The very next real story that comes up in the Torah (after a bunch of "begats") is the story of Abraham.[8] In other words, it could be that we are meant to see the career of Abraham the Patriarch as an antidote to this spirit of "making oneself a name." Something interesting about the career of Abraham, perhaps more than any other patriarch, is that three times in his career he makes a certain gesture which pertains to the structure of "making a name" through the Tower of Babel.

Genesis 12

8 And he removed from there to the mountain on the east of Beth-el, and pitched his tent, having Beth-el on the west, and Ai on the east; and he built an altar there for the LORD, and **called in the name of the LORD.**

ח וַיַּעְתֵּק מִשָּׁם הָהָרָה מִקֶּדֶם לְבֵית-אֵל–וַיֵּט אָהֳלֹה: בֵּית-אֵל מִיָּם וְהָעַי מִקֶּדֶם וַיִּבֶן-שָׁם מִזְבֵּחַ לַיי וַיִּקְרָא בְּשֵׁם יי.

This is shortly after Abraham's arrival in the land of Canaan. What does it mean to "call in the name of the Lord"?

Rashi explains that he prays. That makes sense. Nachmanides (Ramban), however, says something else. He says no, it is not praying. He says to "call in God's name" is not something that's cast *upwards*, it is cast *outwards*. Ramban contextualizes the phrase as: proclaiming God's greatness.[9] Abraham makes an altar and spreads the good word about God's reputation.

It is interesting to examine at which junctures Abraham performs this gesture of building something and glorifying God's name.

The next instance this occurs is just a few verses further, when Abraham has just returned to Canaan from Egypt, after his great victory over Pharoah:

Genesis 13

1 And Abram went up out of Egypt, he, and his wife, and all that he had, and Lot with him, into the South.

א וַיַּעַל אַבְרָם מִמִּצְרַיִם הוּא וְאִשְׁתּוֹ וְכָל-אֲשֶׁר-לוֹ וְלוֹט עִמּוֹ–הַנֶּגְבָּה.

2 And Abram was very rich in cattle, in silver, and in gold.

ב וְאַבְרָם כָּבֵד מְאֹד: בַּמִּקְנֶה בַּכֶּסֶף וּבַזָּהָב.

3 And he went on his journeys from the South even to Beth-el, to the place where his tent had been at the beginning, between Beth-el and Ai;

ג וַיֵּלֶךְ לְמַסָּעָיו מִנֶּגֶב וְעַד-בֵּית-אֵל: עַד-הַמָּקוֹם אֲשֶׁר-הָיָה שָׁם אָהֳלֹה בַּתְּחִלָּה בֵּין בֵּית-אֵל וּבֵין הָעָי.

4 to the place of the altar, which he had made there at the first; and **Abram called there in the name of the LORD**.

ד אֶל-מְקוֹם הַמִּזְבֵּחַ אֲשֶׁר- עָשָׂה שָׁם בָּרִאשֹׁנָה: וַיִּקְרָא שָׁם אַבְרָם בְּשֵׁם יי.

The third and final place that we see this is just before the binding of Isaac. Abraham has an encounter with Avimelekh, King of the Philistines.[10] Avimelekh comes to Abraham and says, "I see that God is with you and I never want to be oppose you in any type of encounter, so let us make a covenant."

After this the text says:

---

9   *vayikra be-shem Hashem, hodi'ah Elokuto vigadluto livnei adam*. Ramban on Genesis 12:8

10   Genesis 21:22-32

Genesis 21

33 And Abraham planted a
tamarisk-tree in Beersheva, and
**called there in the name of the
LORD,** the Everlasting God.

לג וַיִּטַּע אֶשֶׁל בִּבְאֵר שָׁבַע:
וַיִּקְרָא-שָׁם–בְּשֵׁם יְיָ אֵל עוֹלָם.

Abraham only calls in God's name under select circumstances. The
first occasion may reflect Abraham's entry into the land of Canaan. What
do the other two instances of Abraham calling God's name have in common? Victory over other kings.

When Abraham returns to Canaan from Egypt, people say: "Gee, he
did well for himself abroad!" It is the same story with Avimelekh. Each
episode represents a moment where Abraham is at the top of his game.
Abraham calls out God's name at times when he is enjoying great stature
in the eyes of others.

What's interesting is that it is *only* at times like these that Abraham
performs this act. One would think that Abraham would want to proclaim God's glory daily. It could well be that Abraham would like to go
out every single day to acknowledge God's greatness and divinity to all
men, but it would not necessarily produce the desired effect.

I am reminded of an experience that I had in the subway when I was
commuting to high school. On a number of occasions the following thing
happened. The subway would be moving and this figure would suddenly
enter through the doors between the cars. It would be this fellow with a
toga and dreadlocks and he would start at the top of his voice, "I've come
to proclaim the name of the Lord..." The rest of us would sort of stare
blankly and secure our wallets, and nobody really paid much attention
to him. This happened a number of times during the course of my four
years of high school. Some figure with a toga and dreadlocks would come
through wanting to proclaim the name of the Lord and nobody would
listen to him.

By contrast, I recall a pitcher for the Los Angeles Dodgers named Orel
Hershiser, who set a record in the late 80's for consecutive scoreless in-
nings pitched. It was a big record in baseball. After he set this record,
Hershiser said in an interview, "I just want to thank the good Lord for
letting me play the game of baseball." Reportedly, church attendance rose
after that.

Why is it that when someone in a toga on the subway proclaims the
name of the Lord, everyone shrinks away in horror, but Orel Hershiser
receives a positive response? People like to listen to a winner and not to a
loser.

Abraham understood this implicitly. When they're dragging Sarah away from him, it is not time to say: God is great, look, He's so amazing. That would not be too impressive. Abraham calls God's name precisely at those moments when he feels a sense of accomplishment. Abraham might always want to proclaim the name of the Lord but knows he had better be doing pretty well if he wants to get that message across.

What does this have to do with David's request to build the Temple, or the phrasing about God resting His name that we see in Deuteronomy, or even David's son building a house for God's name?[11]

The connection is the following: Abraham is only one man. To truly proclaim God's greatness and His sovereignty beyond the life span of one man, you need a nation. And just as Abraham could only perform this act when at the top of his game, so too the nation of Israel will only truly be able proclaim God's greatness when they are at the top of *their* game.

The Temple, as a place designed to broadcast God's greatness and sovereignty, can only be built at specific times. Let us look at one of the first places in Deuteronomy where the Temple is discussed. We are introduced here to the conditions that need to be in place in order for the Temple to be built.

Deuteronomy 12

10 But when you go over the Jordan, and dwell in the land which the LORD your God causes you to inherit, and He gives you rest from all your enemies round about, so that you dwell in safety;

י וַעֲבַרְתֶּם אֶת־הַיַּרְדֵּן וִישַׁבְתֶּם בָּאָרֶץ אֲשֶׁר־יְיָ אֱלֹהֵיכֶם מַנְחִיל אֶתְכֶם: וְהֵנִיחַ לָכֶם מִכָּל־אֹיְבֵיכֶם מִסָּבִיב וִישַׁבְתֶּם־בֶּטַח.

11 then it shall come to pass that the place which the LORD your God shall choose to cause His name to dwell there, there shall you bring all that I command you: your burnt-offerings, and your sacrifices, your tithes, and the offering of your hand, and all your choice vows which you vow unto the LORD.

יא וְהָיָה הַמָּקוֹם אֲשֶׁר־יִבְחַר יְיָ אֱלֹהֵיכֶם בּוֹ לְשַׁכֵּן שְׁמוֹ שָׁם שָׁמָּה תָבִיאוּ אֵת כָּל־אֲשֶׁר אָנֹכִי מְצַוֶּה אֶתְכֶם: עוֹלֹתֵיכֶם וְזִבְחֵיכֶם מַעְשְׂרֹתֵיכֶם וּתְרֻמַת יֶדְכֶם וְכֹל מִבְחַר נִדְרֵיכֶם אֲשֶׁר תִּדְּרוּ לַייָ.

First of all, it is not enough that the people of Israel be in the land– they have to be settled there. A loose collection of nomadic tribes is

---

11   II Samuel 7:13

not very impressive. Moreover, the Torah lays out the proper diplomatic climate for the building of the Temple. It is not enough to dwell in the land if one is constantly fighting invaders. The Temple does not belong in such an environment. The Torah says there has to be a certain foundation of stability in order for the Temple to serve its function as the place which will properly advertise God's reputation.

Now the context required for the Temple-building enterprise is brought into sharper focus. If we question why the Temple wasn't built until the time of David or Solomon, we can begin to understand. Joshua couldn't build it because he was too busy fighting. And in the time of the Book of Judges, war was a constant, people were starving, so that wasn't the proper time either. The very first time that it was even conceivable to think of building a temple is our present chapter – of the book, and of Jewish history.

Re-reading the Chapter

I would like to go back and reread the passage with which we began, II Samuel 7, in light of the ideas that we have been developing here. We will notice many relevant details.

The first thing that comes into focus now is verse 1:

II Samuel 7

1 And it came to pass, when the king dwelt in his house, and the LORD had given him rest from all his enemies round about,	א וַיְהִי כִּי-יָשַׁב הַמֶּלֶךְ בְּבֵיתוֹ: וַיי הֵנִיחַ-לוֹ מִסָּבִיב מִכָּל-אֹיְבָיו.

This verse identifies for us at precisely what juncture David conceives the idea to build a temple, and it says two things. The first, David is sitting in his big house. Saul apparently never built a palace. A palace is a monumental project and as such signifies prosperity and stability. It bespeaks the ability to marshal great resources, material, as well as human. So, for David, the building of a palace means having attained a certain stature.

What is the second thing this verse tells us? "The Lord had given him rest from his enemies all about." Does that sound familiar? Deuteronomy 12:10! In other words, David is sitting there in his palace learning the Book of Deuteronomy and he sees this verse, and sees that all these requirements have been met. In the land. Check. Peace all around. Check. And David says, "That's now!" It is clear. He is seeing the fulfillment of that verse in Deuteronomy in his own time and so he has this natural question. Maybe it is time to build? So he puts in the request. But of course, we end up with our original question: Why does God reject David's request?

I'd like to start from verse 5. One can clearly see that God is not upset because He refers to David as, "my servant," an intimate phrase when discussing relationship to God.

So what is the problem?

God tells David, "Your intuition is good. We are approaching the proper time to build a temple. I have given you leadership over the people and (verse 9) cut off your enemies from before you. You're right. When you were reading Deuteronomy 12:10 and you read that verse, you read it true. Yes, David. Your reputation and My reputation are joined and the great honor that you receive can be translated into great honor for My name. You're right. There's unprecedented tranquility now. And... (verses 11-12) you're going to have a dynasty."

What is missing? It is clear that God agrees. There is peace and secure borders. You have a palace which indicates power, stability and the support of the people. What is missing? Let's put aside the Tanakh and think.

What attributes does a country have to have in our time in order to be respected by others? Morals, laws, security, great leaders and... order of succession. For example, many of us might recall a situation in Russia, in the 1990s. The economy was in an upswing and it was one of the strongest countries in the world. But there was one big problem with Russia. And that was President Boris Yeltsin and the bottle. One drink too many and the guy could have a heart attack. It wasn't quite clear what would happen in Russia if a president (a new thing there) suddenly died. The issue of orderly transfer of succession is one of the hallmarks of a stable society. Even in Israel, it is a sign of strength. When there was a terrible assassination, nobody doubted that there would be an orderly transfer of government. There is perpetual chaos but the government functions by rules and everyone knows that is the case.

Coming back to Tanakh, if we think about the history of Israel until this point, no issue has been a perennial sore point greater than the issue of succession.

When Moses passes on, he makes sure that Joshua will take the helm. But when Joshua passes way, it is not at all clear who will be in charge. The judges, by and large, are not national leaders. They are regional leaders. And as we all know, every time a judge passes on, a power vacuum is created and everything reverts to chaos.

The same situation still exists for David. Saul doesn't transfer the king-ship. What is supposed to happen after Saul? A gray period follows and then David comes to the fore. Maybe David is being told the following: You want to build a temple. You're on the right track. What is missing is a system, a way of ensuring that when one great leader passes on, that, yes, there will be continuity and a secure transfer of leadership. And that is called a dynasty.

So Solomon's great qualification for building the Temple is not his wisdom, not the political peace and tranquility of his reign. His great qualification is that he is second in a dynasty, because, by definition, it is the second member of the dynasty that creates the dynasty. Solomon's qualification is that he rules by virtue of an orderly transfer of power.

And that really explains everything. That is why David does not re-spond with disappointment. David understands that this gift of dynasty, coming precisely when he had asked for the Temple, is God's way of in-forming him of what is missing. God is telling David that "You are the first in the dynasty, but the Temple needs to be built by number two."

This is very evident for Solomon when he builds the Temple:

I Kings 8

17 Now it was in the heart of David my father to build a house for the name of the LORD, the God of Israel.

יז וַיְהִי עִם-לְבַב דָּוִד אָבִי: לִבְנוֹת בַּיִת לְשֵׁם יְיָ אֱלֹהֵי יִשְׂרָאֵל.

18 But the LORD said to David my father: Whereas it was in your heart to **build a house for My name**, you did well that it was in your heart.

יח וַיֹּאמֶר יְיָ אֶל-דָּוִד אָבִי יַעַן אֲשֶׁר הָיָה עִם-לְבָבְךָ לִבְנוֹת בַּיִת לִשְׁמִי: הֱטִיבֹתָ כִּי הָיָה עִם-לְבָבֶךָ.

19 nevertheless you shall not build the house; but your son that shall come forth out of your loins, **he shall build the house for My name**.

יט רַק אַתָּה לֹא תִבְנֶה הַבָּיִת: כִּי אִם-בִּנְךָ הַיֹּצֵא מֵחֲלָצֶיךָ הוּא-יִבְנֶה הַבַּיִת לִשְׁמִי.

Solomon forcefully emphasizes these points. He acknowledges that his father really wanted to build the Temple. Solomon perceives a great thing has happened in Israel: an orderly transfer of rule. He understands that he merits building the Temple not for his own devotion, but because he embodies the continuity of David's reign.

The idea that the Temple's primary purpose is to proclaim God's greatness and sovereignty is evident throughout the account of Solomon and the Temple in Kings.

When Solomon sets up the Temple, he orates the "Prayer of Solomon."[12] In his prayer, Solomon envisions circumstances in which people will pray toward the Temple. Most are fairly predictable: times of war, of famine, of drought.

Let us look further:

I Kings 8

41 Moreover concerning the stranger that is not of Your people Israel, when he shall come out of a far country for **Your name's sake–**

מא וְגַם אֶל-הַנָּכְרִי אֲשֶׁר לֹא-מֵעַמְּךָ יִשְׂרָאֵל הוּא: וּבָא מֵאֶרֶץ רְחוֹקָה לְמַעַן שְׁמֶךָ.

42 for they shall hear of **Your great name**, and of Your mighty hand, and of Your outstretched arm – when he shall come and pray toward this house;

מב כִּי יִשְׁמְעוּן אֶת-שִׁמְךָ הַגָּדוֹל וְאֶת-יָדְךָ הַחֲזָקָה וּזְרֹעֲךָ הַנְּטוּיָה: וּבָא וְהִתְפַּלֵּל אֶל-הַבַּיִת הַזֶּה.

43 hear You in heaven Your dwelling-place, and do according to all that the stranger calls to You for; that all the peoples of the earth **may know Your name, to fear You, as do Your people Israel**, and that they may know that **Your name is called upon this house which I have built.**

מג אַתָּה תִּשְׁמַע הַשָּׁמַיִם מְכוֹן שִׁבְתֶּךָ וְעָשִׂיתָ כְּכֹל אֲשֶׁר-יִקְרָא אֵלֶיךָ הַנָּכְרִי: לְמַעַן יֵדְעוּן כָּל-עַמֵּי הָאָרֶץ אֶת-שְׁמֶךָ לְיִרְאָה אֹתְךָ כְּעַמְּךָ יִשְׂרָאֵל וְלָדַעַת כִּי-שִׁמְךָ נִקְרָא עַל-הַבַּיִת הַזֶּה אֲשֶׁר בָּנִיתִי.

In the Temple, all peoples are fully welcome. Maybe they can not bring every variety of sacrifice, but all the nations are expected to visit to pay homage to God's great name. The Temple is absolutely open to all. This is also the reason we are told the story of the Queen of Sheba.

I Kings 10

1 And when the Queen of Sheba heard of the fame of Solomon because of **the name of the LORD**, she came to test him with hard questions.

א וּמַלְכַּת-שְׁבָא שֹׁמַעַת אֶת-שֵׁמַע שְׁלֹמֹה לְשֵׁם יְיָ וַתָּבֹא לְנַסֹּתוֹ בְּחִידוֹת.

She hears of Solomon's reputation and comes out of curiosity, perhaps to challenge Solomon, perhaps to receive his advice on governance.

I Kings 10

2 And she came to Jerusalem with a very great train, with camels that bore spices and gold very much, and precious stones; and when she was come to Solomon, she spoke with him of all that was in her heart.

ב וַתָּבֹא יְרוּשָׁלַמָה בְּחַיִל כָּבֵד מְאֹד גְּמַלִּים נֹשְׂאִים בְּשָׂמִים וְזָהָב רַב-מְאֹד וְאֶבֶן יְקָרָה וַתָּבֹא אֶל-שְׁלֹמֹה וַתְּדַבֵּר אֵלָיו אֵת כָּל-אֲשֶׁר הָיָה עִם-לְבָבָהּ.

3 And Solomon told her all her questions; there was not any thing hid from the king which he told her not.

ג וַיַּגֶּד-לָהּ שְׁלֹמֹה אֶת-כָּל- דְּבָרֶיהָ: לֹא-הָיָה דָּבָר נֶעְלָם מִן-הַמֶּלֶךְ אֲשֶׁר לֹא הִגִּיד לָהּ.

Now, let us look at what this outsider sees:

I Kings 10

4 And when the Queen of Sheba had seen all the wisdom of Solomon, and **the house** that he had built,

ד וַתֵּרֶא מַלְכַּת-שְׁבָא אֵת כָּל-חָכְמַת שְׁלֹמֹה וְהַבַּיִת אֲשֶׁר בָּנָה.

5 and the food of his table, and the sitting of his servants, and the attendance of his ministers, and their apparel, and his cupbearers, and his burnt-offering which he offered in the house of the LORD, there was no more spirit in her.

ה וּמַאֲכַל שֻׁלְחָנוֹ וּמוֹשַׁב עֲבָדָיו וּמַעֲמַד מְשָׁרְתָו וּמַלְבֻּשֵׁיהֶם וּמַשְׁקָיו וְעֹלָתוֹ אֲשֶׁר יַעֲלֶה בֵּית יְיָ: וְלֹא-הָיָה בָהּ עוֹד רוּחַ.

6 And she said to the king: 'It was a true report that I heard in mine own land of thine acts, and of your wisdom.

ו וַתֹּאמֶר אֶל-הַמֶּלֶךְ אֱמֶת הָיָה הַדָּבָר אֲשֶׁר שָׁמַעְתִּי בְּאַרְצִי: עַל-דְּבָרֶיךָ וְעַל-חָכְמָתֶךָ.

7 And I believed not the words, until I came, and mine eyes had seen it; and, behold, the half was not told me; you have wisdom and prosperity exceeding the fame which I heard.

ז וְלֹא-הֶאֱמַנְתִּי לַדְּבָרִים עַד אֲשֶׁר-בָּאתִי וַתִּרְאֶינָה עֵינַי וְהִנֵּה לֹא-הֻגַּד-לִי הַחֵצִי: הוֹסַפְתָּ חָכְמָה וָטוֹב אֶל-הַשְּׁמוּעָה אֲשֶׁר שָׁמָעְתִּי.

8 Happy are your men, happy
are these your servants, that
stand continually before you,
and that hear your wisdom.

ח אַשְׁרֵי אֲנָשֶׁיךָ אַשְׁרֵי עֲבָדֶיךָ
אֵלֶּה: הָעֹמְדִים לְפָנֶיךָ תָּמִיד
הַשֹּׁמְעִים אֶת-חָכְמָתֶךָ.

What we have here is the impression of a tourist. What is it that she
sees in Solomon and in his empire? First of all, the House. What does
that indicate? Prosperity, technology. Then there is the food – quite a
smorgasbord, which also indicates prosperity. The clothing impresses her
as well. So, she's impressed with the wisdom, with the technology, with
the prosperity.

I Kings 10

9 Blessed be the LORD your God,
who delights in you, to set you
on the throne of Israel; because
the LORD loves Israel for ever,
therefore made He you king, to
do justice and righteousness.'

ט יְהִי יי אֱלֹהֶיךָ בָּרוּךְ אֲשֶׁר חָפֵץ בְּךָ
לְתִתְּךָ עַל-כִּסֵּא יִשְׂרָאֵל: בְּאַהֲבַת
יי אֶת-יִשְׂרָאֵל לְעֹלָם וַיְשִׂימְךָ
לְמֶלֶךְ לַעֲשׂוֹת מִשְׁפָּט וּצְדָקָה.

And the final thing that impresses her is that there seems to be moral
and equal treatment of citizens, and care of the poor.

This story of the Queen of Sheba belongs here because this is what the
Temple is all about. It is about creating a central place that broadcasts
God's greatness and God's sovereignty. This atmosphere can be created
only in the life of a nation at the top of its game – as reflected in the life
of the individual Abraham when he was at his most successful. When he
was at the top, he called out in God's name. This also holds true, for the
nation Israel.

As religious Zionists, we tend to view our age with great excitement,
as "the beginning of the flower of our Redemption."[13] But it is important
to see the half of the cup that is empty. What does it mean that we do not
have a Temple in our time? It is almost a tease. It is as if God is telling
us: "I am going to bring you back into the parking lot, but I am not going to let you into the House." It is a statement. The fact is that we have
not yet perfected ourselves to the point that God is comfortable with us
proclaiming His greatness and His sovereignty.

Our task now is a different kind of building. This building has nothing
to do with wood and with gold and with silver. It is the institution of

---

13   From the Prayer for the State of Israel

a society that's worthy of having a Temple. This is the task of our own time.

The Queen of Sheba is not impressed because Solomon has strict standards for his kosher meat, or is meticulous in observing the laws of ritual purity. She is impressed because he makes a great society. Therefore, it is a religiously charged endeavor to make Israel a better place in all facets: education, welfare and science. And it is only through making the land of Israel a great place, founded on Torah and good works, that it will be ready to become a proper place to glorify God, and a place to rest His name.[14]

---

14   This material has appeared in a different form in a book called *The Temple: Its Symbolism and Meaning, Then and Now.* (Jason Aronson, 1995). I wrote this book in close association with Rabbi Menachem Leibtag from whom I received almost all of this material. He, in turn, received it from Rabbi Yoel Bin Nun.

YCT Tanakh Companion

David and Batsheva:
Echoes of Saul and the gift of forgiveness
II Samuel 11-12

Rabbi Shmuel Herzfeld

The David and Batsheva narrative stands as the turning point in David's fortunes.

Prior to David's sin with Batsheva, his life is enchanted. He is a success.

After the sin, his kingdom falls apart, his children rebel against him, and his life becomes a punishment.

After this episode, David stops functioning as a king. His next royal act is to arrange for Solomon to be anointed as his successor.[1] When Absalom dies, Yo'av has to drag David out just so the people can see that their king is alive.[2] It seems as if David has had a breakdown.

As we will see, David's fall reminds us of the fall of his predecessor, King Saul. This juxtaposition starkly conveys a central theological message of the Book of Samuel: Monarchy in Israel is a tragic experiment destined to end in overthrow and exile. No matter how pure of heart the leader, power will corrupt.

At the same time, this story also teaches a lesson about repentance and atonement.

II Samuel 11

1 And it came to pass, at the return of the year, at the time when kings go out to battle, that David

א וַיְהִי לִתְשׁוּבַת הַשָּׁנָה לְעֵת צֵאת הַמַּלְאָכִים וַיִּשְׁלַח דָּוִד

---

1   Fact noted by Rabbi Yaaqov Medan in his *David U' Batsheva: HaHet, HaOnesh V'HaTikkun* (Hebrew): Yeshivat Har Etzion

2   II Samuel 19:8

sent Yo'av, and his servants with him, and all Israel; and they destroyed the children of Ammon, and besieged Rabbah. But David tarried at Jerusalem.	אֶת-יוֹאָב וְאֶת-עֲבָדָיו עִמּוֹ וְאֶת-כָּל-יִשְׂרָאֵל וַיַּשְׁחִתוּ אֶת-בְּנֵי עַמּוֹן וַיָּצֻרוּ עַל-רַבָּה: וְדָוִד יוֹשֵׁב בִּירוּשָׁלָם.

It is the season when kings go out to battle, but David stays home. (Later on the people will beseech David to retire from battle permanently.[3] Here, however, this is clearly the wrong choice.)

This is more than just a misjudgment on David's part. His inaction actually negates the very reason for David's kingship. Remember, the people have asked for a monarch, "that our king may judge us, and go out before us, and fight our battles."[4]

In failing to lead the battle, David negates his mission, and loses kingly legitimacy. If David is not living up to his responsibility to go to war, perhaps he is no longer fit to judge, either. David's abuse of his role casts into doubt whether David, or perhaps any king, is the most appropriate person to preside over the people of Israel.

David's dereliction of duty starts a chain of events which culminates in his affair with Batsheva. As we'll see, this story repeatedly highlights David's moral failure and foreshadows his political doom.

Up on the Roof

First, the sense of the text is that David's absence is not an innocent mistake.

II Samuel 11

2 It was toward the evening; David arose from his slumber and wandered **on the roof** of the king's house; and **from on the roof** he saw a woman bathing; and the woman was very beautiful to look upon.	ב וַיְהִי לְעֵת הָעֶרֶב וַיָּקָם דָּוִד מֵעַל מִשְׁכָּבוֹ וַיִּתְהַלֵּךְ עַל-גַּג בֵּית-הַמֶּלֶךְ וַיַּרְא אִשָּׁה רֹחֶצֶת מֵעַל הַגָּג: וְהָאִשָּׁה טוֹבַת מַרְאֶה מְאֹד.

The indolent tone to this wandering is disturbing when we consider that David's soldiers are at war serving him. After sleeping the afternoon

---

3   II Samuel 18:3-4
4   I Samuel 8:20

away, David wakes toward evening, walks on the roof of the palace, and spots beautiful Batsheva bathing.

There is an implication that there is a lot more to this simple evening stroll than the wanderings of a tired man. The words "on the roof," *al gag*, and then, *me'al ha-gag*, "from on the roof" appear in this one verse.

These words remind us of Saul whose downfall came from not killing Agag – whose name sounds very much like *al ha-gag*. Moreover, we are also reminded of the place where Saul is first anointed.

I Samuel 9

25 And when they were come down from the high place into the city, he spoke with Saul **on the roof**.

כה וַיֵּרְדוּ מֵהַבָּמָה הָעִיר: וַיְדַבֵּר עִם-שָׁאוּל עַל-הַגָּג.

26 And they arose early; and it came to pass about the break of day, that Samuel called to Saul **on the roof**, saying: 'Up, that I may send you away.' And Saul arose, and they went out both of them, he and Samuel, abroad.

כו וַיַּשְׁכִּמוּ וַיְהִי כַּעֲלוֹת הַשַּׁחַר וַיִּקְרָא שְׁמוּאֵל אֶל-שָׁאוּל הַגָּג לֵאמֹר קוּמָה וַאֲשַׁלְּחֶךָ: וַיָּקָם שָׁאוּל וַיֵּצְאוּ שְׁנֵיהֶם הוּא וּשְׁמוּאֵל הַחוּצָה.

When Samuel anoints Saul for the first time, the text makes a point of telling us that Samuel takes Saul out onto the roof, *al ha-gag*, and this phrase is repeated. Reading the stories of Saul and Samuel, we wonder: Why does the text keep referring to the roof? The answer may lie in the connection between the two roofs. Saul's anointment on the roof, *al ha-gag*, comes full circle with the beginning of David's descent, which begins on another roof. Saul's sin with Agag signals the end of his kingdom. David's sin, *al ha-gag*, "on the roof," will also be his undoing. This language at the very beginning of the David/Batsheva story alerts us to a major turning point in David's career.

In this way, the failure of the monarchy in Israel is foreshadowed from its very inception. In anointing Saul *al ha-gag*, the Book of Samuel points to Saul's downfall with Agag. Normally, we would expect an anointment to be filled with great hope. In retrospect we see its portentous aspect.

We have also touched upon David's wandering. The phrase, "and he walked" (or: wandered), "*va-yithalekh,*" appears many times throughout the David narrative in a way that conveys a lot of meaning. For example, Nathan later reproves David for his sin with Batsheva using imagery of a wanderer, a *helekh*.[5]

---

5   II Samuel 12:4

Another "wanderer" story appears after Saul has just killed the entire city of Nov[6] in a rage. Saul finds it intolerable that someone from the city has aided David by supplying him with food and a sword.

David runs to the city of Ke'ilah and saves the city from the Philistines. When David hears that Saul is coming to attack Ke'ilah for harboring him, David turns to God and asks whether the people of Ke'ilah will hand him over to Saul. God answers "Yes," so David leaves the city.

I Samuel 23

13 Then David and his men, who were about six hundred, arose and departed out of Ke'ilah, and **wandered where they could wander**. And it was told Saul that David was escaped from Ke'ilah; and he forbore to go forth.	יג וַיָּקָם דָּוִד וַאֲנָשָׁיו כְּשֵׁשׁ-מֵאוֹת אִישׁ וַיֵּצְאוּ מִקְּעִלָה וַיִּתְהַלְּכוּ בַּאֲשֶׁר יִתְהַלָּכוּ וּלְשָׁאוּל הֻגַּד כִּי-נִמְלַט דָּוִד מִקְּעִילָה וַיֶּחְדַּל לָצֵאת.

They wander aimlessly. This is David's finest moment. Rather than put innocent people at risk, he leaves the city he has just saved, a city he might have used as a fortress to protect himself against Saul. He chooses to wander instead.

In our chapter, David, entrenched as king, again wanders aimlessly; only now it is not a wandering of courage, but a wandering of corruption. His wandering on the roof leads him to look through the oncoming darkness and see Batsheva.

As many have pointed out, each sin in this story leads to another sin.

The act of seeing Batsheva leads to sleeping with her, which in turn leads to recalling Uriah from battle in order to cover up David's role in Batsheva's pregnancy. This leads to lying to Uriah, which leads to throwing lavish parties in order to entice Uriah to go home and sleep with Batsheva to account for her pregnancy. When Uriah doesn't comply, David arranges for Uriah's death in battle – and ultimately the death of many other innocent soldiers, as well.

II Samuel 11

25 Then David said to the messenger: 'Thus shall you say to Yo'av: Let not this thing be bad **in your eyes**, for the	כה וַיֹּאמֶר דָּוִד אֶל-הַמַּלְאָךְ כֹּה-תֹאמַר אֶל-יוֹאָב אַל-יֵרַע בְּעֵינֶיךָ

---

6   I Samuel 22:17-19

sword devours in one manner
or another; make your battle
more strong against the city, and
overthrow it; and encourage him.'

26 And when the wife of
Uriah heard that Uriah her
husband was dead, she made
lamentation for her husband.

27 And when the mourning was
past, David sent and took her
home to his house, and she
became his wife, and bore
him a son. But the thing that
David had done was evil in
the **eyes** of the LORD.

אֶת-הַדָּבָר הַזֶּה-כִּי-כָזֹה וְכָזֶה
תֹּאכַל הֶחָרֶב: הַחֲזֵק מִלְחַמְתְּךָ
אֶל-הָעִיר וְהָרְסָהּ וְחַזְּקֵהוּ.

כו וַתִּשְׁמַע אֵשֶׁת אוּרִיָּה כִּי-מֵת
אוּרִיָּה אִישָׁהּ: וַתִּסְפֹּד עַל-בַּעְלָהּ.

כז וַיַּעֲבֹר הָאֵבֶל וַיִּשְׁלַח דָּוִד
וַיַּאַסְפָהּ אֶל-בֵּיתוֹ וַתְּהִי-לוֹ
לְאִשָּׁה וַתֵּלֶד לוֹ בֵּן: וַיֵּרַע הַדָּבָר
אֲשֶׁר-עָשָׂה דָוִד בְּעֵינֵי יי.

As a result of sinning with his eyes by looking at Batsheva, David now commits the terrible sin of rationalizing the murders for which he is accountable. David slides from the realm of human error and temptation into that of real evil, and in doing so he crosses the line of what offends God. Of course, we are told that although to David's own eyes he has done nothing wrong – in the eyes of God David *has* done wrong. In that sense this sin comes full circle; starting with David's wandering eyes, it ends with God's disapproving ones.

Political motivation?

There is some suggestion that David's sin with Batsheva may have been motivated by political ambition on David's part. Before summoning Batsheva, David inquires as to her identity:

II Samuel 11

3 And David sent and inquired
after the woman. And one
said: 'Is not this Batsheva,
the daughter of Eli'am, the
wife of Uriah the Hittite?'

ג וַיִּשְׁלַח דָּוִד וַיִּדְרֹשׁ לָאִשָּׁה:
וַיֹּאמֶר הֲלוֹא-זֹאת בַּת-שֶׁבַע
בַּת-אֱלִיעָם-אֵשֶׁת אוּרִיָּה הַחִתִּי.

Whether David knows her or not, one thing is clear, David *does* know her husband. How do we know this? If you look at the end of II Samuel, Uriah the Hittite is listed as one of the 37 warriors who, in a sense, make up David's cabinet.[7] Uriah is an officer of David's. Another on that list is Eli'am, who we assume is the father of Batsheva. (Eli'am is a rare name which does not appear elsewhere in Tanakh.) And Eli'am's father is Achitofel, the prized adviser. Some say that David's intrigue with Batsheva is the reason that Achitofel ultimately turns against David.[8]

Throughout the Book of Samuel, women are sought after for their beauty, their love of Torah, their homemaking abilities, and for their political position. This is the case with Avigayil, the wife of Naval, and with Michal, daughter of Saul. Michal is sent back and forth between husbands numerous times. Right after David marries Avigayil, Saul immediately withdraws Michal from David. There is a sense that David is becoming too powerful through his marital alliances. It is possible, and here I'll admit it's circumstantial evidence, that the sin with Batsheva is not only one of lust, but there may be an element of cold, premeditated ambition on the part of David as he tries to strengthen his kingdom through another alliance with a very powerful woman, the daughter of Eli'am, and granddaughter of Achitofel.

As a result of this lustful (or perhaps not so lustful) alliance, David ends up not only sinning against God but also sinning against his most loyal supporters, the people of Israel. He abuses his power by lying in sin with the wife and daughter of the fiercest warriors of Israel, his own inner circle. So, King David, whom we first meet as someone who is *tov ro'i* and *ro'eh tzon* – or, in the less lyrical English, someone who looks good,[9] and somebody who is careful to watch his sheep,[10] now becomes someone who is not really looking out for his own flock. Or perhaps he is watching them too closely, like a wolf. It is clear that he is no longer protecting them, he is betraying them.

II Samuel 11

4 And David sent messengers, and took her; and she came in to him, and he lay with her; for she was purified from her uncleanness; and she returned unto her house.

ד וַיִּשְׁלַח דָּוִד מַלְאָכִים וַיִּקָּחֶהָ וַתָּבוֹא אֵלָיו וַיִּשְׁכַּב עִמָּהּ וְהִיא מִתְקַדֶּשֶׁת מִטֻּמְאָתָהּ: וַתָּשָׁב אֶל-בֵּיתָהּ.

---

7   II Samuel 23:39

8   A commonly cited modern opinion is that Achitofel should have protected David because his great grandson would have been a future king.

9   I Samuel 16:12: "Now he was ruddy, and withal of beautiful eyes, and goodly to look upon (*tov ro'i*)."

10   I Samuel 16:11: "There remains yet the youngest, and, behold, he keeps the sheep (*ro'eh tzon*)."

5 And the woman conceived; ה וַתַּהַר הָאִשָּׁה: וַתִּשְׁלַח וַתַּגֵּד
and she sent and told David, לְדָוִד וַתֹּאמֶר הָרָה אָנֹכִי.
and said: 'I am with child.'

After David's sin with Batsheva, it dawns on us that David has long been a seducer. David seduced the daughters of Israel. They transferred their allegiance from Saul and fell in love with David:

I Samuel 18

7 And the women sang one to ז וַתַּעֲנֶינָה הַנָּשִׁים הַמְשַׂחֲקוֹת
another in their play, and said: וַתֹּאמַרְןָ: הִכָּה שָׁאוּל
Saul has slain his thousands, בַּאֲלָפָו וְדָוִד בְּרִבְבֹתָיו.
and David his ten thousands.

8 And Saul was very wroth, and ח וַיִּחַר לְשָׁאוּל מְאֹד וַיֵּרַע בְּעֵינָיו
this saying displeased him; and הַדָּבָר הַזֶּה וַיֹּאמֶר נָתְנוּ לְדָוִד
he said: 'They have ascribed to רְבָבוֹת וְלִי נָתְנוּ הָאֲלָפִים:
David ten thousands, and to me וְעוֹד לוֹ אַךְ הַמְּלוּכָה.
they have ascribed but thousands;
and all he lacks is the kingdom!'

He seduced Avigayil, who transferred her allegiance from Naval to David. He took back Michal, even after she married Palti ben Layish. Again he betrayed somebody else's love. And, finally, in perhaps the greatest seduction of the entire story, David seduced Saul's son, Jonathan. Jonathan fell in love with David to the detriment of his father and himself.

This time, however, David doesn't get away with his seduction. The tragedy of David's sin with Batsheva is highlighted when one views the hardship of David's closing years, and contrasts it with David's early brilliance and potential. The text makes this point in a number of ways.

Within the David/Batsheva story, there are a number of parallels to earlier stories. Parallels to the Avigayil story are particularly poignant. If the David and Batsheva story marks a turning point for the worse in David's life, the Avigayil interlude signals the onset of David's ascension to the throne.

I Samuel 25:2

2 And there was a man in Ma'on, ב וְאִישׁ בְּמָעוֹן וּמַעֲשֵׂהוּ בַכַּרְמֶל
whose possessions were in וְהָאִישׁ גָּדוֹל מְאֹד וְלוֹ צֹאן
Carmel; and the man was
very great, and he had

three thousand sheep, and a thousand goats; and he was shearing his sheep in Carmel.	שְׁלֹשֶׁת־אֲלָפִים וְאֶלֶף עִזִּים: וַיְהִי בִגְזֹז אֶת־צֹאנוֹ בַּכַּרְמֶל.

Avigayil was married to Naval, a man of great wealth. Her subsequent marriage to David gives him status. David, once a nomadic warrior, becomes a powerful force.

(One of the reasons that we know that Avigayil has such great wealth besides the account of Naval's 4,000 animals, and the description of him as "very great" is that throughout Tanakh, even later on, Avigayil is always referred to as the wife of Naval Ha-Carmeli.[11] If marriage to a woman is clearly an alliance which catapults a man to power, people always remember where the woman comes from. That is almost the whole point of marrying into influence or wealth. Another striking example of this from history is Eleanor of Aquitaine. Her very name is that of her land holding. She was very sought after for her great wealth and she was, in fact, a bigger landowner than the king of England and the king of France.)

Looking closely at the David and Batsheva story and the David and Avigayil story, we notice many points of stark contrast.

David could easily have had an adulterous relationship with Avigayil. He had plenty of incentive to do so. Naval was ready to kill David, and Avigayil betrayed her husband on behalf of David. She secretly ran to David, beseeching him. Yet, in that instance, David refrained. In the case of Batsheva, circumstantial evidence notwithstanding, David sins without any apparent incentive.

The text clearly invites us to draw a parallel between the two stories. Both stories begin with David sending messengers. Messengers dominate the David and Batsheva story. (Most likely, the messengers are the reason that the prophet Nathan hears of the deed. There are too many of them going back and forth to actually keep things secret.)

In both stories, David begins the conversations with his adversaries with disingenuous calls for peace.

II Samuel 11

6	And David sent to Yo'av,[saying]: 'Send me Uriah the Hittite.' And Yo'av sent Uriah to David.	ו וַיִּשְׁלַח דָּוִד אֶל־יוֹאָב שְׁלַח אֵלַי אֶת־אוּרִיָּה הַחִתִּי: וַיִּשְׁלַח יוֹאָב אֶת־אוּרִיָּה אֶל־דָּוִד.

---

7 And when Uriah came to
him, David asked of him after
the **peace** of Yo'av; and the
peace of the people, and the
welfare (**peace**) of the war.

ז וַיָּבֹא אוּרִיָּה אֵלָיו: וַיִּשְׁאַל
דָּוִד לִשְׁלוֹם יוֹאָב וְלִשְׁלוֹם
הָעָם וְלִשְׁלוֹם הַמִּלְחָמָה.

David begins his discussion with Uriah with three expressions of peace.
What does David say in his message to Naval?

I Samuel 25

5 And David sent ten young
men, and David said to the
young men: 'Get you up to
Carmel, and go to Naval,
and greet him in my name;

ה וַיִּשְׁלַח דָּוִד עֲשָׂרָה נְעָרִים:
וַיֹּאמֶר דָּוִד לַנְּעָרִים עֲלוּ
כַרְמֶלָה וּבָאתֶם אֶל-נָבָל
וּשְׁאֶלְתֶּם-לוֹ בִשְׁמִי לְשָׁלוֹם.

6 and thus you shall say: All hail!
and **peace** be both to you, and
peace be to your house, and
peace be to all that you have.'

ו וַאֲמַרְתֶּם כֹּה לֶחָי: וְאַתָּה שָׁלוֹם
וּבֵיתְךָ שָׁלוֹם וְכֹל אֲשֶׁר-לְךָ שָׁלוֹם.

It is the exact same threefold statement of peace. Since, however, Naval
and Uriah both die at the end of their respective stories, the utterance of
peace becomes meaningless. It is the parallels between the stories that are
meaningful; we are being told to compare the two.

When Nathan the prophet comes to reproach King David, after his sin
with Batsheva, he says:

II Samuel 12

12 For you didst it in **hiding**; but
I will do this thing before all
Israel, and before the sun.

יב כִּי אַתָּה עָשִׂיתָ בַסָּתֶר: וַאֲנִי
אֶעֱשֶׂה אֶת-הַדָּבָר הַזֶּה נֶגֶד
כָּל-יִשְׂרָאֵל וְנֶגֶד הַשָּׁמֶשׁ.

Does Avigayil act in secret? Of course she does.

I Samuel 25

19 And she said unto her young
men: 'Go on before me; behold,
I come after you.' But she told
not her husband Naval.

יט וַתֹּאמֶר לִנְעָרֶיהָ עִבְרוּ
לְפָנַי הִנְנִי אַחֲרֵיכֶם בָּאָה:
וּלְאִישָׁהּ נָבָל לֹא הִגִּידָה.

20 And it was so, as she rode on
her ass, and came down by the
hidden side of the mountain,
that, behold, David and his
men came down towards
her; and she met them.

כ וְהָיָה הִיא רֹכֶבֶת עַל-הַחֲמוֹר וְיֹרֶדֶת
בְּסֵתֶר הָהָר וְהִנֵּה דָוִד וַאֲנָשָׁיו
יֹרְדִים לִקְרָאתָהּ: וַתִּפְגֹּשׁ אֹתָם.

And how does Avigayil arrange for Naval to die?

I Samuel 25

36 And Avigayil came to Naval;
and, behold, he held a feast in
his house, **like the drink of a
king**; and Naval's heart was
merry within him, for he was
very drunken; wherefore she
told him nothing, less or more,
until the morning light.

לו וַתָּבֹא אֲבִיגַיִל אֶל-נָבָל וְהִנֵּה-לוֹ
מִשְׁתֶּה בְּבֵיתוֹ כְּמִשְׁתֵּה הַמֶּלֶךְ
וְלֵב נָבָל טוֹב עָלָיו וְהוּא שִׁכֹּר
עַד-מְאֹד: וְלֹא-הִגִּידָה לּוֹ דָּבָר
קָטֹן וְגָדוֹל-עַד-אוֹר הַבֹּקֶר.

First she gives Naval wine at night "like the drink of the king." Notice,
later on when David tries to convince Uriah to go to Batsheva, he *literally*
gives him the kingly wine to drink, the *mishteh hamelekh*,[12] and makes
him drunk.

Whereas Naval receives the wine from Avigayil for David's betterment,
David is of course sinning when he gives Uriah *his* kingly wine.

When David hears Naval has rejected him, he girds up his sword in
anger and prepares to fight Naval.[13] Similarly, when David hears about
the deaths sustained by his troops in his attempt to kill Uriah,[14] David
says: "People are eaten by the sword in battle, but don't let it bother you."

The sword in the Avigayil story symbolizes David's strength and
restraint in eschewing battle. It also showcases David's decisiveness; although girded for war, he decides against it. In the Batsheva story, David's
weakness and his future impotence are foreshadowed.

And that, by the way, is the curse of Nathan.

II Samuel 12

10 Now therefore, the **sword** shall
never depart from your house;
because you have despised Me,

י וְעַתָּה לֹא-תָסוּר חֶרֶב
מִבֵּיתְךָ-עַד-עוֹלָם: עֵקֶב כִּי

---

12 II Samuel 11:13
13 I Samuel 25:13
14 As above, II Samuel 11:25

and taken the wife of Uriah the Hittite to be your wife.	בְזִתָּנִי וַתִּקַּח אֶת-אֵשֶׁת אוּרִיָּה הַחִתִּי לִהְיוֹת לְךָ לְאִשָּׁה.

The sword, which is a symbol of David's strength in the Avigayil story, degenerates into the symbol of his curse.

The Avigayil story represents David's rise to power. Not only did he acquire financial and political power through this marriage, but it was through Avigayil (probably more than any other person) that David gained moral strength. By persuading David to withhold the sword from Naval, Avigayil guided him to greatness. David exuded strength in conquering his rage and withholding his attack of Naval. And all this occurred right after Saul brutally murdered the inhabitants of Nob, the city of priests.

Saul's great sins are failing to kill Agag, and not waiting for Samuel before bringing the sacrifice – but the people really only turn against Saul after the destruction of Nob. Avigayil, through her moral guidance, saved David from committing the sin of Saul. Thanks to Avigayil, David did not allow his rage to lead him to murder.

Another Parallel

In her attempt to temper David's anger, Avigayil gave David certain gifts.

I Samuel 25

18 Then Avigayil made haste, and took **two hundred loaves**, and **two bottles of wine**, and **five sheep ready dressed**, and five measures of parched corn, and a hundred clusters of raisins, and two hundred cakes of figs, and laid them on asses.	יח וַתְּמַהֵר אבוגיל (אֲבִיגַיִל) וַתִּקַּח מָאתַיִם לֶחֶם וּשְׁנַיִם נִבְלֵי-יַיִן וְחָמֵשׁ צֹאן עשוות (עֲשׂוּיוֹת) וְחָמֵשׁ סְאִים קָלִי וּמֵאָה צִמֻּקִים וּמָאתַיִם דְּבֵלִים וַתָּשֶׂם עַל-הַחֲמֹרִים.

Why are we told the specifics of these gifts? What is their symbolism? Of course, they are very generous gifts, but this book is so brilliant that every single point carries with it deep significance. If you look closely throughout the Book of Samuel, these gifts symbolize the promise of kingship. Similar gifts appear when Saul learns from Samuel that he will be king.

I Samuel 10

3 Then shall you go on forward from there, and you shall come to the terebinth of Tabor, and you shall find there three men going up to God to Beth-el, one carrying **three kids**, and another carrying **three loaves of bread**, and another carrying a **bottle of wine**.

4 And they will salute you, and give you two cakes of bread; which you shall take from their hand.

ג וְחָלַפְתָּ מִשָּׁם וָהָלְאָה וּבָאתָ
עַד-אֵלוֹן תָּבוֹר וּמְצָאוּךְ שָּׁם
שְׁלֹשָׁה אֲנָשִׁים עֹלִים אֶל-הָאֱלֹהִים
בֵּית-אֵל: אֶחָד נֹשֵׂא שְׁלֹשָׁה
גְדָיִים וְאֶחָד נֹשֵׂא שְׁלֹשֶׁת כִּכְּרוֹת
לֶחֶם וְאֶחָד נֹשֵׂא נֵבֶל-יָיִן.

ד וְשָׁאֲלוּ לְךָ לְשָׁלוֹם: וְנָתְנוּ לְךָ
שְׁתֵּי-לֶחֶם וְלָקַחְתָּ מִיָּדָם.

Samuel provides several signs to indicate that Saul's rise to power will actually take place. Saul is told that he will receive a gift of bread, wine, and kid goats. The threefold symbols reappear in the story with Avigayil. (In one instance it is goats, and in the other, it is sheep, but it is the same concept of receiving livestock, bread and wine.)

This motif recurs in the story of the Egyptian. David, on the road to rescue the women and children of his city, comes upon an Egyptian who very clearly symbolizes Saul at that moment. David gives certain gifts to this Egyptian.

I Samuel 30

11 And they found an Egyptian in the field, and brought him to David, and gave him bread, and he did eat; and they gave him water to drink;

12 and they gave him a piece of a cake of figs, and two clusters of raisins; and when he had eaten, his spirit came back to him; for he had eaten no bread, nor drunk any water, three days and three nights.

יא וַיִּמְצְאוּ אִישׁ-מִצְרִי בַּשָּׂדֶה
וַיִּקְחוּ אֹתוֹ אֶל-דָּוִד: וַיִּתְּנוּ-לוֹ
לֶחֶם וַיֹּאכַל וַיַּשְׁקֻהוּ מָיִם.

יב וַיִּתְּנוּ-לוֹ פֶלַח דְּבֵלָה וּשְׁנֵי צִמֻּקִים
וַיֹּאכַל וַתָּשָׁב רוּחוֹ אֵלָיו: כִּי
לֹא-אָכַל לֶחֶם וְלֹא-שָׁתָה מַיִם
שְׁלֹשָׁה יָמִים וּשְׁלֹשָׁה לֵילוֹת.

The raisins and figs remind us of Avigayil's gifts, but notice that the wine and the meat are missing.

Even without the symbolism and the comparison to the promise of the kingship, it is very clear that Avigayil's gifts are a conferral of blessing. By giving these gifts to David and by asking David to recognize his lot, she tells David that she knows he will be king of Israel.

The contrast between Avigayil and Batsheva could not be greater. Following Batsheva leads David away from the heights he has reached with Avigayil and into utter failure. Avigayil saves David from killing innocent men, and due to Batsheva, David causes the deaths of innocent men. Avigayil uses food and drink to prevent David from becoming a criminal. In the Batsheva story, food and drink are used in the context of David attempting to cover up his crime. Through Batsheva, David loses all of the grace that he has gained from his association with Avigayil.

Woolly Parable

With this in mind, I would like to shift to the parable of Nathan, which is central to the David/Batsheva story:

II Samuel 12

1 And the LORD sent Nathan to David. And he came to him, and said to him: 'There were **two men** in one city: **the one rich**, and **the other poor**.

א וַיִּשְׁלַח יי אֶת־נָתָן אֶל־דָּוִד: וַיָּבֹא אֵלָיו וַיֹּאמֶר לוֹ שְׁנֵי אֲנָשִׁים הָיוּ בְּעִיר אֶחָת אֶחָד עָשִׁיר וְאֶחָד רָאשׁ.

2 The **rich** had exceeding many flocks and herds;

ב לְעָשִׁיר הָיָה צֹאן וּבָקָר־הַרְבֵּה מְאֹד.

3 but the **poor** had nothing save one little ewe lamb, which he had bought and reared; and it grew up together with him, and with his children; it did eat of his own morsel, and drank of his own cup, and lay in his bosom, and was to him as a daughter.

ג וְלָרָשׁ אֵין־כֹּל כִּי אִם־כִּבְשָׂה אַחַת קְטַנָּה אֲשֶׁר קָנָה וַיְחַיֶּהָ וַתִּגְדַּל עִמּוֹ וְעִם־בָּנָיו יַחְדָּו: מִפִּתּוֹ תֹאכַל וּמִכֹּסוֹ תִשְׁתֶּה וּבְחֵיקוֹ תִשְׁכָּב וַתְּהִי־לוֹ כְּבַת.

4 And there came a **wanderer** unto the **rich man**, and he spared to take of his own flock and of his own herd, to dress for the **visitor** that was come unto him, but took the **poor man**'s lamb, and dressed it for the **man that came to him.**'

ד וַיָּבֹא הֵלֶךְ לְאִישׁ הֶעָשִׁיר וַיַּחְמֹל לָקַחַת מִצֹּאנוֹ וּמִבְּקָרוֹ לַעֲשׂוֹת לָאֹרֵחַ הַבָּא־לוֹ: וַיִּקַּח אֶת־כִּבְשַׂת הָאִישׁ הָרָאשׁ וַיַּעֲשֶׂהָ לָאִישׁ הַבָּא אֵלָיו

5 And David's anger was greatly
kindled against the **man**; and
he said to Nathan: 'As the
LORD lives, the **man** that has
done this deserves to die;

ה וַיִּחַר-אַף דָּוִד בָּאִישׁ מְאֹד: וַיֹּאמֶר אֶל-נָתָן חַי-יְיָ כִּי בֶן-מָוֶת הָאִישׁ הָעֹשֶׂה זֹאת.

6 and he shall restore the
lamb fourfold, because
he did this thing, and
because he had no pity.'

ו וְאֶת-הַכִּבְשָׂה יְשַׁלֵּם אַרְבַּעְתָּיִם: עֵקֶב אֲשֶׁר עָשָׂה אֶת-הַדָּבָר הַזֶּה וְעַל אֲשֶׁר לֹא-חָמָל.

7 And Nathan said to David:
'**You are the man**. Thus says
the LORD, the God of Israel:
I anointed you king over
Israel, and I delivered you
out of the hand of Saul;

ז וַיֹּאמֶר נָתָן אֶל-דָּוִד אַתָּה הָאִישׁ: כֹּה-אָמַר יְיָ אֱלֹהֵי יִשְׂרָאֵל אָנֹכִי מְשַׁחְתִּיךָ לְמֶלֶךְ עַל-יִשְׂרָאֵל וְאָנֹכִי הִצַּלְתִּיךָ מִיַּד שָׁאוּל.

Our initial assumption is that David is being compared to the rich man – the one who takes the sheep. But in the parable, the rich man gives the sheep away to the wanderer. If we assume that David is the rich man with many sheep, and Batsheva is the stolen ewe, the parable breaks down because David does not give Batsheva away. He keeps her for himself. So what does the wanderer have to do with anything? There are many problems with this parable, but this is the most basic one. The parable has four characters (rich man, poor man, wanderer, sheep), while David's sin only has three (David, Uriah, Batsheva).

Many commentators simply explain away the details as literary technique. Nathan is building up the story. The point is to teach the parable, and not every detail has to jibe. But I think that's giving up before we even start. So let me ask: When Nathan tells David, "You are the man," exactly *which* man is Nathan referring to?

Shadowing Saul

Before we try making sense of the parable's details, however, let us review some of the details of David's career up to this point, paying particular attention to how it intertwines with Saul's.

For starters, both Saul and David were selected from obscurity and chosen to be kings of Israel.

Probably the best example of transposition between the lives of Saul and David is when David considers chasing after the Amalekites who plundered Ziklag. David, the decisive hero of the fight with Goliath and

Israel's champion against the Philistines, is suddenly indecisive; he's unsure of what to do. He turns to the *ephod*[15] and asks if he should pursue the Philistines in battle.[16] Consulting the *ephod*, rather than going out to fight, is not the way one imagines David, but it actually reminds us of another person who is indecisive about battle – Saul.

In I Samuel, chapter 14, we have a story that clearly delineates Saul's ambivalence. While Jonathan calmly sets out to battle with only one other soldier and brilliantly defeats a whole garrison of Philistines, Saul sits under a pomegranate tree, consulting the ephod, trying to figure out whether or not he should go out to battle. Saul's terrible character flaw, indecisiveness, now plagues David. David's early resolve disappears.

Additionally, David captures and divides the booty of Amalek. The people say, "This is David's spoil," *zeh shalal David*.[17] He also allows four hundred youths from Amalek to escape.

So let's get this straight. David is indecisive, he goes after Amalek, does not utterly destroy them, and he takes Amalekite spoil for himself![18]

This should sound familiar. David is now repeating the sins of Saul.

One verse poetically epitomizes the interwoven fates of David and Saul. When David chases Amalek, the text[19] tells us that 200 of David's army of 600 men get tired and don't cross the River Besor. The remaining 400 go on to defeat Amalek without them. Afterwards, there is a discussion. Should any booty go to those who never make it to the battle?

I Samuel 30

24 And who will hearken to you in this matter? **for as is the share of him that goes down to the battle, so shall be the share of him that tarries by the baggage; they shall share alike.'**

כד וּמִי יִשְׁמַע לָכֶם לַדָּבָר הַזֶּה: כִּי כְּחֵלֶק הַיֹּרֵד בַּמִּלְחָמָה וּכְחֵלֶק הַיֹּשֵׁב עַל-הַכֵּלִים יַחְדָּו יַחֲלֹקוּ.

David makes a new law in Israel. The ones who go down to fight, and the ones who remain with the baggage, will share equally.

In the Book of Samuel, who is known for going down into battle? King David, the warrior who attacks the Philistines. Who is the one described as hiding in the baggage? Saul, of whom it was said: "Saul was hiding

---

15	I Samuel 30:7-8
16	I Samuel 30:8
17	I Samuel 30:20
18	I Samuel 15:8
19	I Samuel 30:10

amongst the baggage."[20] David's law is an inadvertent declaration that he (the one who does battle) and Saul (the one who tarries by the baggage) will share a common lot. And they do – their kingships both end tragically.

Many Men

With this in mind, let us turn back to Nathan's parable.

Remember we noted the many messengers in the Batsheva story? All of these other messengers now give way to the messenger of God who brings forth the true message.

As we mentioned before, on the surface it seems like Nathan's parable is a simple one – with the rich man standing in for David and the poor man for Uriah. However, let's look closely at the text again. (This interpretation is not original; it is very heavily influenced by a commentary that I read by Robert Polzin.[21] He lives in Ottawa, Canada. Once you read his commentary, it is very difficult to read the text differently.)

Before we get to Nathan's accusation, "You are the man," let us see which of the parable's three men – rich man, poor man, wanderer – are called man, אִישׁ, "*ish*."

The rich man shows up in verses 1 and 2. The first describes two "**men**... one rich"; the second refers just to the "rich."

The poor man also shows up in verse 1 ("two **men**... and one poor") and in verse 3, he is merely identified as the "poor" one.

The wanderer enters the story in verse 4 as simply a "wanderer." Later in the verse, he is referred to as "the **man** that came to him." Verse 4 also refers to both "the rich **man**" and "the poor **man**."

In short: All three are referred to *without* the prefix "man," *ish*, and *with* the prefix "man," *ish*.

So that when Nathan says "You are the **man**," even though David might understand himself to be the rich man, it's very possible that this is coming to teach us something much deeper.

Perhaps David is being told that he has fulfilled all *three* of these roles in his life.

---

20   I Samuel 10:22

21   Polzin, Robert *David and the Deuteronomist*, 1993: Indiana University Press. 120-130

God tells David:

II Samuel 12

11 Thus says the LORD: Behold, I
will raise up evil against you out
of your own house, and I will take
your wives before your eyes, and
give them unto your neighbor,
and he shall lie with your
wives in the sight of this sun.

יא כֹּה אָמַר יְי הִנְנִי מֵקִים עָלֶיךָ
רָעָה מִבֵּיתֶךָ וְלָקַחְתִּי אֶת-נָשֶׁיךָ
לְעֵינֶיךָ וְנָתַתִּי לְרֵעֶיךָ: וְשָׁכַב
עִם-נָשֶׁיךָ לְעֵינֵי הַשֶּׁמֶשׁ הַזֹּאת.

This recalls what God said earlier,

II Samuel 12

8 and I gave you your master's
house, and your master's wives
into your bosom, and gave you
the house of Israel and of Judah;
and if that were too little, then
would I add to you so much more.

ח וָאֶתְּנָה לְךָ אֶת-בֵּית אֲדֹנֶיךָ
וְאֶת-נְשֵׁי אֲדֹנֶיךָ בְּחֵיקֶךָ וָאֶתְּנָה לְךָ
אֶת-בֵּית יִשְׂרָאֵל וִיהוּדָה: וְאִם-
מְעָט וְאֹסִפָה לְךָ כָּהֵנָּה וְכָהֵנָּה.

Here it sounds as if it is God who is the rich man who takes from
the poor man to give to David. God, who has so many wives, who has
the entire world, decides to take the wives from David's masters and give
them to David.

This may be a metaphoric reference to God handing David the kingship, or it may be a literal statement: God gave Avigayil, the wife of Naval, to David as it says, "And God smote Naval."[22] Similarly, God took
Michal from Saul and gave her to David.

The giving may allude to God's role in the transfer of loyalties of the
daughters of Israel. God even takes the kingdom from Saul and gives it to
David. In this sense, God's role parallels that of the rich man of Nathan's
parable. Saul, is, in this sense, the poor man, and David, *va-yithalekh al
hagag*, the **wanderer** on the roof, now becomes the *helekh*, wanderer, of
the parable. So, perhaps David is the wanderer – we recall that David has
also been referred to as *va-yithalekh* in many key places in the text.

But as Nathan continues to speak, it seems that David becomes the
rich man, having sinned in this case by taking Batsheva. Remembering
back to the First Book of Samuel, David refers to himself as somebody
who will become rich. As the one who felled Goliath, David stood to

22   I Samuel 25:38

earn many riches.[23]

So who is David in this parable?

He is the wanderer.

He is also the rich man because he killed Goliath, and because he took Batsheva in a sinful way.

And David is also the poor man. David refers to himself as a poor man when Saul taunts him, sending his servants with a ruse to get David to admit his wish to be the king's son-in-law, thereby revealing David's ambition to be king. David responds: I can't marry the king's daughter, I am a poor man.[24] David will one day become like the poor man in that he will be exiled, or his kingdom will one day be exiled from the land. As the poor man's ewe was taken, so too, David's wives will be taken by his son Absalom; his kingdom by Jeroboam, then Assyria, and then Babylonia.

Polzin extends the metaphor of the parable beyond the life of David. He comments that it can be viewed also as a parable for the life of Saul.

Saul too is the wanderer on the road. Very clearly he is a wanderer on his way to Samuel, when he first learns of his own kingly destiny.

I Samuel 9

6 And he said to him: 'Behold now, there is in this city a man of God, and he is a man that is held in honor; all that he says comes surely to pass; now **let us go** there; perhaps he can tell us concerning our journey whereon **we go**.'

ו וַיֹּאמֶר לוֹ הִנֵּה-נָא אִישׁ-אֱלֹהִים
בָּעִיר הַזֹּאת וְהָאִישׁ נִכְבָּד כֹּל
אֲשֶׁר-יְדַבֵּר בּוֹא יָבוֹא: עַתָּה
נֵלְכָה שָּׁם-אוּלַי יַגִּיד לָנוּ אֶת-
דַּרְכֵּנוּ אֲשֶׁר-הָלַכְנוּ עָלֶיהָ.

Saul, too, in turn acts like the rich man, when he takes Michal away from David in the beginning of chapter 26, and gives her to Palti Ben Layish. And in the end, Saul, too, becomes the poor man, as God strips him of the kingdom to confer it upon David.

I Samuel 15

28 And Samuel said unto him: 'The LORD has torn the kingdom of Israel from you this day, and

כח וַיֹּאמֶר אֵלָיו שְׁמוּאֵל קָרַע יְיָ
אֶת-מַמְלְכוּת יִשְׂרָאֵל מֵעָלֶיךָ

---

23   I Samuel 17:25
24   I Samuel 18:23

has given it to **a neighbor of
yours**, who is better than you.'

הַיּוֹם: וּנְתָנָהּ לְרֵעֲךָ הַטּוֹב מִמֶּךָּ.

So God is taking away the kingdom from Saul because he finds a different man – David. Now remember back when Saul was first anointed:

I Samuel 10

6 And the spirit of the LORD will
come mightily upon you, and you
shall prophesy with them, and
will be turned into another man.

ו וְצָלְחָה עָלֶיךָ רוּחַ יְיָ וְהִתְנַבִּיתָ
עִמָּם: וְנֶהְפַּכְתָּ לְאִישׁ אַחֵר.

That is what happens. Saul becomes another man. Saul, who had been the wanderer, becomes the rich man, and will, in the end, become another man – the poor man.

Ultimately, this parable extends even beyond David and Saul to become a meditation on the very notion of kingship in Israel.

Early on, the people receive a stern warning from Samuel as to what they can realistically expect from a king.[25] Kings take the sons and daughters of the people. Kings take the riches of the kingdom and use them for personal benefit. Is this not what David does by sinning with Batsheva? Does David not plunder riches? Does he not take the people's sons for the army, and their daughters for himself? We see this, too, in the way David dines and wines Uriah with the riches of the palace for his own benefit. This is what the kingdom has become. All the words of Samuel on the subject of kingship have come to pass. So this parable of Nathan may be seen as a reflection on kingship in general.

Lastly, Polzin applies this parable to the Jewish people. At first, they too are wanderers on the road. God takes Canaan from the other nations and gives the land to the Jewish people:

Judges 6

9 and I delivered you out of the
hand of the Egyptians, and
out of the hand of all that
oppressed you, and drove
them out from before you,
and **gave you their land**.

ט וָאַצִּל אֶתְכֶם מִיַּד מִצְרַיִם וּמִיַּד
כָּל-לֹחֲצֵיכֶם: וָאֲגָרֵשׁ אוֹתָם
מִפְּנֵיכֶם וָאֶתְּנָה לָכֶם אֶת-אַרְצָם.

---

25   I Samuel 8:10-18

At that point, the Jewish people are like the rich man. But although they have everything, they lust after the very concept of kingship. They lust after idolatry. They lust after what's not theirs. They want to be like other nations:

I Samuel 8

4 Then all the elders of Israel gathered themselves together, and came to Samuel to Ramah.

ד וַיִּתְקַבְּצוּ כֹּל זִקְנֵי יִשְׂרָאֵל: וַיָּבֹאוּ אֶל-שְׁמוּאֵל הָרָמָתָה.

5 And they said to him: 'Behold, you are old, and your sons walk not in your ways; now make us a king to judge us like all the nations.'

ה וַיֹּאמְרוּ אֵלָיו הִנֵּה אַתָּה זָקַנְתָּ וּבָנֶיךָ לֹא הָלְכוּ בִּדְרָכֶיךָ: עַתָּה שִׂימָה-לָּנוּ מֶלֶךְ לְשָׁפְטֵנוּ–כְּכָל-הַגּוֹיִם.

David's adultery reminds us of the betrayal that the Jews perpetrate against God. In the end, the Jewish nation resembles the poor man. The people will be exiled and God will transfer the land of promise to the people of Assyria.

Hannah, the great Hannah, has foretold all of this from the very beginning:

I Samuel 2

7 The LORD makes poor, and makes rich; He brings low, He also lifts up.

ז יְיָ מוֹרִישׁ וּמַעֲשִׁיר: מַשְׁפִּיל אַף-מְרוֹמֵם.

So David, Saul, and the people of Israel, each having received their promised kingdom, will ultimately all be exiled. The best that any one of them can hope for, at this point, is some measure of personal forgiveness from God.

II Samuel 12

9 Wherefore have you **despised** the word of the LORD, to do that which is evil in My sight? Uriah the Hittite you have smitten with the sword, and his wife you have taken to be your wife, and him you have slain with the sword of the children of Ammon.

ט מַדּוּעַ בָּזִיתָ אֶת-דְּבַר יְיָ לַעֲשׂוֹת הָרַע בעינו (בְּעֵינַי) אֶת אוּרִיָּה הַחִתִּי הִכִּיתָ בַחֶרֶב וְאֶת-אִשְׁתּוֹ לָקַחְתָּ לְּךָ לְאִשָּׁה: וְאֹתוֹ הָרַגְתָּ בְּחֶרֶב בְּנֵי עַמּוֹן.

The only other time this root *bazaz*, (בזז), "despise," appears in the Book of Samuel is when the man of God comes to rebuke Eli the Priest about his sons, and to tell Eli that a new, faithful priest, Samuel, will arise to assume the priesthood.

I Samuel 2

30 Therefore the LORD, the God of Israel, says: I said indeed that your house, and the house of your father, should walk before Me for ever; but now the LORD says: Be it far from Me: for them that honour Me I will honour, and **they that despise Me** shall be lightly esteemed.

ל לָכֵן נְאֻם-יְיָ אֱלֹהֵי יִשְׂרָאֵל
אָמוֹר אָמַרְתִּי בֵּיתְךָ וּבֵית
אָבִיךָ יִתְהַלְּכוּ לְפָנַי עַד-עוֹלָם:
וְעַתָּה נְאֻם-יְיָ חָלִילָה לִּי
כִּי-מְכַבְּדַי אֲכַבֵּד וּבֹזַי יֵקָלּוּ.

Fates Diverge

In the end, the greatest lesson that David teaches comes to us by way of his sin – and it is his penitence. According to the Talmud,[26] David sins only in order to teach us about how to repent. With David's words, "I have sinned to the Lord,"[27] it seems at first glance, that all is forgiven. Yet, the limitations of repentance are evident in David's subsequent suffering. His first child with Batsheva dies. His son, Absalom, lies with David's own concubines before all of Israel – a direct fulfillment of the curse of Nathan.[28] So although David gains personal absolution, he suffers deeply for the remainder of his life.

This theme of contrition connects the lives of Saul and David. Nathan tells David that he is forgiven for his sin. Why isn't Saul forgiven?

I Samuel 15

24 And Saul said unto Samuel: 'I have sinned; for I have transgressed the commandment

כד וַיֹּאמֶר שָׁאוּל אֶל-שְׁמוּאֵל
חָטָאתִי כִּי-עָבַרְתִּי אֶת-פִּי-יְיָ

---

26   See Talmud Bavli, Avodah Zarah 4b, with Rashi's interpretation. See also the Comments of Shlomo Golvenshitz, *Seyag Ve-Siach Be-Neviim*, Shmuel Bet, 127.

27   חָטָאתִי לַיְיָ II Samuel 12:13

28   II Samuel 12:11

of the LORD, and your words;
because I feared the people,
and hearkened to their voice.

וְאֶת-דְּבָרֶיךָ: כִּי יָרֵאתִי
אֶת-הָעָם וָאֶשְׁמַע בְּקוֹלָם.

25 Now therefore, I pray
you, pardon my sin, and
return with me, that I may
worship the LORD.'

כה וְעַתָּה שָׂא נָא אֶת-חַטָּאתִי:
וְשׁוּב עִמִּי וְאֶשְׁתַּחֲוֶה לַיי.

26 And Samuel said to Saul: 'I will
not return with you; for you have
rejected the word of the LORD,
and **the LORD has rejected you**
from being king over Israel.'

כו וַיֹּאמֶר שְׁמוּאֵל אֶל-שָׁאוּל
לֹא אָשׁוּב עִמָּךְ: כִּי מָאַסְתָּה
אֶת-דְּבַר יי וַיִּמְאָסְךָ יי
מִהְיוֹת מֶלֶךְ עַל-יִשְׂרָאֵל.

Samuel tells Saul that his repentance will not be accepted.

I Samuel 15

29 And also the Glory of Israel will
not lie nor repent; for He is not
a man, that He should repent.'

כט וְגַם נֵצַח יִשְׂרָאֵל לֹא יְשַׁקֵּר וְלֹא
יִנָּחֵם: כִּי לֹא אָדָם הוּא לְהִנָּחֵם.

God will not change his mind. With these words, Samuel seems to be rejecting the concept of repentance.

But we know from the Book of Samuel that God *does* believe in return. Samuel, it seems, accepts some measure of Saul's penitence.

I Samuel 15

30 Then he (Saul) said: 'I have
sinned; yet honor me now, I
pray you, before the elders of
my people, and before Israel,
and return with me, that I may
worship the LORD your God.'

ל וַיֹּאמֶר חָטָאתִי עַתָּה כַּבְּדֵנִי נָא
נֶגֶד זִקְנֵי-עַמִּי וְנֶגֶד יִשְׂרָאֵל: וְשׁוּב
עִמִּי וְהִשְׁתַּחֲוֵיתִי לַיי אֱלֹהֶיךָ.

31 So Samuel returned after Saul;
and Saul worshiped the LORD.

לא וַיָּשָׁב שְׁמוּאֵל אַחֲרֵי שָׁאוּל:
וַיִּשְׁתַּחוּ שָׁאוּל לַיי.

Although Samuel and Saul return together, God tells Samuel that He is finished with Saul — the repentance has not been accepted by God. Although the possibility for repentance always exists, God is not bound to accept it.

But as Jonathan says, the possibility that God will show us favor always exists.

I Samuel 14

6 And Jonathan said to the young
man that bore his armor:
'Come and let us go over to the
garrison of these uncircumcised;
**it may be that the LORD
will work for us**; for there is
no restraint to the LORD to
save by many or by few.'

ו וַיֹּאמֶר יְהוֹנָתָן אֶל-הַנַּעַר נֹשֵׂא כֵלָיו
לְכָה וְנַעְבְּרָה אֶל-מַצַּב הָעֲרֵלִים
הָאֵלֶּה אוּלַי יַעֲשֶׂה יְיָ לָנוּ: כִּי אֵין
לַיְיָ מַעְצוֹר לְהוֹשִׁיעַ בְּרַב אוֹ בִמְעָט.

And so we ask the question, why does God accept David's return even
partially, and reject the return of Saul entirely? I think this reflects the
fundamental nature of David's sin – he tries to conceal it, as though he
can hide from God.

When Yo'av is out in the battlefield sending messages to David,[29] he
tells the messenger to anticipate certain questions on David's behalf. David never asks these questions. However, Yo'av anticipates that David will
say certain things:

II Samuel 11

19 and he (Yo'av) charged the
messenger, saying: 'When you
have made an end of telling
all the things concerning
the war to the king,

20 it shall be that, if the king's wrath
arise, and he (David) says to you:
**Why did you go so close to the
city to fight? Knew you not that
they would shoot from the wall?**

21 **Who smote Avimelekh the
son of Jerubbesheth? Did not a
woman cast an upper millstone
upon him from the wall, that
he died at Thebez? Why did
you go so close to the wall?**
Then shall you say: Your servant
Uriah the Hittite is dead also.'

יט וַיְצַו אֶת-הַמַּלְאָךְ לֵאמֹר:
כְּכַלּוֹתְךָ אֵת כָּל-דִּבְרֵי
הַמִּלְחָמָה לְדַבֵּר אֶל-הַמֶּלֶךְ.

כ וְהָיָה אִם-תַּעֲלֶה חֲמַת הַמֶּלֶךְ
וְאָמַר לְךָ מַדּוּעַ נִגַּשְׁתֶּם אֶל-הָעִיר
לְהִלָּחֵם: הֲלוֹא יְדַעְתֶּם אֵת
אֲשֶׁר-יֹרוּ מֵעַל הַחוֹמָה.

כא מִי-הִכָּה אֶת-אֲבִימֶלֶךְ בֶּן-יְרֻבֶּשֶׁת
הֲלוֹא אִשָּׁה הִשְׁלִיכָה עָלָיו פֶּלַח
רֶכֶב מֵעַל הַחוֹמָה וַיָּמָת בְּתֵבֵץ
לָמָה נִגַּשְׁתֶּם אֶל-הַחוֹמָה: וְאָמַרְתָּ–
גַּם עַבְדְּךָ אוּרִיָּה הַחִתִּי מֵת.

---

29   II Samuel 11:18-25

We are left wondering, why does the text include this passage? Furthermore, what is Yo'av getting at? What is it that Avimelekh tried to do? Let us look:

Judges 9

51 But there was a strong tower within the city, and there fled all the men and women, even all they of the city, and shut themselves in, and went up to the **roof** of the tower.

נא וּמִגְדַּל-עֹז הָיָה בְתוֹךְ-הָעִיר וַיָּנֻסוּ שָׁמָּה כָּל-הָאֲנָשִׁים וְהַנָּשִׁים וְכֹל בַּעֲלֵי הָעִיר וַיִּסְגְּרוּ בַּעֲדָם: וַיַּעֲלוּ עַל-גַּג הַמִּגְדָּל.

53 And a certain woman cast an upper millstone upon Avimelekh's head, and broke his skull.

נג וַתַּשְׁלֵךְ אִשָּׁה אַחַת פֶּלַח רֶכֶב עַל-רֹאשׁ אֲבִימֶלֶךְ: וַתָּרִץ אֶת-גֻּלְגָּלְתּוֹ.

54 Then he called hastily to the young man his armor-bearer, and said to him: 'Draw your sword, and kill me, that men say not of me: A woman slew him.' And his young man thrust him through, and he died.

נד וַיִּקְרָא מְהֵרָה אֶל-הַנַּעַר נֹשֵׂא כֵלָיו וַיֹּאמֶר לוֹ שְׁלֹף חַרְבְּךָ וּמוֹתְתֵנִי פֶּן-יֹאמְרוּ לִי אִשָּׁה הֲרָגָתְהוּ: וַיִּדְקְרֵהוּ נַעֲרוֹ וַיָּמֹת.

Eye in the Sky

On one hand, Yo'av tells David, you are not the only king who ever risked losing his kingdom because of a woman on a roof. Moreover, although Avimelekh also tried to cover up his humiliation, it couldn't be kept secret, either.

Every time David sins, he tries to cover it up. That is the nature of his sin. However, Yo'av tells him that the truth will always be revealed. And David finally gets it. This central point, that sin cannot be concealed from God, is what David grasps as the essential teaching of Nathan.

II Samuel 12

13 And David said to Nathan: '**I have sinned against the LORD.**' And Nathan said to David: 'The LORD also has put away your sin; you shall not die.

יג וַיֹּאמֶר דָּוִד אֶל-נָתָן חָטָאתִי לַיָי: וַיֹּאמֶר נָתָן אֶל-דָּוִד גַּם-יְי הֶעֱבִיר חַטָּאתְךָ-לֹא תָמוּת.

While Saul sins in full view of everyone – paradoxically, he tries to hide his sin. In contrast, David sins in secret, yet he reveals his sin to all. This speaks to David's greatness, and it is this acceptance of the yoke of God which leads to David's forgiveness.

As Yehudah Eleetzur[30] points out, when Nathan comes to David, there are many excuses that David can offer. He can tell Nathan it was just one night. He can say that Uriah's death is a terrible accident. He can make up any story. But he recognizes the futility of trying to continue the cover-up and fully admits his sin.

David's approach contrasts with Saul's initial justification of his actions.[31]

Further, if you look at chapter 12 closely, you see David repenting for his earlier sins at every single step. Rabbi Jack Riemer pointed out to me[32] that David even names one of his sons Nathan.[33] It is very clear that David honors Nathan, and seeks to incorporate the message of Nathan into his life.

When David's son with Batsheva is sick,[34] David does not eat. As soon as the child dies, David eats.[35] How does this show repentance? Remember when Uriah says to David:

II Samuel 11

11 And Uriah said to David: 'The ark, and Israel, and Judah, abide in booths; and my lord Yo'av, and the servants of my lord, are encamped in the open field; shall I then go into my house, to eat and to drink, and to lie with my wife? as you live, and as your soul lives, I will not do this thing.'

יא וַיֹּאמֶר אוּרִיָּה אֶל-דָּוִד הָאָרוֹן וְיִשְׂרָאֵל וִיהוּדָה יֹשְׁבִים בַּסֻּכּוֹת וַאדֹנִי יוֹאָב וְעַבְדֵי אֲדֹנִי עַל-פְּנֵי הַשָּׂדֶה חֹנִים וַאֲנִי אָבוֹא אֶל-בֵּיתִי לֶאֱכֹל וְלִשְׁתּוֹת וְלִשְׁכַּב עִם-אִשְׁתִּי חַיֶּךָ וְחֵי נַפְשֶׁךָ אִם-אֶעֱשֶׂה אֶת-הַדָּבָר הַזֶּה.

As part of his repentance, David learns from Uriah's actions, and withholds from attending to his own needs while his child is battling for his life. When his son dies, David recognizes that the battle is done, and he begins to eat.

---

30   *Iyyunim b'Sefer Shmuel*, ed. B.Z. Luria (Jerusalem, 1992), vol. I, 187
31   See Samuel 13: 8-14; and I Samuel 15: 14-23
32   In private communication
33   II Samuel 5:14
34   II Samuel 12:15
35   II Samuel 12:22

On another level, this whole story takes place because David has absented himself from battle. Once he repents, David resumes his place at the head of his troops.[36]

At the close of the Batsheva episode, David returns with the people to Jerusalem, victorious. [37] More than that, David really returns to God.

Witnessing David's repentance process we learn about the power of repentance.

In Psalm 51, David says, "God, hide your face from my sin." In saying that, David is recognizing that God's face *is* toward his sin – it is impossible to hide from God. David prays for the miracle of grace, and hopes that perhaps God will decide to look away and forgive.

When we think about David, the enchanted warrior is not the persona with which we generally identify. Most of us are more like the David who sometimes sins. We connect with the David who messes up like we do all too often. David's true greatness is in his repentance.

There are two different ways to repent. The Talmud[38] discusses this and Rabbi Abraham Isaac Kook and Rabbi Joseph B. Soleveitchik write frequently about it: One repentance is from fear; we are worried about the punishment we are going to get. Repentance which comes from love is on a higher level. It comes with an awareness that sin creates a barrier between us and God. More than anything, repentance from love seeks to remove that barrier and once again allow the penitent to cleave to God.

David is punished. The punishment isn't going to be removed. The kingdom disintegrates. There are points of elevation, but there is a steady deterioration until the exile at the end of the Book of Kings. Yet, despite the numerous punishments, despite the fact that his concubines are taken by his own son in front of the eyes of all of Israel, despite David's manipulative and rebellious children, David seeks closeness with God. He seeks the repentance of love. He does not aim to remove the punishment, but rather to remove the barrier between himself and God.

And this is why the Talmud[39] states that in the world to come, when all of the righteous ones sit at one table, the one honored with performing the blessing on the cup of blessing will be David.

By sinning and returning, David has taught us all about the power of hope and faith and about the never ending ability to return to God.

---

36   II Samuel 12:29
37   II Samuel 12:31
38   Yomah 86a. As cited and discussed by Medan, 156-161.
39   Pesachim 119b

YCT Tanakh Companion

Anarchy and Monarchy Part Two
II Samuel 21-24

based on a lecture by **Rabbi David Silber**

What do the final chapters of the Book of Samuel teach us?

Had the narrative simply ended with the death of David, we might not search for further meaning. However, since David's story continues into the Book of Kings, we are left with a question: Why does this book end where it does, and what are we to learn from it?

To answer this question, let us first take a look at the beginning of the final chapter:

II Samuel 24

1 **And the anger of the LORD was continued against Israel,** and He incited David against them, saying: 'Go, number Israel and Judah.'

א וַיֹּסֶף אַף-יְיָ לַחֲרוֹת בְּיִשְׂרָאֵל:
וַיָּסֶת אֶת-דָּוִד בָּהֶם לֵאמֹר לֵךְ
מְנֵה אֶת-יִשְׂרָאֵל וְאֶת-יְהוּדָה.

On this phrase, Rashi asks: What is God angry about?

I have a further question: what does the word "continued" mean here? "God continued to be angry with Israel" – from when?

Here, the commentaries[1] point out the *previous* story where God is angry – chapter 21. There it says:

II Samuel 21

1 And there was a famine in the days of David three years, year after year; and David sought the

א וַיְהִי רָעָב בִּימֵי דָוִד שָׁלֹשׁ שָׁנִים
שָׁנָה אַחֲרֵי שָׁנָה וַיְבַקֵּשׁ

---

1   Metzudot, II Samuel 24:1

face of the LORD. And the LORD said: 'It is for Saul, and for his bloody house, because he put to death the Give'onites.'

דָּוִד אֶת־פְּנֵי יְיָ: וַיֹּאמֶר יְיָ אֶל־שָׁאוּל וְאֶל־בֵּית הַדָּמִים עַל־אֲשֶׁר־הֵמִית אֶת־הַגִּבְעֹנִים.

God's anger is expressed in a three-year famine. Its cause: Saul's massacre of the Give'onites. We first hear of of the Give'onites in the Book of Joshua.[2] Deathly afraid of the Israelites, the Give'onites pretend that they have come from afar to make a covenant of peace with the Israelites, when in fact they represent one of the indigenous peoples that Joshua is prepared to destroy. Duped, Israel takes an oath not to harm them – and that is the last we hear of them until this verse.

Saul's apparent persecution of the Give'onites is not in the text, but God's resulting anger *is* documented.

Chapter 21 is about a sin that Saul committed by violating an oath taken in God's name and about how David subsequently sets things right. Although Saul was being zealous for his people,[3] violating the oath was still a sin.

Here, in chapter 24, God *continues* to be angry for Saul's sin, and we learn details concerning a different sin committed by his successor, David:

II Samuel 24

1 And the anger of the LORD continued to be kindled against Israel, and He incited David against them, saying: 'Go, number Israel and Judah.'

א וַיֹּסֶף אַף־יְיָ לַחֲרוֹת בְּיִשְׂרָאֵל: וַיָּסֶת אֶת־דָּוִד בָּהֶם לֵאמֹר לֵךְ מְנֵה אֶת־יִשְׂרָאֵל וְאֶת־יְהוּדָה.

2 And the king said to Yo'av the captain of the host that was with him: 'Go now to and fro through all the tribes of Israel, from Dan even to Beer-sheba, and number the people, that I may know the count of the people.'

ב וַיֹּאמֶר הַמֶּלֶךְ אֶל־יוֹאָב שַׂר־הַחַיִל אֲשֶׁר־אִתּוֹ שׁוּט־נָא בְּכָל־שִׁבְטֵי יִשְׂרָאֵל מִדָּן וְעַד־בְּאֵר שֶׁבַע וּפִקְדוּ אֶת־הָעָם: וְיָדַעְתִּי אֵת מִסְפַּר הָעָם.

God incites David against the people[4] saying, "Count them," take a census. David instructs his general to be involved in the count and Yo'av,

---

2   Joshua 9

3   II Samuel 21:2

4   An interesting topic beyond the scope of our present discussion.

who realizes that this is wrong, asks David to reconsider:

II Samuel 24

3 And Yo'av said to the king: 'Now the LORD your God add to the people, however many they may be, a hundredfold, and may the eyes of my lord the king see it; but why does my lord the king delight in this thing?'

ג וַיֹּאמֶר יוֹאָב אֶל-הַמֶּלֶךְ וְיוֹסֵף יְיָ אֱלֹהֶיךָ אֶל-הָעָם כָּהֵם וְכָהֵם מֵאָה פְעָמִים וְעֵינֵי אֲדֹנִי-הַמֶּלֶךְ רֹאוֹת: וַאדֹנִי הַמֶּלֶךְ לָמָּה חָפֵץ בַּדָּבָר הַזֶּה?

But the king insists. The Tanakh describes how Yo'av and his men go throughout the land to take a census and they come back after nine months and twenty days[5] to give the count to David.

David is very contrite afterwards:

II Samuel 24

10 And David's heart smote him after that he had numbered the people. And David said to the LORD: 'I have sinned greatly in what I have done; but now, O LORD, put away, I beseech You, the iniquity of Your servant; for I have been greatly foolish.'

י וַיַּךְ לֵב-דָּוִד אֹתוֹ אַחֲרֵי-כֵן סָפַר אֶת-הָעָם: וַיֹּאמֶר דָּוִד אֶל-יְיָ חָטָאתִי מְאֹד אֲשֶׁר עָשִׂיתִי וְעַתָּה יְיָ הַעֲבֶר-נָא אֶת-עֲוֹן עַבְדְּךָ כִּי נִסְכַּלְתִּי מְאֹד.

What is David's sin? David's sin is counting the people, and he realizes it on his own.

David says: "I have sinned *greatly*. I have been *greatly* foolish." He talks about his behavior as sinful and foolish, and uses the word "greatly." Only a few chapters earlier, David's response to Nathan the prophet regarding his sin with Batsheva is: "I have sinned against the Lord."[6] He doesn't say, "greatly." *That* was only adultery, a cover-up, and mass murder. That does not rate the term "greatly." But here, David reaches for even more emphatic phraseology.

What is the grievous sin? Counting the people. Why is this so awful?

---

5   II Samuel 24:8
6   II Samuel 12:13

Epilogue in Four Chapters

To understand the significance of these two breaches committed by the first two kings, let us take a step back and examine the overall structure of the end of the Book of Samuel.

Chapters 21 and 24, as we have seen, describe the sins of the kings. The sin of Saul (and David's response) occupies 21, the sin of David, 24.

What follows is an outline of these four chapters, divided into two sets of three:

A: chapter 21 (first half)   Sin of King Saul (Give'onites)
B: chapter 21 (second half)   Description of David's warriors
C: chapter 22   The song of David

C: chapter 23 (first half)   Another song of David
B: chapter 23 (second half)   More warriors of David
A: chapter 24   Sin of King David (census)

Here we have what is called a chiastic structure, where the themes in the first half, ABC, are mirrored in the second: CBA.

This elaborate structure suggests that these chapters are a separate entity from the rest of the work. Thus, what we are looking at is no longer a chronological presentation, but a thematic presentation. Appropriately, the structure highlights the three personas of David: David the psalmist, David the warrior, and David the sinner. Essentially, the end of the Book of Samuel is a kind of epilogue with its own internal structure, and its own message.

As such, I would say, it is parallel to the end of the Book of Judges, which works the same way. Incorporated in the last five chapters of Judges are two stories[7] with a recurring *leitmotif* connecting them: "In those days there was no king."[8]

These last four chapters of the Book of Samuel have their own particular construction which carries its own message. It is a message that provides an answer to Rashi's question: What *is* God angry about in chapter 24?

---

7   The idol of Micah (Judges 17-18), and the concubine of Give'ah (Judges 19-21)

8   Judges 17:6; 18:1; 19:1; 21:5

Supplanting God/Reflecting God

Every book has its own agenda. The issue of the Book of Kings and the Book of Samuel is monarchy: the kingship of Israel, and its relationship to the kingship of God. The end of the Book of Samuel raises the question: Can kingship in Israel work? When God tells Samuel to give the people what they want and anoint a king,[9] God is giving Israel a chance to create a monarchy that will either supplant God or reflect God.

This epilogue returns us to kingship, the core issue of the Book of Samuel, which has been all but forgotten in the dramas of David and Saul and Absalom.

Here at the end of the Book of Samuel, we find that David has performed the ultimate crime – counting the people without God.

What would have been the proper way to count the people?

Exodus[10] is clear: A census must be performed by means of the half-shekel head count associated with the Tabernacle (*mishkan*). The people should be counted through God because counting means ownership: Israel is God's people.

David's act of counting without permission is therefore a direct affront to God. It makes the statement: These people are mine. The Bible says: "No, Israel is *God's* people, and *you* work for God, too." Seen this way, counting the people is certainly more serious than David's sin with Batsheva, which was an indulgence that spiraled out of control.

David recognizes his sin, and sets about trying to resolve it.

First, the prophet Gad comes to reprove David for taking the census:

II Samuel 24

13 So Gad came to David, and told him, and said to him: 'Shall seven years of famine come to you in your land? or will you flee three months before your foes while they pursue you? or shall there be three days' plague in your land? now advise you, and consider what word I shall return to Him who sent me.'	יג וַיָּבֹא-גָד אֶל-דָּוִד וַיַּגֶּד-לוֹ: וַיֹּאמֶר לוֹ הֲתָבוֹא לְךָ שֶׁבַע שָׁנִים רָעָב בְּאַרְצֶךָ אִם-שְׁלֹשָׁה חֳדָשִׁים נֻסְךָ לִפְנֵי-צָרֶיךָ וְהוּא רֹדְפֶךָ וְאִם-הֱיוֹת שְׁלֹשֶׁת יָמִים דֶּבֶר בְּאַרְצֶךָ עַתָּה דַּע וּרְאֵה מָה-אָשִׁיב שֹׁלְחִי דָּבָר.
14 And David said to Gad: 'I am in a great strait; let us fall now into the hand of the LORD; for	יד וַיֹּאמֶר דָּוִד אֶל-גָד צַר-לִי מְאֹד: נִפְּלָה-נָּא בְיַד-יי

---

9   I Samuel 8:22
10 Exodus 30:12-16

His mercies are great; and let me
not fall into the hand of man.'

כִּי-רַבִּים רַחֲמָו וּבְיַד-
אָדָם אַל-אֶפֹּלָה.

15 So the LORD sent a pestilence
upon Israel from the morning
even to the time appointed;
and there died of the people
from Dan even to Beer-sheba
seventy thousand men.

טו וַיִּתֵּן יְיָ דֶּבֶר בְּיִשְׂרָאֵל מֵהַבֹּקֶר
וְעַד-עֵת מוֹעֵד וַיָּמָת מִן-הָעָם מִדָּן
וְעַד-בְּאֵר שֶׁבַע שִׁבְעִים אֶלֶף אִישׁ.

The prophet Gad presents David with a Hobson's choice, an apparently
free choice that is in fact no choice at all. What is going on here? What is
God's message in offering David so many bad choices?

Solomon's Choice

God's offer to David of an array of choices brings to mind a subsequent
story in the beginning of the Book of Kings:

I Kings 3

5 In Give'on the LORD appeared
to Solomon in a dream by
night; and God said: 'Ask
what I shall give you.'

ה בְּגִבְעוֹן נִרְאָה יְיָ אֶל-שְׁלֹמֹה
בַּחֲלוֹם הַלָּיְלָה: וַיֹּאמֶר אֱלֹהִים
שְׁאַל מָה אֶתֶּן-לָךְ.

God appears to Solomon and asks him what he would like. Solomon
requests wisdom in order to guide the people. That was a good answer.

I Kings 3

10 And the speech pleased
the LORD, that Solomon
had asked this thing.

י וַיִּיטַב הַדָּבָר בְּעֵינֵי יְיָ: כִּי שָׁאַל
שְׁלֹמֹה אֶת-הַדָּבָר הַזֶּה.

11 And God said to him: 'Because
you asked for this thing, and
have not asked for long life;
neither have you asked riches
for yourself, nor have asked
the life of your enemies;
but have asked for yourself
understanding to discern justice;

יא וַיֹּאמֶר אֱלֹהִים אֵלָיו יַעַן אֲשֶׁר
שָׁאַלְתָּ אֶת-הַדָּבָר הַזֶּה וְלֹא-שָׁאַלְתָּ
לְּךָ יָמִים רַבִּים וְלֹא-שָׁאַלְתָּ לְּךָ
עֹשֶׁר וְלֹא שָׁאַלְתָּ נֶפֶשׁ אֹיְבֶיךָ:
וְשָׁאַלְתָּ לְּךָ הָבִין לִשְׁמֹעַ מִשְׁפָּט.

12 behold, I have done according to your word: lo, I have given you a wise and an understanding heart; so that there have been none like you before, neither after you shall any arise like unto you.	יב הִנֵּה עָשִׂיתִי כִּדְבָרֶיךָ: הִנֵּה נָתַתִּי לְךָ לֵב חָכָם וְנָבוֹן אֲשֶׁר כָּמוֹךָ לֹא-הָיָה לְפָנֶיךָ וְאַחֲרֶיךָ לֹא-יָקוּם כָּמוֹךָ.
13 And I have also given you that which you have not asked, both riches and honor–so that there have not been any among the kings like you–all your days.'	יג וְגַם אֲשֶׁר לֹא-שָׁאַלְתָּ נָתַתִּי לָךְ גַּם-עֹשֶׁר גַּם-כָּבוֹד: אֲשֶׁר לֹא-הָיָה כָמוֹךָ אִישׁ בַּמְּלָכִים כָּל-יָמֶיךָ.

God ends up giving Solomon all the other good things as well. It was a test. By asking for discernment to lead the people rather than seeking personal comfort, Solomon demonstrates that is already wise.

Plagued by Choice

David now undergoes a similar challenge. In this object lesson, the prophet walks through the door, and says: "Okay, you are the boss. Tell God what you want."

Of course, the choices Gad offers David are false choices. All the alternatives are bad. And the funny thing is, the reader knows the answer also. This test is about the *illusion* of control – the illusion of leadership, when true leadership ultimately rests with God.

There is only one answer to Gad's question, because the Bible describes the rules for counting the people:

Exodus 30

12 When you take the census of the children of Israel, according to their number, then every man shall give a ransom for his soul unto the LORD– when you number them; so that **there be no plague among them when you number them**.	יב כִּי תִשָּׂא אֶת-רֹאשׁ בְּנֵי-יִשְׂרָאֵל לִפְקֻדֵיהֶם וְנָתְנוּ אִישׁ כֹּפֶר נַפְשׁוֹ לַיי בִּפְקֹד אֹתָם: וְלֹא-יִהְיֶה בָהֶם נֶגֶף בִּפְקֹד אֹתָם.

Counting without giving God His due incurs a plague. Only one of the choices is plague, which is *"dever"* (דבר). Further, David has already *had* the other punishments. Chapter 21 is about the famine, and David has already experienced war. Been there, done that.

Also, the verse itself points to the answer with a play on words:

II Samuel 24

13 So Gad came to David, and told him, and said to him: 'Shall seven years of famine come to you in your land? or will you flee three months before your foes while they pursue you? or shall there be three days' **plague** in your land? now advise you, and consider what **word** I shall return to He that sent me.'

יג וַיָּבֹא־גָד אֶל־דָּוִד וַיַּגֶּד־לוֹ: וַיֹּאמֶר לוֹ הֲתָבוֹא לְךָ שֶׁבַע שָׁנִים רָעָב בְּאַרְצֶךָ אִם־שְׁלֹשָׁה חֳדָשִׁים נֻסְךָ לִפְנֵי־צָרֶיךָ וְהוּא רֹדְפֶךָ וְאִם־הֱיוֹת שְׁלֹשֶׁת יָמִים דֶּבֶר בְּאַרְצֶךָ עַתָּה דַּע וּרְאֵה מָה־אָשִׁיב שֹׁלְחִי דָּבָר.

"What **word** shall I return to He that sent me," "*Mah ashiv sholchi davar*" (דָּבָר) is a play on *dever* (דֶּבֶר), "plague." In effect, Gad is saying to David: "Say the **word**."

The Two Lessons of Leadership

David gives a brilliant answer, which is: "I eliminate the middle possibility. I have had enough of wars in my life. As for the rest, it's in God's hands." And the plague begins.

With this answer, David passes test number one, the recognition that a king works for God, which is what the Bible says about kingship.[11]

But then David sees the people dying. Why are *they* being punished? Because the sin is theirs. It is the people who have requested a king. David is an ambitious person. He wants to be king, yes. But the request for kingship came from the people who wanted to be "like all the nations,"[12] not from David.

And now, seeing the avenging angel hovering above Jerusalem, David objects:

II Samuel 24

17 And David spoke to the LORD when he saw the angel that smote the people, and said: 'Lo, I have sinned, and I have done

יז וַיֹּאמֶר דָּוִד אֶל־יְיָ בִּרְאֹתוֹ אֶת־הַמַּלְאָךְ הַמַּכֶּה בָעָם וַיֹּאמֶר הִנֵּה אָנֹכִי חָטָאתִי וְאָנֹכִי הֶעֱוֵיתִי

11 Deuteronomy 17:18-20
12 I Samuel 8:5

iniquitously; but these sheep,
what have they done? let Your
hand, I pray You, be against me,
and against my father's house.'

וְאֵלֶּה הַצֹּאן מֶה עָשׂוּ: תְּהִי
נָא יָדְךָ בִּי וּבְבֵית אָבִי.

David, the most ambitious man who ever lived says to God: "I abdicate. If my being king means that they suffer, forget me. I give up the kingship."

The prophet returns to him and says: "David, you've just passed God's second test."

And what is the second test? David finally understands the biblical requirement: the king is "one of the people."[13] At last, David understands both of his kingly tasks. The king works for God, *and* the king works for the people. David says, "I am in the hands of God. Moreover, the people come first and I come second." That is the point of kingship.

II Samuel 24

18 And Gad came that day to
David, and said unto him:
'Go up, rear an altar unto the
LORD in the threshing-floor
of Araunah the Jebusite.'

יח וַיָּבֹא-גָד אֶל-דָּוִד בַּיּוֹם הַהוּא:
וַיֹּאמֶר לוֹ עֲלֵה הָקֵם לַיי מִזְבֵּחַ
בְּגֹרֶן ארניה (אֲרַוְנָה) הַיְבֻסִי.

David is then instructed to go and build a permanent altar for God. Because he passed the second test, David is shown the place in his own city where God will dwell permanently.

Relearning his lessons

David displays understanding of both kingship concepts in an earlier story from the Book of Samuel, when returning the Ark to Jerusalem:

II Samuel 6

20 Then David returned to bless
his household. And Michal
the daughter of Saul came out
to meet David, and said: 'How
did the king of Israel get him
honor today, who uncovered
himself today in the eyes of

כ וַיָּשָׁב דָּוִד לְבָרֵךְ אֶת-בֵּיתוֹ: וַתֵּצֵא
מִיכַל בַּת-שָׁאוּל לִקְרַאת דָּוִד
וַתֹּאמֶר מַה-נִּכְבַּד הַיּוֹם מֶלֶךְ
יִשְׂרָאֵל אֲשֶׁר נִגְלָה הַיּוֹם

---

13   Deuteronomy 17:15

the handmaids of his servants,
as one of the vain fellows
shamelessly uncovers himself!'

21 And David said unto Michal:
'Before the LORD, who chose
me above your father, and above
all his house, to appoint me
prince over the people of the
LORD, over Israel, before the
LORD will I make merry.

22 And I will be yet more vile than
this, and will be base in my own
sight; and with the handmaids
whom you hast spoken of, with
them will I get me honor.'

לְעֵינֵי אַמְהוֹת עֲבָדָיו כְּהִגָּלוֹת
נִגְלוֹת אַחַד הָרֵקִים.

כא וַיֹּאמֶר דָּוִד אֶל־מִיכַל לִפְנֵי יְיָ
אֲשֶׁר בָּחַר־בִּי מֵאָבִיךְ וּמִכָּל־
בֵּיתוֹ לְצַוֹּת אֹתִי נָגִיד עַל־עַם יְיָ
עַל־יִשְׂרָאֵל: וְשִׂחַקְתִּי לִפְנֵי יְיָ.

כב וּנְקַלֹּתִי עוֹד מִזֹּאת וְהָיִיתִי
שָׁפָל בְּעֵינָי: וְעִם־הָאֲמָהוֹת
אֲשֶׁר אָמַרְתְּ עִמָּם אִכָּבֵדָה.

There is a nasty side to David in the Book of Samuel. This is how he talks to the woman who saved his life! He says to her: "Lady, goodbye, I don't need you anymore." That is quintessential David. But though he behaves badly, he is right. David *has* brought glory upon himself. Michal misunderstands the point of kingship.

David is saying: "I dance before the God who chose me to lead God's people. It is not about me, I have a job to do, to serve God, and lead God's people, and since you don't understand that, I cannot find glory with *you*."

And at that moment, we know that Michal will not be the mother to the next king of Israel. David is saying: I cannot be an extension of Saul. If Michal has a baby, the grandfather would be Saul, and the house of Saul and David would be united. David knows that glory will not come from Michal daughter of Saul, because she, like her father, misses the whole point of the kingship.

David finds his own place… and God's

David finally understands. (The problem with David is that he sometimes loses track of what is important because he gets blinded by the promise of power.)

Ultimately, the answer of the Book of Samuel is that, *ideally*, kingship can work. From a pragmatic standpoint, it *did* work in history – that is the subject of the Book of Kings – although, for the most part, it doesn't work very *well*. In theory, it can work, but only if you have a king who understands the kingly role – who understands that God makes the choices.

When David shows he understands that God is the true king, David is rewarded with the task of building God's altar.

The Book of Samuel begins with the destruction of Shiloh and the capture of the Ark by the Philistines.[14] The book now ends with God being restored to God's place. Saul may not accomplish this task: He never figures out what is required from him as king. Initially, it can't be David either, until he internalizes his mission to serve God.

In the last chapter, David is the one who installs the Ark in its permanent place. And where is the permanent place for the Ark? The threshing place of Aravnah the Jebusite, *"goren Aravnah"* (גֹּרֶן אֲרַוְנָה). *Aron* (ארון) is the Hebrew word for the Ark. The words *goren Aravnah* can be read: "the threshold of the Ark," therefore it is the ideal place for God's spirit to dwell. This is ultimately the site of the future Temple.

In other words, the Ark has returned, God has found God's place, and this coincides with David being chosen eternally.

The lesson of the chiasm at the end of the Book of Samuel is that, in an ideal world, kingship can work. The Ark can find its place, and the king and God can live together. But this can only happen if the king understands one thing: Israel's king is chosen by God to serve Him faithfully.

---

14   I Samuel 4:11

YCT Tanakh Companion

Rabbi Hayyim Angel is Rabbi of Congregation Shearith Israel of New York City (the Spanish-Portuguese Synagogue, founded in 1654) and teaches advanced Tanakh courses at Yeshiva University. He has published articles on Tanakh in journals such as *Tradition, Nahalah, Jewish Thought, Jewish Bible Quarterly, Or HaMizrah,* and in several collections of essays. He recently published *Through an Opaque Lens,* a collection of twenty of his biblical studies.

Rabbi Joshua Berman studied at Yeshivat Har-Etzion, Princeton University and holds a doctorate in Bible from Bar-Ilan University. He is a lecturer in Tanach at Bar-Ilan University, and is the author of *The Temple: Its Symbolism and Meaning Then and Now* (Jason Aronson, 1995), currently in its second printing. His articles on contemporary issues have appeared in the pages of *Tradition, L'Eylah, Midstream, Judaism* and the *Jerusalem Post.* His most recent book, *Narrative Analogy in the Hebrew Bible,* was published by Brill Academic Publishers in the spring of 2004. He is currently a fellow at the Shalem Center in Jerusalem where he is working on a book about the revolution in social and political thought witnessed in the Tanakh relative to the surrounding cultures of the ancient Near East.

Rabbi Jack Bieler was ordained by the Rabbi Isaac Elchanan Theological Seminary in 1974. He served on the faculty of Yeshivat Ramaz from 1974-88 during which time he was also permanent Scholar-in-Residence at Congregation Kehillat Jeshurun. Since 1988, Rabbi Bieler has served as Lead Teacher, Chairman of the Judaic Studies Department and Assistant Principal for Judaic Studies at the Hebrew Academy of Greater Washington, now the Melvin J. Berman Hebrew Academy in Rockville, MD. In 1993 he was appointed Rabbi of the Kemp Mill Synagogue in Silver Spring, MD. He has published and given presentations on Jewish education and on issues facing Judaism today, especially concerning Modern Orthodoxy.

Rabbi Dr. Yehuda Felix studied at Yeshivat Mercaz HaRav in Jerusalem, where he was ordained by Rav Avraham Shapira, Rav Simcha Kook and the late Rav Betzalel Zolti. He received his doctorate from Bar Ilan University. He founded and for 25 years headed Orot College in Israel and is currently the Jewish Agency for Israel's educational director for North America.

Leeor Gottlieb, a graduate of Yeshivat Sha'alvim and Beit Morasha, is a Ph.D. candidate and an instructor of Bible in Hebrew University's Department of Bible. His work focuses on the transmission of the Biblical text, the inner-development of Biblical Hebrew and the ancient translations of the Bible.

Rabbi Nathaniel Helfgot is the Chair of the Bible and Jewish Thought Departments at Yeshivat Chovevei Torah Rabbinical School. He previously served as Judaic Studies Curriculum Coordinator at the Maayanot Yeshiva High School and on the Judaic Studies faculty of the Frisch Yeshiva High School. He is a long-time member of the Drisha Institute for Jewish Education Faculty and a widely sought out lecturer in communities throughout North America and beyond on areas of Jewish Studies. He has authored dozens of essays in Hebrew and English, serves as co-editor of the Hebrew journal *Or ha-Mizrach* and most recently served as editor of the volume *Community, Covenant and Commitment: Selected Letters and Communications of Rabbi Joseph B. Soloveitchik* (Toras HoRav Foundation/Ktav, 2005).

Rabbi Shmuel Herzfeld is spiritual leader of Ohev Sholom—The National Synagogue, located on 16th street in Washington, DC. His articles and Divrei Torah are archived on his website, www.rabbishmuel.com.

Rabbi David Silber is the founder and dean of Drisha Institute for Jewish Education (www.drisha.org), internationally recognized as the creative force for women's advanced study of classical Jewish texts. Rabbi Silber has introduced groundbreaking initiatives that continue to change the way people regard Jewish education in general, and the leadership role of women in particular. Rabbi Silber is a pre-eminent Bible scholar and sought-after speaker whose *shiurim* and CD recordings are distributed worldwide. He received ordination from the Rabbi Isaac Elchanan Theological Seminary, and is a recipient of the Covenant Award.

Rabbi Avraham (Avi) Weiss is Founder and Dean of Yeshivat Chovevei Torah – the Open Orthodox Rabbinical school. He is Senior Rabbi of the Hebrew Institute of Riverdale, a modern and open Orthodox congregation of 850 families. He has authored two books – *Women at Prayer*, a halakhic analysis of women's prayer groups, and *Principles of Spiritual Activism*. He is also the editor of the *Haggadah for the Yom HaShoah* seder.

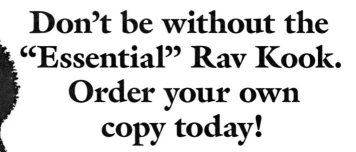

Don't be without the "Essential" Rav Kook. Order your own copy today!

Check your favorite bookseller, or order here:

[ ] **YES,** I want ___ copies of *The Essential Writings of Abraham Isaac Kook* at $19.95 each, plus $3 shipping per book (New Jersey residents please add $1.40 sales tax per book). Canadian orders must be accompanied by a postal money order in U.S. funds. Allow 2-4 weeks for delivery.

My check or money order for $_____ is enclosed.
Please charge my [ ] Visa [ ] MasterCard

Name _____

Organization _____

Address _____

City/State/Zip_____

Phone _____ Email _____

Card # _____Exp. Date _____

Signature _____Security code _____

Please return to: **Ben Yehuda Press**
430 Kensington Rd.   Teaneck, NJ 07666
email: sales@BenYehudaPress.com
buy online at http://www.BenYehudaPress.com

Books make great gifts! We'll happily enclose a card, inscribe the book to the recipient, and wrap it. Just let us know the details!

Acquire a Companion!
Order your own copy of the Yeshivat Chovevi Torah Tanakh Companion to the Book of Samuel

Check your favorite bookseller, or order direct:

[ ] **YES,** I want ___ copies of *The Yeshivat Chovevei Torah Rabbinical School Tanakh Companion: Book of Samuel* at $19.95 each, plus $3 shipping per book (New Jersey residents please add $1.40 sales tax per book). Canadian orders must be accompanied by a postal money order in U.S. funds. Allow 2-4 weeks for delivery.

My check or money order for $_____ is enclosed.
Please charge my [ ] Visa [ ] MasterCard

Name _____

Organization _____

Address _____

City/State/Zip_____

Phone _____ Email _____

Card # _____Exp. Date _____

Signature _____Security code _____

Please return to: ***Ben Yehuda Press***
430 Kensington Rd.   Teaneck, NJ 07666
fax: (201) 917-1278 phone: (800) 809-3505
email: sales@BenYehudaPress.com
buy online at http://www.BenYehudaPress.com

Books make great gifts! We'll happily enclose a card, inscribe the book to the recipient, and wrap it. Just let us know the details!

YCT Tanakh Companion: Samuel
Road-Ready Audio Edition
12 cassette tapes, featuring the original lectures from the YCT *yemei iyun.*
Only $85.

[ ] YES, I want ___ sets of *The YCT Tanakh Companion for the Road: The Book of Samuel* at $85 each, shipping included. (New Jersey and New York residents, please add $6.00 sales tax per set.) Canadian orders must be accompanied by a postal money order in U.S. funds. Allow 3-6 weeks for delivery.

My check or money order for $_____ is enclosed.
Please charge my [ ] Visa [ ] MasterCard

Name _____

Organization _____

Address _____

City/State/Zip_____

Phone _____ Email _____

Card # _____Exp. Date _____

Signature _____Security code _____

Please return to: **Ben Yehuda Press**
430 Kensington Rd.   Teaneck, NJ 07666
email: sales@BenYehudaPress.com
fax: (201) 917-1278 phone: (800) 809-3505
buy online at http://www.BenYehudaPress.com

CPSIA information can be obtained at www.ICGtesting.com
Printed in the USA
243677LV00002B/77/A

9 780976 986249